NEW HORIZONS IN THEOLOGY

NEW HORIZONS
IN THEOLOGY

Terrence W. Tilley
Editor

**THE ANNUAL PUBLICATION
OF THE COLLEGE THEOLOGY SOCIETY
2004
VOLUME 50**

ORBIS BOOKS

Maryknoll, New York 10545

Founded in 1970, Orbis Books endeavors to publish works that enlighten the mind, nourish the spirit, and challenge the conscience. The publishing arm of the Maryknoll Fathers and Brothers, Orbis seeks to explore the global dimensions of the Christian faith and mission, to invite dialogue with diverse cultures and religious traditions, and to serve the cause of reconciliation and peace. The books published reflect the views of their authors and do not represent the official position of the Maryknoll Society. To learn more about Maryknoll and Orbis Books, please visit our website at www.maryknoll.org.

Published by Orbis Books, Maryknoll, New York 10545-0308.
Manufactured in the United States of America.

Library of Congress Cataloging-in-Publication Data

College Theology Society. Meeting (50th : 2004 : The Catholic University of America)
    New horizons in theology / Terrence W. Tilley, editor.
      p. cm.
    Includes bibliographical references and index.
    ISBN 1-57075-597-3 (pbk.)
    1. Catholic Church—Doctrines—Congresses.   I. Tilley, Terrence W. II. Title.
      BX1751.3.C39 2004
      230'.2—dc22
                                    2004027718

To all the saints who from their labors rest
and
all the saints who in their labors teach

This volume is dedicated
to all the members, past and present,
who have formed the community called the
Society of Catholic College Teachers
of Sacred Doctrine
continuing today as the
College Theology Society

Contents

PART III
NEW HORIZONS IN TEACHING THEOLOGY

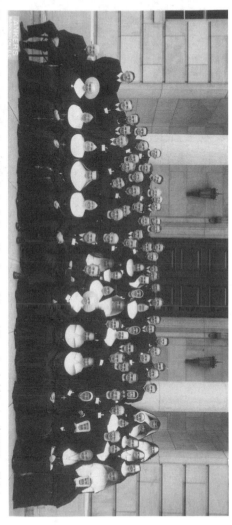

The first meeting of the Society of Catholic College Teachers of Sacred Doctrine held in April 1955 at Trinity College in Washington, D.C. (Credit: CTS Archives at The Catholic University of America)

The fiftieth meeting of the College Theology Society was held in June 2004 at The Catholic University of America, Washington, D.C. (Credit: CTS Archives)

From left, Keith J. Egan, Francis J. Buckley, s.j., Terrence W. Tilley, M. Theresa Moser, r.s.c.j, William M. Shea, Gerard S. Sloyan, William P. Loewe, Brennan R. Hill, Robert L. Masson, Loretta M. Devoy, o.p.

Presidents of the College Theology Society

Eugene Burke, C.S.P. (1955)

John J. Fernan, S.J. (1956)

Thomas C. Donlan, O.P. (1957)

Alban of Mary, F.S.C. (1958)

Bernard Cooke, S.J. (1960)

Urban Voll, O.P. (1962)

Rev. Raymond A. Parr (1964)

Rev. Gerard S. Sloyan (1966)

Mark Heath, O.P. (1968)

James Wieland (1970)

Francis J. Buckley, S.J. (1972)

Matthew C. Kohmescher, S.M. (1974)

Rev. James J. Flanagan (1976)

William Cenkner, O.P. (1978)

Vera Chester, C.S.J. (1980)

Roger Van Allen (1982)

William M. Shea (1984)

Dolores L. Greeley, R.S.M. (1986)

Mary Lea Schneider, O.F.M. (1988)

Keith J. Egan (1990)

Joan A. Leonard, O.P. (1992)

Brennan R. Hill (1994)

Terrence W. Tilley (1996)

M. Theresa Moser, R.S.C.J. (1998)

William P. Loewe (2000)

Loretta M. Devoy, O.P. (2002)

Robert L. Masson (2004)

Introduction

The College Theology Society celebrated its fiftieth annual meeting at The Catholic University of America in Washington, D.C., in June 2004. How much has changed since the first meeting of the Society of Catholic College Teachers of Sacred Doctrine fifty years earlier! The United States elected its first Catholic president, Vatican II met and redirected the practice and teaching of the church, and other cultural and ecclesial shifts unimaginable in 1954 have affected us deeply. Many of the papers in this volume address in a special way the changes in *who* is doing theology (layfolk more than clerics and religious) and *where* academic theology is centered (more in the universities and colleges than in the seminaries). Yet much remains the same: we still teach (mostly) undergraduates, we still teach (mostly) in colleges and universities, and we still are committed to excellence in both teaching and research as a service to the church, the Society, and the academy.

Not every "new horizon" can be covered in one volume. Indeed, each of the previous volumes of the College Theology Society reveals one or more of the "cutting edges" in theology at the time they were published. The more recent volumes remain important indicators of the evolution of contemporary theology, with an emphasis on Catholic theology in the United States—as might be expected, given the membership of the CTS.

The present volume includes papers that offer perspectives on how we got here, where we are, and where we're going as theological and ecclesial communities.

Part I, "*Tour d'Horizon*," begins with two papers given as stirring plenary addresses to the convention. Elizabeth Johnson discerns the emergence of new voices in the ongoing conversation that is theology and Joseph Komonchak reminds us both of how theology was done at the birth of our Society and of how we can and should do it today. Then two papers trace the evolution of contemporary trends in theology. Norbert Rigali limns the evolution of Catholic moral theology, and J. Matthew Ashley reveals the multiple shapes that a "mystical-political" theology takes. This section might well have been titled "*Gaudium et Spes*" as it shows how theology done in and for the church has been shaped by and has tried to shape our world.

In the second part, "Expanding the Horizon," seven papers explore and expand specific points on our theological horizons. Elizabeth Groppe's exciting paper reflects on a collaborative way for Jews and Christians to influence the interpretation of scripture—with a remarkable focus on the dietary laws in the Hebrew Bible. Michael Barnes mounts historical and theological arguments to show that contemporary "physicalist" notions of the soul can be understood to preserve what has been important in traditional Christian concepts of the soul. Steven Harmon's paper was given in a session co-sponsored with the National Association of Baptist Professors of Religion (whose "regional meeting" has been part of the CTS meetings in most years since our first associated meeting in 1996). He shows the happy result of the *Horizontverschmelzung* occurring between Catholics and Baptists in regard to "tradition" as a theological topic in the Baptist communities.

Colleen Mallon explores "tradition" in another contemporary context: that of globalization. Using emergent explorations in the social sciences, Mallon argues for an important theological refiguring of the concept of tradition. Anne Clifford reminds us that the global issues of religious diversity are also quite local and shows how this "local" concern makes a real difference in understanding the face-to-face encounter of interreligious dialogue. Sally Kenel reshapes the traditional understanding of the eco*nomy* of salvation in reflections on the eco*logy* of salvation to show how we can rethink christology and soteriology ecologically. Randall Woodard calls attention to an emerging question in the practical theology of marriage: how can we understand and how should we work with the increasing number of cohabiting couples who seek to enter into a sacramental marriage? Given the immense changes in how we understand and engage in human relationships over the past fifty years, Woodard's historical and theological contribution reminds us that all theology is done with and for those who seek ways to live in and live out the ancient creeds in the new horizons of our contemporary world. *Dignitatis humanae personae* is the heart of the work we do *ad majorem dei gloriam*.

The College Theology Society has always kept its focus on the theory and practice of teaching theology and religious studies. The final part of the volume reflects on the new horizons in teaching that face us after fifty years as a society. A set of papers from a plenary panel begins this section. Sandra Yocum Mize, whose new history of the College Theology Society will appear in 2005, discusses the differing contours of the horizons within which we theologized in the mid-twentieth century and in the present. Miguel Díaz reminds us of the new voices emerging from the U.S. Hispanic community and explores what it means to theologize *latinamente*. Mary Ann Hinsdale highlights the significance of the changes in the ecclesial status and social locations of the practitioners of theology for the teaching of theology today. James Donahue reflects on the practices of graduate and undergraduate teaching in a globalized, diverse, and plural world. Suzanne Toton and Ismael Muvingi conclude with a report on a fascinating experiment in putting our theological commitments into educational practice. Their exciting and creative approach, which presents an attractive model for excellence in teaching, provides a fitting conclusion to this annual volume. Education is indeed *"ex corde ecclesiae,"* for we who learn and teach theology do so from the heart.

The editor owes so much thanks to so many people that his debts can only be hinted at in what follows. To the Society as a whole, to whom this volume is dedicated, he owes the shape of his academic life: without the CTS, it would have been much different and far less satisfying. To William Loewe, Shannon Schrein, and their associates, many thanks for doing all the tedious work that made the meeting at Catholic University possible. To our terrific editor at Orbis Books, Susan Perry, he gives thanks for all she has done for the Society in particular and for theologians in general. To the authors of papers in this volume, a great round of applause for exceptionally fine papers and remarkably quick responsiveness to editorial demands, requests, and adjustments.

And to the referees—especially those who read two or three of the essays submitted and all of whom worked quickly and exceedingly carefully to help me discern which essays most deserved publication and to make those essays as good as possible—a huge thank you: Matt Ashley, Mike Barnes, Joe Bracken, Bill Burrows, Lisa Sowle Cahill, Frank Clooney, Nancy Dallavalle, Carol Dempsey, John Downey, Dennis Doyle, Orlando Espín, Dan Finucane, Zeni Fox, Curtis Freeman, George Gilmore, Tony Godzieba, Barbara Green, Joann Heaney-Hunter, Jim Heft, Kelly Johnson, Brad Kallenberg,

Mike Lawler, Therese Lysaught, Tim Matovina, Sandra Yocum Mize, Theresa Moser, Tim Muldoon, Nancey Murphy, Tim O'Connell, Beth Newman, Bill Portier, Elena Procario-Foley, Bill Roberts, Susan Ross, Bill Shea, Tom Shannon, Dave Stagaman, Pam Thimmes, Mil Thompson, Maureen Tilley, Phyllis Zagano, and anyone I have managed to omit inadvertently!

Sandra Yocum Mize suggested taking the photographs at the 2004 convention that form the composite on p. ix and juxtaposing this composite with the photo of the 1954 meeting of the Society. I assembled the 2004 composite with the assistance of Chris Conlon, S.M.

And to the College Theology Society: *ad multos annos!*

Terrence W. Tilley
University of Dayton
All Souls Day, 2004

Part I

TOUR D'HORIZON

Horizons of Theology

New Voices in a Living Tradition

Elizabeth A. Johnson

Happy 50th Anniversary to the College Theology Society!

Happy 30th Anniversary to *Horizons: Journal of the College Theology Society*!

Originally founded in 1954 as the Society of Catholic College Teachers of Sacred Doctrine (and God bless those who changed the name), this Society has grown from the original dream of Rose Eileen Masterman, Gerard Sloyan, and their colleagues, to a vibrant community of almost one thousand professors who teach and research in the area of theology and religious studies.[1] We join a group such as this to gain intellectual and emotional nourishment for our personal and professional lives. In doing so, together we also make a communal contribution beyond ourselves to theology's three publics of academy, church, and society. Celebrating fifty years of the College Theology Society hails, in Bernard Cooke's inimitable words, "a committed community of responsible scholarship that is powerful enough to sustain honest and fearless pursuit and teaching of the truth about the God revealed in Jesus, about the church's people and institutions and history,"[2] and about what life in the Spirit requires of us now.

A jubilee is a time to celebrate. It is also a time to take stock and set directions for the half century to come. Carrying out the jubilee theme of "new horizons," I would like to consider the emergence of "new voices" in the living tradition of Christian faith. In short, these are an American voice, a global voice, and the voice of the earth. All of these overlap.

American Voices

An American voice is emerging in theology. By this adjective "American" I do not mean a superior, nationalistic voice, one that promotes imperialistic claims to be "number 1," gets high on the hubris of pre-emptive war, and conducts economic policy for the benefit of the rich. I do not mean an uncritical, "flag-waving" voice. Rather, the voice I refer to is a complex voice reflecting the experience of the church in this country, where something new is happening that has not occurred before in history. Let me explain.

If the founders of this Society had fallen asleep fifty years ago and just awakened, these Rip Van Winkles would be astonished at the changed situation in which we do theology today. Consider first, in the context of the academy, who is teaching theology, and where. Half a century ago, theology was taught mostly in seminaries to candidates for the priesthood. The professors were ordained priests, the best and brightest of whom received their degrees in Rome, or, in the case of some, at The Catholic University of America. What they taught was mostly neo-scholastic theology organized according to the schema of the manuals. The method employed was deductive reasoning from stated theses. Theology in this country had a Roman voice. Let it be noted that in those days the only place in this country where women could receive an advanced degree in theology was St. Mary's College in South Bend, Indiana, thanks to Sister Madeleva Wolff.

Today, every aspect of that picture has shifted. In addition to seminaries, theology is also taught in colleges and universities. Those under Catholic auspices number more than 230. It is fair to say that nowhere else in the world does a more complete, varied, excellent system of independent Catholic higher education exist. The students who receive this teaching are mainly young adults, thousands of undergraduate and graduate lay students. And the professors teaching them include not only ordained priests but also lay persons, women and men. The institutions where these professors received their doctoral education have also shifted, beyond Rome, to universities in Europe and North America, some Catholic, but also divinity schools and departments of religion in private, non-denominational, Ivy League, and state universities. Methods of doing theology have expanded commensurate with this diversity of education. Varieties of transcendental, process, political, radically orthodox, theologically aesthetic, neo-Thomist, feminist/womanist/*mujerista*, liberation, ecological, postliberal, and postmodern constructs, along with interreligious dialogue, now make pluralism in theology seem entirely normal.

These shifts in the academic social location of theology have happened in a church itself undergoing major transitions due to the Second Vatican Council. This Society was not even a decade old when the Council began, and most of its history has been interwoven with the reception of the Council and its reverberating effects. The picture is complicated, with a conflict of interpretations over what the Council actually meant, and with the current effort of the highest ecclesiastical authorities to restore one interpretation over all.

Out of these swirling currents in academy and church is emerging, I wager, a distinctive American voice, or better, voices, in theology. In 1979 Karl Rahner, responding to an honorary degree awarded him at Marquette University, memorably envisioned the future of theology. He said:

> I am thinking of a theology which can no longer be uniform in a neo-scholastic approach. . . . I envisage a theology which in the Church at large must be the theology of a worldwide Church. That means a theology which does not only recite its own medieval history, but one that can listen to the wisdom of the East, the longing for freedom in Latin America, and also to the sound of African drums.[3]

Notice what is missing geographically: any mention of theology dancing to an American beat. At that point in time, most North American theologians were still absorbing the wisdom of European theologians who had pioneered the breakthroughs of the Second Vatican Council, including that of Rahner himself. We might say that theology in this country had a German voice—Barth, Bonhoeffer, Pannenberg, Moltmann, Balthasar, Rahner, Metz, Küng, Kasper—although some French like de Lubac and Congar, and some Flemish or Dutch like Schillebeeckx and Schoonenberg varied the accent. But that was twenty-five years ago.

Since then there has been rapid maturing of the community of biblical, historical, foundational, systematic, and moral theologians in this country. In terms of numbers, there are now close to two thousand academically trained people teaching, researching, and writing Catholic religious scholarship across this country, a critical mass unmatched in any other country on earth. This is largely due to our system of higher education, which requires professors in great numbers. In terms of practitioners, for the first time in history the majority of this critical mass of credentialed teacher-scholars is composed of women and men who have *not* been through seminary training, who may well be married, with children and other commitments in society, and who bring a distinctively lay experience into the profession. This number includes people (not yet enough) of different races and ethnic communities, whose voices contribute insight that enhances the pluralistic picture.

All of this brings precision to the idea that a new voice to notice at this Jubilee is theology done in an emerging, genuine, diverse American idiom. It is not a Roman voice, not a German voice, not someone else's voice, but our voice and we need to claim it. Remember that Christian theology's two-thousand-year history of development shows not only that theology inevitably takes on cultural forms. It also makes clear that theology works best when fertilized by the philosophical assumptions, patterns of thought, and pressing questions of its own time and place, and when energized by the dynamic moral resources of the Christian tradition to challenge violations of the gospel occurring in its own culture. Utilizing the lived experience that this American life provides for understanding faith, we are already newly engaged in "naming grace," in Mary Catherine Hilkert's beautiful term, and in the process "inventing Catholic tradition," in Terrence Tilley's provocative phrase.[4] It is a sign of the growing maturity of the church community in this country that it can generate such reflection, and a sign of the hunger of so many adults for a mature faith that this work is being so well received.

One hundred years from now, how will historians describe the characteristics of theology done in American voices? If the past is prologue, let it be noted that the first time the American experience affected universal church teaching was when John Courtney Murray's work on religious freedom and the value of separation of church and state flowed into the conciliar document *Dignitatis humanae*, on the dignity of the human person, which requires that the exercise of religion in society be free. I suggest that the experience of living in a pluralistic, more or less democratic society replete with American philosophical and cultural resources, along with efforts to be self-critical of the consumerist, selfishly narrow, violent, and amnesiac streams in our own culture, will bear fruit in ways yet to be envisioned that will benefit the world church.

But there is ever so much more involved. We live today in one world where national borders do not limit consciousness; a world where beautiful advances in human dignity interact with gross violations of human rights; a world where immense striving seems to put only a dent in flagrant inequity and poverty; a world where heroic efforts for peace have not ended violence, terror, and war; a world where growing ecological consciousness co-exists with species extinction and the natural world itself under threat. If theology done in an American voice does not responsibly heed the voices arising from these concerns, both at home and abroad, it will end up as little more than elegant frittering.

Global Voices

Consider, then, the wider world, marked by an interdependence that is entirely new in history. Globalization is the term that pinpoints the increasingly interconnected character of political, economic, and social life of the peoples on this planet. To cite key examples: the world-wide expansion of market capitalism is creating a single world economy, now reigning almost everywhere, with dramatically different effects on rich and poor nations; technology such as the Internet compresses time and space, enabling the rapid global transfer of ideas and information beyond the ability of any hierarchy, civil or religious, to control it; the migration of millions fleeing war and poverty mixes peoples together at an unprecedented rate, so that multicultural experience is to be had practically everywhere. Nineteen-fifty-four seems a long, long time ago, not only in the academy and in the church, but also in the world.

In his book *The New Catholicity*, Robert Schreiter proposes that these changes have produced "global information flows," that is, circulations of insight across geographical and cultural boundaries that change every local landscape. Commensurate with this, theology everywhere in our day is also affected by global currents that spread beyond their point of origin to address issues that affect everyone.[5] Theological discourse in the world church is increasingly interlinked, for example, by liberation, feminist, and human rights concerns. Insofar as these flows carry a holistic vision of what is essential for life's flourishing, along with protest against how this is being violated, they form a chorus of new voices crying out for the reign of God. From the many sources of new religious insight, take note of at least four.

Voices of the Poor

The struggle for life waged by billions of economically poor people has given rise to liberation theologies on various continents. There is deep wisdom here, arising from the underside of history, about divine compassion and the liberating way God acts with the world as revealed in Jesus Christ. Partnering this wisdom is a challenge to conscience. This voice calls us well-off theologians, who have enough to eat, to listen to the voiceless hungry people of the world, struggling through short lives of immense misery. It calls us to attend to the quiet, searing pain of the dying poor. Making a preferential option for the poor, taking their side, brings into view the suffering caused by the devastation of war and by structurally unjust economic policies, for example, transnational corporations that are not accountable to the people affected by their policies but seek mainly to maximize profit for their own shareholders. Hearing these voices causes theology to reflect in a way that will challenge oppression and promote the justice that benefits the disenfranchised.

Voices of Women

The struggle for women's equal human dignity has taken on distinctive theological shapes among women with diverse racial, ethnic, class, and cultural identities, as the adjectives feminist, womanist, and *mujerista* indicate. There is deep wisdom here, arising from women's religious experience, about divine compassion and the liberating way God acts with the world as revealed in Jesus Christ. Partnering this wisdom is a challenge to conscience. Many aspects of society and religion are structured according to the norms of patriarchy. The majority of the world's women still lack goods that Western women take for granted: access to basic education, nutrition, and health care, the right to consent to marriage and to sexual acts, the right to own property and to legal protection from domestic violence. Defined by their feminine nature as a breed of human beings different from men, women in the church are barred from sacramental ministry and governance of the community and directed to secondary resources for their spirituality. Hearing these voices calls theology to promote the human flourishing of all women in every systemic dimension of life because women, too, are beloved of God.

Voices of Black, Hispanic, and Asian Peoples

The struggle for equality by communities in this country whose racial or ethnic heritage differs from mainstream Euro-Americans is giving rise to new theologies coherent with each group's history. There is deep wisdom here, drawn from resistance to slavery, lynchings, and discrimination, and drawn from popular religious practices in the home and neighborhood, about divine compassion and the liberating way God acts with the world as revealed in Jesus Christ. Partnering this wisdom is a challenge to conscience. Made invisible or cast as "Other" by the racism of traditional theology, minority groups today still wrestle with the exclusion dictated by the prejudice of the white majority. Hearing these voices calls theology to promote inclusion of all peoples in the promise of the reign of God, in both thought and practice.

Voices of World Religious Traditions

Encounters with people of the world's religions enhanced by interreligious dialogue are giving rise to a sea-change in the way the Christian church views other religions and itself in relation to them. There is deep wisdom here, about divine compassion and the liberating way God acts with the world as revealed in religious paths *beyond* the historical following of Jesus Christ. Partnering this wisdom is a challenge to conscience. The devotion of adherents of the world's religious traditions shows Christians that while in Jesus Christ, crucified and risen, we have a unique encounter with the incarnate God's ways in the world, we do not have a monopoly on either truth or holiness. Hearing these voices causes theology to try to "get right" the Holocaust and build a relationship with the Jewish people grounded, finally, in mutual respect. Stretching us even further, these voices call theology to attend to what God has been up to in the traditions that address the God of Abraham, Sarah, and Hagar, the God of Jesus and Mary Magdalene, as Krishna, Buddha, and Allah.

Watered by these global theological flows, the work of trying to "name the grace" of God's presence in *this* global era and not some other moves theology beyond parochial horizons and narrow interests. Circling back to the earlier question of what characterizes theology done in a distinctive American idiom, it now becomes clear that attending to these previously unheard voices is essential for the vitality of any long-term contribution. Though these voices may create a taxing dissonance with traditional stances, doing justice to them must be part of our normal practice as we research, write, read, and teach theology. Blocking them out would undermine the very service theology intends to render, starting with service to the American Catholic community itself.

Here is a Jubilee hope: that a North American theology will come forth that is a genuine contribution to the conversation emerging from these new global flows because it remembers and serves those outside our own privileged circles. Steeped in a love of freedom, this theology would be intelligible, credible, flexibly normative, full of affirmation, and adequate to praxis and to ritual (for "a tradition that is not celebrated is dying") precisely by listening generously to the voices of those who demand of us a new mode of working and relating to them. Such a theology, as it affects our local church through teaching and preaching, would light the way to meaning at the same time that it challenged the conscience of those who have more than they realize. Such a theology in an American voice would be worth its weight in gold.

There is yet another voice to be heard, one that calls our thought and care beyond the human race to consider the entire community of life with whom we share this planet as a matter of faith and ethics.

The Voice of the Earth

At the start of this third millennium, a new awareness of the magnificence of life on planet Earth is growing among peoples everywhere—another sign of globalization. We have seen the image of Earth from space, a blue marble swirled around with white clouds, the only spot of life in a vast black sea of space. Contemporary science has taught us about the origin of the universe in the unimaginable Big Bang some fourteen billion years ago; and about the formation of our sun and planet from an exploding star; and about the flaring forth of life in the ancient seas; and its evolution from single-celled to multiple-celled creatures, and from plant to animal life, including *homo sapiens*, we human mammals whose brains are so richly complex that we enjoy self-reflective consciousness and freedom. This new cosmology makes clear that humans are part and parcel of the envelope of life on this planet, true earthlings, who share genetic ancestry and the material of existence with all other creatures on the planet.

The present moment is marked by a strange paradox. While we grow in wonder at life on this planet, we are at the same time engaged in death-dealing actions that ravage and deplete, even wipe out, the natural world. Two major engines of destruction are over-consumption and overpopulation. Every year, 20 percent of Earth's people in the rich nations use 75 percent of the world's resources and produce 80 percent of the world's waste. An example: Chicago with three million people consumes as much raw material in a year as Bangladesh with ninety-seven million people. Such over-consumption is driven by a consumer economy that must constantly grow in order to be viable, one whose greatest goal is a bottom line in the black. It does not factor in the ecological cost. Simultaneously, human numbers multiply exponentially. In 1950 the world numbered two billion people; at the turn of the millennium, six billion. Current projections envision that by the year 2030 there will be ten billion persons on the planet. Earth's human population will have multiplied five times during the average lifetime of a Westerner born in 1950. To translate these statistics into a vivid image: another Mexico City is added every sixty days; another Brazil is added every year.

The capacity of the planet to carry life is being exhausted by these human habits. Not only is our species gobbling up resources faster than Earth's ability to replenish itself, but our practices are causing damage to the very systems that sustain life itself: holes in the ozone layer, polluted air, acid rain, clear-cut forests, drained wetlands, denuded soils, poisoned rivers and lakes, fouled patches of ocean. Appallingly, this widespread destruction of habitats has as its flip side the death of creatures that thrive in these ecosystems. By a conservative estimate, in the last quarter of the twentieth century, at least 10 percent of all living species have gone extinct. When these creatures, these magnificent plants and animals, large and small, go extinct, they never come back again. We are killing birth itself, wiping out the future of fellow creatures who took millions of years to evolve.

A moral universe limited to the human community no longer serves the future of life. Countering the sins of ecocide, biocide, and geocide, theology must listen to the voice of the Earth and take action on behalf of the natural world, even if this goes counter to powerful economic and political interests—and it does. In 1990, Pope John Paul II offered a radical principle: "Respect for life and for the dignity of the human person extends also to the rest of creation."[6] We owe love and justice, in other words, not only to humankind but also to "otherkind." In such ethical reflection, the great commandment to love your neighbor as yourself extends to include all members of the life community. "Save the rain forest" becomes a concrete moral application of the commandment, "Thou shalt not kill." This in turn requires us to probe the deep connections between social injustice and ecological devastation, laying bare how ravaging the land and exploiting the poor go hand in hand. Whether or not theology contributes to a sustainable Earth community is now a matter of life and death.

Doing theology with an ear attuned to the voice of the Earth requires that theology dive deep and find love for the Earth at the very core of Christian faith.

Think of creation: In the beginning God created the heavens and the earth, and pronounced everything *good*. But God did not just create the world and then depart. The Spirit of God, who moved over the original chaos to bring forth the world, continues to dwell within the world, vivifying it, even renewing the face of the Earth. The Earth, it is clear, is the Lord's with all its fullness (Ps 24:1). In Jewish and Christian tradition, the truth of the world is this inner dwelling of the Spirit of God within it. To craft an a-cosmic theology of God is to be ignorant of the divine relationship of transcendent immanence.

Think of incarnation: This same creative Spirit of God overshadowed a young girl in the poor, peasant community of Nazareth. The Word became flesh and dwelt among us! What else does this mean but that God is no longer satisfied to be with us in Word and Spirit only, but becomes one of us in the flesh. The material of this Earth, coalesced from an exploding star and evolved through eons of deep time into life and the human species, becomes God's own body present in history. From now on, God in the flesh becomes part of the history of this cosmos.

Think of resurrection: By the power of the Creator Spirit, the crucified Jesus died not into nothing, but into the hands of the living God. God had the last word, and it was the same as the first: Let there be life! Death now has no more dominion, for his destiny is a pledge of the future for the rest of us. This has cosmic significance. As

Karl Rahner preached in a homily on Easter as the feast of the future of the earth, in Christ risen a piece of this earth, real to the core, is now forever with God in glory. "His resurrection is like the first eruption of a volcano which shows that in the interior of the world God's fire is already burning, and this will bring everything to blessedness in its light. He has risen to show that it has already begun."[7] The future will be on a cosmic scale what has already happened to him.

I rehearse these Christian doctrines, among others, because they hold powerful implications for the meaning of the natural world in a faith context. They coalesce in the view that the world is a *sacrament*, a tangible, material being vivified by the living Spirit, "charged with the grandeur of God," as Gerard Manley Hopkins put it.[8] Seen in this light, the value of creation, now under duress, becomes an intrinsic part of Christian belief, not something added on. And the practice of virtue, which in Christian teaching has always called for love of neighbor and resistance to harm, broadens to include the whole community of life and the ecosystems that make life possible on this planet. A flourishing humanity on a thriving Earth in an evolving universe, all together filled with the glory of God: such is the global vision and praxis theology must work for in this critical age of Earth's distress. Only thus will people be encouraged to become partners rather than unwitting destroyers of the great ongoing saga of life.

Conclusion

The multiple voices emerging in our own society and around the world require tending. Being new, in some cases fragile, tentative, challenging, perhaps filled with anguish, they may tempt us to shut our ears. Such voices require, in Nelle Morton's famous phrase, that we "hear each other into speech."[9] Even attempting to do this opens up new horizons for our theological work. "Horizons" is a wonderful metaphor. The horizon surrounds us all the time, but even in the fastest plane we can never catch it. Moving toward the horizon, though, opens up previously unseen vistas, rich understandings of God and God's gracious ways with the world that bear fruit in loving praxis.

I feel a passionate urgency about the need for theology to engage the real questions of our day. Studying the history of religions, the

German theologian Wolfhart Pannenberg was struck by how many of the religions of the past have disappeared. Who worships Jupiter any more, or Athena or Ra or Baal and Ashtarte? Probing for reasons why, he coined a memorable axiom: *Religions die when their lights fail, that is, when they lose their power to convince.*[10] History is dynamic. In every generation, people have new experiences. If the god they believe in cannot keep up with this ongoing experience, if such a deity cannot unlock a meaningful life in this new context, then people eventually lose heart and let go of the old religious pattern, seeking elsewhere for something that makes more sense. Pannenberg sees the early Christian theological shift from Hebrew to Hellenistic categories as profound evidence that the God of Jesus Christ is the true God who, as Lord of history, can keep pace with the current historical experience of the community.

I put this question to the College Theology Society as a challenge for the next fifty years: Is the God of Jesus Christ so true as to be able to keep pace with twenty-first-century experiences of people in postmodern American society; with the struggles of the materially disenfranchised, of women, of racial and ethnic minorities; with the appreciation of other great religious traditions; with the awakening of ecological care? If not, Christianity will fade away. If yes, it is the work of theology to show how this is the case.

My wager is that we are up to the task. May it be so.

Notes

[1] See Sandra Yocum Mize, "On Writing a History of the College Theology Society," *Horizons: Journal of the College Theology Society* 31/1 (Spring 2004): 94-104.

[2] Bernard Cooke, "Retreat and Advance" (Twenty-Fifth Anniversary Essays), *Horizons: Journal of the College Theology Society* 26/2 (Fall 1999): 276-78; quotation at 277.

[3] Karl Rahner, "Foreword," *Theology and Discovery: Essays in Honor of Karl Rahner, S.J.*, ed. William Kelly, S.J. (Milwaukee: Marquette University Press, 1980), vii.

[4] Mary Catherine Hilkert, *Naming Grace: Preaching and the Sacramental Imagination* (New York: Continuum, 1997); Terrence W. Tilley, *Inventing Catholic Tradition* (Maryknoll, N.Y.: Orbis Books, 2000).

[5] Robert J. Schreiter, *The New Catholicity: Theology between the Global and the Local* (Maryknoll, N.Y.: Orbis Books, 1997), 15.

[6] John Paul II, "The Ecological Crisis: A Common Responsibility," *And*

God Saw That It Was Good: Catholic Theology and the Environment, ed. Drew Christiansen and Walter Grazer (Washington, D.C.: U.S. Catholic Conference, 1996), 222.

[7]Karl Rahner, "Easter: A Faith That Loves the Earth," *The Great Church Year*, ed. Albert Raffelt (New York: Crossroad, 2001), 192-97.

[8]Gerard Manley Hopkins, "God's Grandeur," *A Hopkins Reader*, ed. John Pick (Garden City: Doubleday, 1966), 47.

[9]Nelle Morton, *The Journey Is Home* (Boston: Beacon, 1985), 128.

[10]Wolfhart Pannenberg, "Toward a Theology of the History of Religions," in his *Basic Questions in Theology*, vol. II (Philadelphia: Fortress, 1971): 65-118.

The Future of Theology in the Church

Joseph A. Komonchak

Ordination does not usually carry with it the charism of prophecy, nor does a doctorate in theology or in religious studies. "I am not a prophet or the son of a prophet." I am not going, then, to offer predictions about the future. I intend to offer instead some reflections on how to think about a theology in service to the church in the future. I want to base them on what I know something about: the recent history of theology within the Roman Catholic tradition. The theme of the convention has to do with horizons. Horizons, of course, are limiting factors: we can't see beyond them; we don't know what lies beyond them. Beyond the horizon is the realm of the unknown unknown, as Bernard Lonergan described it. But perhaps how the horizon of theology has been expanded in the recent past may provide some clues as to how to prepare for expansions of our horizons in the future.

"Theology" at the Birth of the College Theology Society

This Society was born under the unwieldy name of the Society of Catholic College Teachers of Sacred Doctrine. It emerged in the midst of a debate as to what to teach undergraduate students and how to teach it. In the discussion one side favored a strictly "scientific," that is, "scholastic" or "academic" approach, by which they meant the same sort of theology that was taught in seminaries at the time, *ad mentem Sancti Thomae*, as it was often put. In fact, this was the only meaning of the word "theology" they were willing to accept. The other side argued instead that religion as taught in Catholic colleges should aim at an existential appropriation of the faith and its application to life. Proponents of this view appeared to have conceded the name "theology" to the other side and spoke instead of teaching "religion" or of "religious education." When this association met for the first time in 1954 and had to decide on a title, to speak of "teachers of theology" would give victory to one side, and so it was decided that the name would be "Society of Catholic College Teachers of Sacred Doctrine."[1]

To describe what was considered theology at the time, permit me an autobiographical reflection. Forty years ago this week students at the Gregorian University in Rome were taking comprehensive examinations for the Licentiate in Sacred Theology. Lesser areas having been disposed of once and for all by exams at the end of each year, this final exam was totally devoted to dogmatic theology. The material covered every course we had taken in the previous four years, all of it neatly made available to us in a little brochure of fifteen pages entitled *Examen peculiare ad Licentiam de universa sacra theologia.*

No fewer than a hundred theses set out the vast area on which we would be examined. For fundamental theology, there were ten theses on Christian revelation; twelve on the church; three on biblical inspiration. Covering the subjects found in the first two parts of the *Summa theologica*, there were eight theses *De Deo uno*, nine *De Deo trino*, and eight *De Deo creante et elevante*, the area where creation and human origins were treated. Covering subjects found in the second and third parts of the *Summa*, there were eleven theses on christology, eight on grace, and six on the virtues. Covering materials found in the third part and in the Supplement to the *Summa*, there were four theses on the sacraments in general, seventeen on the individual sacraments (six on the Eucharist and five on Penance), and four on the last things.

For each of these hundred theses we were expected to be able to defend the proposed thesis and to explain it by defining the terms used, to identify adversaries to it, to provide arguments in favor from Scripture, tradition, the magisterium, and theological reason, to assign it a theological note, and to respond to objections. Four of us went into a room where a Jesuit professor sat in each of the four corners. The exam was oral and conducted, as the course-lectures had been, in Latin. We sat and performed before each of the Jesuits for fifteen minutes until a bell was rung and we moved on to the next examiner. (There are many Jesuits whose time in purgatory has been considerably lessened for having to listen to our babbling, incoherent Latin for eight hours a day for six weeks).

This system has been criticized, not unjustly, on many grounds. (Bernard Lonergan once told me that the pedagogical philosophy of the Gregorian—lectures delivered to hundreds of students in a large hall—was based upon systematic neglect of two inventions: the electric light bulb and the printing press). But before agreeing with some of these criticisms, I would like to mention one or two things that were valuable about this education.

First, it was comprehensive: we learned an awful lot. By the end of four years we had covered just about every area of theology and learned, at however second-hand a level of acquaintance, about the great and lesser controversies that had marked the history of theology from the patristic period on. The general knowledge we gained would provide us with a foundation on which to draw when we went on for further studies. I didn't appreciate how much I had benefited from the education until I found myself doing doctoral studies at Union Theological Seminary in New York alongside students who brought no such general or basic knowledge with them.

Second, the education also emphasized clarity and intellectual rigor, which I continue to think are mental virtues. Distinctions were highly valued,[2] and if at times they were carried to mind-numbing lengths, they also helped cultivate an analytical mind; another benefit was that they could prove useful should a position come under attack for unorthodoxy. Theological notes identified to what degree the church had committed herself to a particular thesis and drove home the point that not all magisterial statements were to be placed on the same level. We were taught by our professors, and saw demonstrated in their own work, how to apply very careful principles for the interpretation of dogmatic statements of councils or popes, what sometimes is dismissed as "minimalism." The whole experience was very beneficial and remains so not least of all when we find ourselves confronted by a revival of maximalism.

On the other hand, and here I enter into a critique, the education was based on textbooks, usually written by our professors, with very little direct contact with the sources. A tradition of two or three hundred years required that certain topics be covered, sometimes, it seemed, simply because they had been covered before. (Karl Rahner noted how little a textbook of 1950 differed from one on the same subject written in 1750, even though "in the last two centuries cultural and spiritual transformations have taken place which, to say the very least, are comparable in depth and extent and power to mould men's lives, with those which took place between the time of Augustine and that of the golden age of scholasticism."³) A premium was placed on clarity of concept and certainty of judgment. Only the exceptional professors, such as Bernard Lonergan, René Latourelle, Juan Alfaro, Zoltan Alszeghy and Maurizio Flick, made personal efforts at systematic understanding. (This sometimes made things difficult at the oral exam. One student had to explain an abstruse thesis of Lonergan to another Jesuit. When he had finished, the examiner said: "*Optime, sed nihil intellexi, neque de tua expositione neque de doctrina patris Lonergan.*" "Very good, but I didn't understand anything, either about your presentation or about the doctrine of Fr. Lonergan."⁴)

The dogmatic theology was built upon a "fundamental theology" that was apologetical in focus, grounding the reasonableness of faith in extrinsic arguments to prove that a divine revelation had taken place in Christ and was now available through the church he had established and endowed with a teaching office that promised the guidance of his Spirit. These arguments provided the only foundations needed—the formal authority of the Scriptures (inspiration and inerrancy) and of the magisterium—for the elaboration of a dogmatic theology over the next three years of study.

Two other criticisms. First, theology was understood to be a "science," an intellectual discipline whose primary purpose was to promote understanding and wisdom. Very little attention was given to drawing out spiritual dimensions of the dogmas treated or their pastoral implications, even though the student body was exclusively seminarians. Second, the theology was meant for domestic consumption within the church. Very little interest was shown in the social, political, and economic realms of contemporary life or in the idea that the church might have a role within them or in their regard. The assumed anthropology was highly individualistic. Redemption meant the salvation of souls for the beatific vision. The relation of Christianity to the collective history of humanity was beyond the horizon of this theology.⁵ Why this was so deserves some reflection.

While Christianity had had enormous consequences for the social, political, and cultural life of the West, no theory of a public transformative role was developed, in part because the sense was lacking that the human race is engaged in a collective self-project in which intelligence and freedom could be exercised for the sake of transforming the physical, economic, social, and cultural conditions in which people live and act. The idea of progress seems to be a modern invention. Unfortunately, it also seems to have emerged at a time when various factors led to the widespread assumption that religion had very little relevance to the task of collective human self-realization in the spheres of science and technology, economics and politics, society and culture. Religion concerned what one did with one's private self. The larger collective self-project could be safely indifferent to the differences among religions and even to those between belief and unbelief, an assumption that, as Henri de Lubac showed in *Surnaturel*, came to be shared by more than a few theologians.

The Catholic Church consistently opposed this privatizing of religion, which it took to be the mortal sin of what it condemned as "liberalism." But, particularly in the century and a half before the Second Vatican Council, its opposition was so global that "progress, liberalism, and recent civilization" could be lumped together, almost as if they were synonyms, in the last proposition condemned in the Syllabus of Errors (1864). This undifferentiated repudiation became the motivating principle of the construction of a sub-culture and sub-society which, in part because it appealed so strongly to the social and cultural reality known as Christendom, seemed to offer only a past ideal as the simple substitute for the liberal idea of human progress. So great was the opposition to this idea and so powerful was the drive to create a countervailing, anti-modern Catholic identity that, paradoxically and often quite contrary to the intentions of popes and bishops, the self-realization of the church at times came to be seen, both inside and outside, as a distinct event, occurring in a separate and differentiated sphere of human life, and without significance for the collective human self-project. Ironically, the Roman Catholicism of the last two centuries was very modern in its anti-modernity.

A classic ecclesiology developed to support this response to modernity. Against the tendency of the modern nation-state to reduce religious groups to simple voluntary associations ultimately subordinate to its own authority to define society and culture, theologians and canonists identified and defended the internal integrity of the church as a separate, autonomous, and self-sufficient—and in that sense "perfect"—society. Against a modern trend toward democracy, they stressed the authority of a hierarchically organized clergy to which they tended to reserve all initiative. To ideas and forces that were international in their appeal and effectiveness, they opposed a universalistic vision of the church as a single people governed from a central headquarters by a sovereign and infallible head in whose hands lay the direction of an increasingly centralized and uniform church polity.

Although this classic ecclesiology was in good part developed in the service of the modern Catholic response to the ideas and forces that were shaping the modern world, it showed surprisingly little interest in the church-world relationship itself. Apart from occasional appendices, *scholia,* or *corollaria* devoted to a rejection of "liberalism," classic ecclesiological treatises treated the church-world relationship in a chapter on church and state. However, right up to the eve of Vatican II, this chapter was devoted to a defense of the church's unique rights, still conceived largely in terms of pre-modern political circumstances ("the Catholic State") and thought to be sufficiently guaranteed by institutional negotiations between the supreme ecclesial and secular authorities (concordats). The larger sphere of church-world relations that includes the responsibilities and activities of Christians in the construction of societies and cultures and in the direction of human history went largely unnoticed in the classical treatises on the church and in the theology constructed for its members.

In this respect the classical modern ecclesiology fell far short of the vision that modern popes had begun to articulate. Under Leo XIII but particularly under Pius XI, the emphasis on church-state relations began to be supplemented by an appeal to Catholic organizations and movements to engage themselves in the effort to win the modern world back to Christ, not only for the sake of the church's freedom to fulfill its distinctive spiritual mission for the salvation of souls but also to address what John Courtney Murray called "the spiritual crisis in the temporal order."[6] The papal support of "Catholic Action," for example, represented an appeal directly to the laity to assume its responsibility for bringing Christian ideas and values to the larger public debate on the character and direction of human history. The church-world relation, in other words, was not to be settled simply by institutional negotiations between sovereign authorities but required an active participation by lay Christians in the collective self-realization of humanity.

It was this appeal that was to inspire and energize the new thinking and new enterprises that would surprise so many people in the debates that defined the drama of the Second Vatican Council. The decade of the 1930s was here crucial.[7] A sense of crisis was nearly universal. Economic depression seemed to confirm the weaknesses of liberal capitalism. The League of Nations collapsed under the weight of revived nationalism. The war fought "to make the world safe for democracy" was followed by the rise of fascist, Nazi, and communist totalitarianisms. With individualism discredited and collectivism threatening, the moment seemed opportune for Catholics to propose a third alternative based upon a distinctive vision of the relationship between person and community derived from a broadened and deepened sense of the scope of Christ's redemptive work and yet not inspired or directed by nostalgia for a pre-modern ideal of Christendom.

Thus it was in the 1930s that Jacques Maritain outlined his notion of a new but "profane" Christendom under the historical ideal of pluralistic and democratic regimes, that Christopher Dawson turned his attention to the relationship between religion and culture, that Marie-Dominique Chenu and Yves Congar began to call for an incarnation of the Gospel into modern milieux from which the church was absent, that Teilhard de Chardin continued to elaborate a cosmic vision of the faith appropriate to the world modern science was revealing, that Henri de Lubac published a book on the social aspects of dogma, that Bernard Lonergan began to sketch a theology of history derived from the Pauline doctrine of the recapitulation of all things in Christ, that John Courtney Murray was imbibing the ideas that would soon lead him to urge upon American Catholics their responsibility for the construction of a Christian culture.

In every one of these cases, an ecclesiology that ignored the church-world relationship, reduced it to pre-modern models of church-state relations, or assigned it principally or even exhaustively to the clergy was implicitly or explicitly criticized. The reality of "the world," of history, began to come to the forefront and to be included in the drama of the human self-project that defines the hermeneutical context in which to communicate and appropriate the Christian Gospel given "for us and for our salvation." This self-project was now understood not merely as the drama of the struggle between sin and grace in an individual's self-realization, but also as including the same dramatic struggle in humanity's collective self-realization. The world was no longer simply the unchanging backdrop against which individual actors played their roles; it was itself the drama that was unfolding. The world was not the stage, but the play itself.

It was the failure of classical theology to contribute to this larger redemptive purpose that explains in part why alternatives were sought, as, for example, in the proposals for a distinct way of teaching the faith in Catholic colleges and universities—the debate with which I began. An early contributor to the debate was John Courtney Murray who himself did not hesitate to call what he was proposing a *theology* for the laity. The two essays in which Murray set out his views in 1944 are still worth reading; even while perhaps disagreeing with Murray's views, readers would benefit from asking themselves what they think a theology for their undergraduate students should be—and whether they have as clear and forceful a vision as he did.[8]

The theology designed to train clerics could not be appropriate for educating lay people, Murray argued. Both kinds stood "in the service of the church," but their forms differed in accordance with the distinct roles of the clergy and the laity. They had distinct finalities. The theology appropriate for the clergy served the need of the church to preserve and defend the faith. Its purpose was primarily intellectual: "the synthesis of all revealed truth, and of revealed truth and philosophic truth."[9] This rigidly logical approach explains its syllogistic style, "the severity of its method," and its polemical edge. A theology for clerics, he concluded, was "that intelligence of faith, especially in its relation to human reason and philosophy, which is required in order that the *magisterium* of the church may be able effectively to preserve, explain, and defend the whole of revealed truth."[10]

What would be a theology in the service of the distinct role of the laity? Murray found that role defined by the tasks assigned to the laity by the modern popes, particularly Pius XI, in their encouragement of various Catholic Action movements. The laity's role was to address "the great 'social transformations' of our times," by which was meant "the secularization of modern life, the gradual development of a complete separation, and, in fact, an active opposition between the spiritual and the temporal, between the church and human society."[11] Unwilling to live a life inwardly directed, the church wanted

an immense penetration of the life of the Church *ad extra*, with the purpose of transforming the total milieu of modern life. Not the isolation of the faithful, nor simply the imposition on them of the duty somehow to live in two separate worlds, but their formation and their organization, according to the very techniques of the milieu they must combat, for the work of recapturing the moral direction of the temporal order, reconstituting a Christian social order, rechristianizing "whole classes" of men, and reanimating with a new spirit the whole complex order of temporal institutions.[12]

Two things were necessary for this to happen: first, "the intensification of the inner life of the church"[13] by drinking as deeply as possible from the sources of her life, the word of God, and the liturgy; second, communicating to the laity the great goal:

> that Christ may reign, not only over men as individuals but over human society in all its groupings . . . through the reconstitution of a social order whose institutions will be conformed to the laws of God and so animated by a Christian dynamism that they will serve at once the eternal salvation of the human person and the stable prosperity of the State.[14]

This task must respect and safeguard both the freedom of the church and the freedom of the secular order, which has a legitimate autonomy. To be avoided are both an " 'angelism' that would consist simply in proclaiming principles and preaching a spirit, without acting toward their incarnation in temporal institutions" and a " 'clericalism' that would involve the immediate shaping of temporal institutions . . . by the sacerdotal order."[15] Hence the distinct role of the laity: "to mediate between the spiritual and temporal." "It is through the layman that there must flow into the world those supernatural energies which, as faith teaches, are necessary in order that man may achieve even his proper humanity—his personal freedom, his social unity."[16]

Murray then encapsulated the differences between the two functions that explain the distinct finalities of the theology they need:

> The ministerial priesthood is to mediate the Holy Spirit to the soul of man; the lay priesthood is to mediate the Christian spirit to the institutions of civil society. The former exercises its mediation in the wholly spiritual order in which the very life of God mysteriously flows into the human soul, to effect its divinization; the latter exercises its mediation in that border-

land of the spiritual and temporal, wherein the life of the Church makes vital contact with the terrestrial life of man, to effect its humanization. The former, as the instrument of Christ, is to bridge the gap created by sin and ignorance between man and God, his Father; the latter, as the instrument of the hierarchy, is to bridge the gap created by secularism between the profane activity of man and the life of the Church, his Mother. The former is instrumentally to rescue man from sin and the peril of losing his soul; the latter is instrumentally to rescue man from social injustice and the peril of losing his humanity on earth.[17]

And another capsule formula sums up the specific finality of a theology for lay people: "That intelligence of faith, especially in its relation to human life and the common good of mankind, which is required in order that the laity of the church may be able effectively to collaborate with the hierarchy in accomplishing the renewal and reconstruction of the whole of modern social life."[18]

Murray insisted that this does not mean "that what the layman needs is a sort of diminished theology, only quantitatively or rhetorically different from that taught in seminaries—a sort of *Summa Theologica* with the hard parts left out."[19] And for that purpose he devoted another lengthy article to the pedagogical implications of a professional course for this distinct lay finality, and here he displayed how familiar he had become with movements of theological and pastoral renewal in the Europe of the late 1930s.

It will be noted that for Murray both types of theology embodied the general notion of theology: "the science of faith in the service of the church."[20] He considered theology "an essentially ecclesiastical science; it is social in its origin, in the collective faith of the church; and it is social in its function—it exists for the benefit of the life of the church, for the building up of her Body."[21] He could not imagine theology as a private exercise, as, perhaps, one might imagine philosophy. One did theology within a community and its tradition and for the sake of that community and its mission.

No doubt we today would have some criticisms to offer to Murray's way of putting things, particularly perhaps too sharp a disjunction between the sacred and the temporal and a corresponding but overly strict differentiation of the roles of clergy and laity. Developments since the Council have seen the collapse of the paradigm of the theology for clerics that Murray described. One of the consequences of the Council's call for the reinvigoration of theology has been that it is seen as far more in the service of the vitality of the church in herself and of the effectiveness of her mission in the world. In addition, theology has moved from being primarily a task undertaken by clerics for clerics, with its typical location in a seminary, to being an activity eagerly undertaken by the laity, women and men alike, with its typical location, perhaps, back in the university. For all these reasons Murray's particular way of characterizing the two functions of theology does not hold up very well today.

At the end of his second article on a theology for lay people, "Towards a Theology for the Layman: The Pedagogical Problem," Murray wondered whether reflection on a lay theology might illuminate the nature of clerical theology as well.[22] One could say that the remark has been vindicated in the meantime. After the difficult trial over the so-called *nouvelle théologie*, which could be described as the last victory of the entrenched notion of theology, the Second Vatican Council transformed the theological scene.

The Second Vatican Council

Pope John XXIII led the way to transforming theology in his opening speech. He declared his disagreement with "prophets of doom" who saw nothing in the modern world but prevarication and ruin; he called the Council at once to preserve the ancient doctrinal heritage and to present it with an eye to contemporary conditions; he distinguished between the substance of the faith and the manner in which it is articulated; he called for a positive presentation of the faith instead of a set of condemnations; he wanted the Council's exercise of the supreme magisterium to be primarily pastoral.

The bishops took up the challenge. By an overwhelming majority (97 percent!), they voted for substantial pastoral reform in the liturgy. By just short of a two-thirds vote they rejected the first of the doctrinal texts brought before them, the schema *De fontibus revelationis*, and by this vote, as their comments made clear, they indicated at least what they did *not* want: texts that did little more than ratify the defensive, suspicious, and even condemnatory attitude that had marked the papal magisterium for the previous century and a half and showed little imprint of the new theological and pastoral orientations that had been surfacing over the previous thirty years. They wanted to say something different in attitude, in content, and in style.

What that something different should be was less easily decided. "The preparatory work was unsatisfactory," Joseph Ratzinger wrote, "and the Council rejected the extant texts. But the question at this point was: What now?"[23] Over the next three sessions, as the Council hammered out its sixteen texts, differences began to be discerned in the so-called progressive majority of bishops and theologians.[24] They became particularly visible during the redaction of *Gaudium et spes*, the Pastoral Constitution on the Church in the Modern World. One group, largely French-speaking, drafted a text that would look at contemporary developments and movements for what one of its inspirers, Marie-Dominique Chenu, called *pierres d'attente*, toothing stones, stones placed in expectation of an eventual addition to a building. In those large social and cultural movements could be discerned aspirations for the Gospel and for the redeemed and reconciled human community that only it could disclose and only God's grace could accomplish through the mediation of the church. These were, Chenu said, the equivalent on the larger public level of what scholastics had called "obediential potency" for the supernatural in the individual.

Another group, largely German-speaking and including such major figures as Karl Rahner and Joseph Ratzinger, found this text far too optimistic, almost Teilhardian in its credulity with regard to modern science and technology. It made use of an uncritical epistemology. It worked with an inadequate understanding of the relation between the natural and the supernatural. It was far from what Rahner called "the necessary Christian pessimism." It minimized the reality and the force of sin and neglected that Christian conversion is by way of the cross. Ratzinger found some of its statements almost Pelagian and he thought the text had purchased dialogue at the expense of the *kerygma*.

A third group, smaller than the other two, one might call evangelical. It was represented by Giuseppe Dossetti, an Italian priest who had played important roles in Italian politics before ordination, and who served at the Council as the chief adviser to Cardinal Lercaro of Bologna. (One will get some sense of his views if one tries to imagine what the agenda of Vatican II might have been like had it been set by Dorothy Day.) Dossetti was fiercely critical of the draft of *Gaudium et spes*. Its analysis of contemporary situations, he said, was journalistic, a set of sociological commonplaces. Christ appears in each chapter almost as an afterthought. What was needed was "the Gospel *sine glossa.*" Only it could loosen the institutional and theological knots that had crippled the church's preaching and life. The timorous approach to the question of war and peace in the document, Dossetti said, typified the Council's failure to go back to the integral Gospel and to undertake the ecclesiastical reforms it demands.

The theological scene as the Council ended, then, was rather more complex than the one often described in Manichean terms of progressives vs. conservatives. Its most dramatic feature was the astoundingly rapid collapse of the neo-scholastic paradigm. And it is very striking to anyone able to look back over fifty years of theological development in the Catholic Church that no paradigm has emerged to take its place. Instead a plurality of approaches to the theological task prevails, as is both described and celebrated in Elizabeth Johnson's essay in this volume.

On the one hand, the Council's refusal of the traditional academic language; its preference for more biblical, patristic, and liturgical emphases and styles; the reduced role it assigned to St. Thomas Aquinas; its stated openness to new methods and forms of thought— all of this served to legitimate the currents of thought that the neo-scholastics had, quite recently, stigmatized for their novelty, when in fact they represented an effort to recover for common Catholic consciousness the ways of thinking and expressing that had prevailed during the first Christian millennium and that Henri de Lubac had said were unfairly dismissed as simply "pre-scientific." The pioneers of the theological revival appeared to have triumphed in Vatican II's constitutions on the liturgy, on the church, and on divine revelation.

On the other hand, another current emerged from the Council that took its main inspiration from the conciliar texts that oriented the church toward the world, particularly the Pastoral Constitution on the Church in the Modern World (*Gaudium et spes*) and the Declaration on Religious Freedom (*Dignitatis humanae*), documents that Yves Congar considered to be distinctively Thomist. The Council had not yet ended when one heard of a theology of secularization, then of a political theology, and then of a liberation theology that itself developed in several directions. A genealogy of these movements would be able to trace some of them back to the thought of bearers of the Thomist tradition such as Karl Rahner and Edward Schillebeeckx. But what might be called "the political turn" that characterized this kind of theology moved the focus of attention to the collective human project and asked what the Gospel of redemption had to say about human development and liberation.

The Church after the Council

Various efforts have been made to characterize these two orientations of post-conciliar Catholic theology. David Tracy has used a distinction between manifestation-theology and correlation-theology.[25] Some have proposed a distinction between a *ressourcement*-approach and an *aggiornamento*-approach. I have floated the hypothesis that they may be traced to the differences between a characteristically patristic or Augustinian orientation and an approach more Thomist in inspiration.

After two decades when the method of correlation dominated, a reaction has set in that favors the epiphanic method. Among graduate students today there is far more interest in the thought of Hans Urs von Balthasar than in that of Karl Rahner or Bernard Lonergan, and the movement that has styled itself "Radical Orthodoxy," of course, runs in the same direction. And, for the moment, in certain circles in Rome an approach prevails that almost denies the need for cultural mediations of the faith and opts instead for "the positivity of Christianity."

It would appear that the two orientations roughly correspond to two dimensions of the church that at the Council were described as the "*Ecclesia ad intra*," the church in her inner life, and the "*Ecclesia ad extra*," the church in her relation to the world. This is not an entirely happy distinction, particularly if it threatens to become a separation, or if one is expected to choose between them. On the other hand, the two dimensions do correspond to the answers to two different questions: "What makes the church the church?" and "What should the church be doing in the world?" But, of course, the fact is that there is no church except in the world. The remainder of this essay will focus on this topic, and what it means for theology.[26]

Both historically and theologically, what we call the Christian Church arose and arises out of the event of Jesus Christ. The church is the *congregatio fidelium*, the assembly of those who believe that Jesus of Nazareth, who was crucified, has been made both Lord and Christ by his resurrection from the dead. This very statement so closely ties the church and Christ as to suggest a clarification of the first sentence in this paragraph. It is not enough to say that the church arose and arises out of the event of Jesus Christ: the emergence of the church, both historically and theologically, is a dimension of the event of Jesus Christ. John Knox was so aware of this as to say something at first very startling: that the emergence of the church *is* the event of Jesus Christ.[27] The only thing one could point to as different in the world before and after Jesus of Nazareth was the existence of the community of believers. The church is the difference Jesus of Nazareth has made and makes in human history. Had the church not arisen, what might count as "the event of Jesus of Nazareth"—if indeed one could speak of such a thing in that case—would have been considerably different from what, both historically and theologically, it did in fact become.

It was in fact through the church that Jesus of Nazareth became an historic figure, an agent of history. It was Christians who preserved the memory of his mere existence, who remembered his words and his deeds, who proclaimed him to have conquered death and to have become Messiah, Lord, and Savior, who interpreted him as the enfleshment of the very Word of God, who understood their own communal experience as a fellowship in his Spirit that made them members of his very Body, who undertook to bring others into communion with him and with his Father, who invited those to whom they spoke to make him the principle and the criterion of a redirected personal and collective history. The church made Jesus of Nazareth an historically significant figure.

Once a narrowly eschatological interpretation of his significance faded and Christians settled in for the long haul of history, the scope of Christ's redemptive influence came to be seen also to transcend the boundaries of the Judaism from which Jesus had come and to require the mission to the Gentiles and the effort to evangelize the society and culture of the Greco-Roman world. From then on, the inward necessity, for the sake of the church's own integrity, to keep alive the memory of Jesus Christ and to proclaim his saving power, has also been an outward engagement with culture and history, and it was always theologically unsound and sociologically naive to think that his significance could be reduced to the sphere of the personal and private or to the dimensions of a sect.

The history of that engagement with history and culture is, of course, as complex and ambiguous as is the history of the encounter of individuals with Christ. More than once, in both histories, the

Gospel and its grace did not succeed in completely overcoming ignorance and embedded sinfulness. Compromise and mediocrity have
never been rare, which is why *heroic* sanctity is required of candidates for canonization. But as this does not deter the church from
continuing to preach Christ and to call for the conversion of individuals, so the ambiguity of past encounters with culture and history
should not suggest that the church leave off the task of the redemption of the entire human project.

The intrinsic link between concern for the integrity of the church
as the *congregatio fidelium* and commitment to the redemption of
history is clear also from a consideration of the process and of the
agents of the church's self-realization. As the church first arose out of
the conviction that Jesus of Nazareth had been raised from the dead,
so it continues to arise from the communication and appropriation
of the word of life: "What we have seen and heard we proclaim to
you so that you too may have fellowship with us, and our fellowship
is with the Father and with his Son, Jesus Christ" (1 Jn 1:3). The
witness of one generation of believers evokes the faith of a new generation and this process reproduces, extends, and widens the communion that first came to be out of the event of Easter and Pentecost.
Everything else about the church—its Scriptures, its creeds, its worship and sacraments, its structures, its laws—exists in order to prepare for, to promote, to safeguard, and to articulate in words, deeds,
and relationships the distinctive communion that arises out of the
witness to and appropriation of the centering grace of God that was
in Christ Jesus.[28]

Now when, as described above, the world is understood not simply as the arena of human history but precisely as the drama of human history, this requires also a corresponding notion of the church.
What does it mean now to speak of the church "in" the world? The
preposition is no longer spatial, as if "the world" means simply the
physical or even social "place" in which the church comes to be.
"The world" in its most significant theological sense means now what
human beings have made of themselves, for good and for ill; and,
since that is never something accomplished once and for all, it means
what human beings are now making of themselves and what they are
about to make of themselves. That is the world "in" which the church
comes to be. The event of the church's self-realization is a moment in
the world's self-realization; it is one of the possible things which human beings can make of themselves, can do with their freedom. The

self-realization of the church as the community that results from the communication and appropriation of the Gospel is an event within, and a choice with regard to, the self-realization of humanity.

The church is also, of course, a *differentiation* within the world's self-realization. This portion of humanity is brought together by the announcement of what God has done in Christ and by the appropriation of that message as the word of life. No other portion of humanity is distinguished by this word and faith, which is what grounds the meaning of the word "world" that associates it with those who have either not yet accepted or have rejected the message of Christ. But in the sense in which I have been using the term above, the church arises within the world and as a differentiation of the world: that portion of the world who believe. With the church the world—history—is different; without the church, the world—history—is different; the church remains the difference Jesus Christ makes in human history, in the world. Through the church he remains an historical agent.

It is not, then, as if there is a first moment in which the church comes to be and then a second moment when it takes a stance in and with regard to the world. The very coming-to-be of the church is already an engagement in history, a decision in the drama that makes the world what it is. In faith, to appropriate the Gospel is to take a stand before the great questions that define any historical moment; it is to identify in the God and Father of the Lord Jesus Christ the origin, center, and goal of human life; it is to recognize the power of sin in oneself and in the world; it is to acknowledge the possibility of forgiveness and reconciliation; it is to have hope that no evil, not even death, not even sin, is stronger or more certain than the power of God; it is to commit oneself to a love that reflects the love of God that has turned one's life around; it is to enter into a community where all this is believed, treasured, celebrated, and made the generative center of common commitments. None of this is simply an individual's experience of transformation; as personal as it is, it is an event that transforms one's interpretation and evaluation of the world, a disclosure of new possibilities for the realization not simply of oneself, but of the world. It is a redefined world that one discovers in the decision of faith.

To what does the church refer in this understanding? Who is the church? The church refers here to the *congregatio fidelium*; it is the whole company of believers who are the church living in distinct local assemblies. The word "church" refers to the totality of people who have been brought into apostolic communion with those who first heard and saw the word of life. The church does not mean first or even chiefly the clergy or the hierarchy: it means the assembly of believers, within which there are, of course, differentiations based on sacraments and charisms. But it is crucial to keep in the foreground of one's mind the comprehensive, inclusive meaning of the word "church" to refer to the whole portion of humanity that has appropriated the Gospel of Christ.

Much ecclesiology presupposes a narrower referent of the word "church," particularly by using it to refer to the clergy, to the canonical structures and institutions, or to the sacramental activities in which its distinctive reality is celebrated in thanksgiving. But an ecclesiology should not be based upon a systematic neglect of the fact that over 99 percent of the members of the church are not ordained leaders of the community of faith and that they live most of their Christian lives outside of formal liturgical services, in what is called "the world." It is there that their Christian lives either do make a difference or do not; it is there and through these Christians that Christ continues to be powerful in human history or does not; it is through them that the world is different because of Christ or is not.

Theologians in and for the Church

Now, how may one describe the role of theologians within the church so conceived? I will assume a very simple definition of Christian theology as critical and systematic reflection on the event of Christ, understanding by the last phrase all those realities that prepared for, constituted, and follow from the event of Jesus of Nazareth confessed as Lord and Savior.

The first thing to note is that the theologian's task is a differentiation within a common enterprise undertaken in many ways and by many other people. There was a church before there were theologians in any strict sense, and, in many circumstances, a church can accomplish its purposes in the world without the presence of theologians.

Second, however, theology arises out of certain exigencies intrinsic to the common Christian enterprise. There is, first, the spontaneous desire to understand as fully as possible what one believes, what one has been given, what one finds oneself loving. Because faith is neither sight nor rationally compelled judgment, it does not quiet our mind's restlessness but urges it on to inquiry and thought.[29] Because faith discloses a new world of great depth and breadth and a new self within it, there is no lack of things about which to ask questions. There is also the need, stated already in the New Testament, "to give an explanation (*apologia*) to anyone who asks you for a reason (*logos*) for the hope that is within you" (1 Pt 3:15). With the Christian church a new praxis is introduced, an existential orientation derived from hope, that poses questions to others, and Christians have an obligation to answer them "with gentleness and respect." Finally, there is the need to defend the Gospel both from misunderstandings of it within the church and from attacks from without. A move toward critical and reflective thought, then, is native to Christian faith and produces the differentiated task that would eventually be called Christian theology.

Third, theology, as I am here discussing it, is in the service of the church's redemptive presence and role in the world. It arises from within a community convinced that Jesus Christ is the Savior of the world, and the event and message on which it reflects is meant to have an effect upon the course of human history. Theology is thus one of the ways in which the church seeks to be the sign and instrument by which Christ continues to be historically effective.

This is a point that needs stressing today. On the one hand, one senses a tendency to loosen the ties of theology to the church, either because of fear of or resentment toward church authorities, because of perceived institutional inertia, because of scandalous actions or failures to act, or because of a desire to be accommodating to broader criteria of intellectual discipline. What one does, then, in one's research or teaching is simply not thought of as ecclesially significant: "church" is something that happens elsewhere. ("I'm doing theology, not catechetics," I once heard a college professor claim—as if catechesis were not a worthwhile life-long project, as if even courses in "remedial Catholicism" were beneath him.) On the other hand, some people defend a notion of theology that relates it nearly exclusively to the domestic service of the church. Justified concern for the substantial integrity of the community of faith takes the appearance of a deliberate defiance of intellectual criteria accepted elsewhere. It can thus appear that the theologian has to choose between primary communities and their respective criteria of loyalty. But if the church is the bearer of a word that is intended for the redemption of human history, this is an impossible choice.

David Tracy has usefully distinguished three audiences to which theologians may address themselves: society and culture, the academy, and the church itself. Primary reference to each of these audiences yields also a distinction between practical, fundamental, and systematic theology.[30] It is clear from his book that Tracy's distinctions are not meant to be taken as separations, something confirmed by simple reflection, first, on the church and, second, on the situation of the theologian. The church is indeed the bearer of the distinctive Christian message from generation to generation, but it is this only by embodying it in the lives of communities engaged in history, society, and culture. In every past age one never encounters the church except as the church-in-the-world, and one never confronts an articulation of the faith that has not been expressed in specific cultural terms and as a response to historical challenges and opportunities. Similarly, in the present moment the church comes to be only in the several local communities living in their several worlds and facing the decision whether or not to differentiate themselves there in a faith and praxis derived from and carrying forward the event of Christ. The church has never been "world-less," and even the most sectarian effort to "go out from among them" is a decision within a world and with respect to that world, a decision that makes that world something different. A theology that is principally concerned to serve the church with systematic reflection on its message must also be an engagement with society and culture.

Furthermore, critical intellectual exigencies are dimensions of a culture, and their institutionalization today in the academy represents a particular historical praxis. In a culture in which these exigencies have developed, a church has no choice but to engage them, something it does even when it is repudiating them, as Tertullian claimed to do when he counterposed Jerusalem and Athens. The broad Catholic tradition has, however, refused that antithesis and chosen to follow rather the examples of Justin Martyr, Clement of Alexandria, and Origen. It is true that after the collapse of the cultural institutions of antiquity, theology was located principally in monasteries, but it should be remembered that these houses were the chief centers of education and learning in the early Middle Ages. Later, when economic, social, and cultural developments led to the establishment of the medieval universities, theology quite appropriately moved there also and became "scholastic," that is, academic. It should also be noted, as Chenu repeatedly stressed, that this move in both the social location and in the methods of theology represented the church's incarnational and redemptive response to the social and cultural transformations known as the renaissance of the twelfth century.[31]

For theologians today to address the concerns of the academy, then, does not represent a new or alien enterprise, nor need it mean a preference for that audience over the other two audiences, the church and society. A modern university represents one practical way in which modern societies have chosen to articulate the social distribution of knowledge. Universities do not only transmit a society's cultural heritage to new generations, they subject it to critical reflection, and through a variety of disciplines they also sponsor research that affects the possibilities of transforming the conditions, from the physical to the cultural, in which their society shall live. Universities, in other words, are part of the constitutive praxis of societies. In the circumstances of modern societies, were the church not engaged in the academy it could not effectively serve its redemptive purpose in history. A theologian's engagement with the academy, then, does not remove him or her from either the church or society. To the contrary, it represents one of the ways in which the church tries to embody in contemporary society the redemptive light and power of the Gospel. Academic excellence is a needed dimension of the work of redemption.

Theologians belong to all three of the worlds represented by Tracy's three audiences. As believers they belong to the church; as dedicated to critical and systematic reflection, they accept certain rational exigencies that define a science or a discipline, which today are institutionalized in the academy; and as individual persons they are not only responsible for what they make of themselves but also participants in the great collective enterprise that forms their society and culture. To withdraw from the church is to cease to be a Christian theologian; to repudiate standards of critical reflection is to cease being a theologian; to think one can abstain from the collective engagement is an illusion only conceivable on indefensible notions of the self, the world, and history.

Perhaps it would be possible to aim one's theology principally at the academic audience or at the larger society, with no interest in the audience that is the church. I do not think, however, that it is possible to put one's theology at the service of the church without also adhering to the canons of scholarship and without engaging the larger world. And the reason is that there is an inner link between the church's distinctive life and discipline and her mission in the world. The church's nature and mission are not separable; the church's nature only exists, is only realized, in its mission in the world. What the church becomes in virtue of its most divine and distinctive principles is an event within and in relationship to the world. And this means that this relationship with the world is an inner dimension and implication both of the hermeneutical event by which the church is reborn in faith each day and of the internal relations that characterize its members. A community is only the church in a redemptive relationship with a world.

This is not to say that it is the world that defines the church. Within the world of human history the church is a differentiation that is defined by normative reference to Jesus Christ. Where this distinctive normative reference is lacking or is compromised, it is something other than the church that emerges within history, and the world lacks the redemptive word and grace of Christ. It is the worst of mistakes to think that concern for the integrity of faith, for the liberating power of hope, and for the comprehensiveness of love is somehow a retreat from the world. What the world needs for the redemption of its historical project is a church that is faithful to its own originating center, proclaimed, interpreted, and appropriated as the word of life for all circumstances and challenges. To be, by one's research and teaching, of service to that event is a worthwhile way of living one's life.

Notes

¹For the context in which the Society was formed, see Philip Gleason, *Contending with Modernity: Catholic Higher Education in the Twentieth Century* (New York: Oxford University Press, 1995), 256-60, which includes a bibliography.

²At his oral examination in moral theology, David Tracy was asked to give the definition of sin and the distinctions in its regard that could be found in our textbook. David proceeded to rattle off the eleven grounds on which Zalba had made his distinctions. By the time he had finished, time had expired, and David was spared any further questions. Zalba distinguished sin on the basis of cause (original and personal), nature (habitual and actual), mode (commission and omission), manifestation (external and internal), constitution (formal and material), responsibility (out of ignorance, weakness, or malice), attention (deliberate and half-deliberate), motive (carnal and spiritual), object sinned against (God, oneself, another person), special disorder (sins against the Holy Spirit, sins crying to heaven or capital sins),

and effect (mortal and venial); see Marcellinus Zalba, *Theologiae Moralis Compendium* (Madrid: Biblioteca de Autores Cristianos, 1958), 424-25. This "compendium" was in two volumes of 1,459 and 1,018 pages.

[3]Karl Rahner, "The Prospect for Dogmatic Theology," *Theological Investigations* (Baltimore: Helicon Press, 1961), I:2.

[4]Severino Dianich a colloquio con Valentino Maraldi, *Una Chiesa dentro la storia* (Milan: Ancora, 2004), 21.

[5]Bernard Lonergan's treatise *De verbo incarnato* did have a cryptic reference to Christ's historical causality, but he never developed it and one has to look to scattered remarks elsewhere in his writings for what it might have become.

[6]John Courtney Murray, "Towards a Theology for the Layman: The Problem of Its Finality," *Theological Studies* 5 (1944): 43-75; "Towards a Theology for the Layman: The Pedagogical Problem," *Theological Studies* 5 (1944): 340-76; quotation at 341.

[7]See Joseph A. Komonchak, "Returning from Exile: Catholic Theology in the 1930s," in *The Twentieth Century: A Theological Overview*, ed. Gregory Baum (Maryknoll, N.Y.: Orbis Books, 1999), 35-48.

[8]See note 6.

[9]Murray, "Towards a Theology for the Layman: The Problem of Its Finality," 57.

[10]Ibid., 63.

[11]Ibid., 66.

[12]Ibid., 67-68.

[13]Ibid., 69.

[14]Ibid.

[15]Ibid., 70.

[16]Ibid., 71.

[17]Ibid., 73-74.

[18]Ibid., 75.

[19]Ibid., 74.

[20]Murray, "Towards a Theology for the Layman: The Pedagogical Problem," 340.

[21]Murray, "Towards a Theology for the Layman: The Problem of Its Finality," 47.

[22]Cf. Murray, "Towards a Theology for the Layman: The Pedagogical Problem," 375.

[23]Joseph Ratzinger, *Theological Highlights of Vatican II* (New York: Paulist Press, 1966), 148; originally published as *Die letze Sitzungsperiode des Konzils* (Cologne: Bachem, 1966).

[24]I have described some of these differences in my 2003 lecture for the Catholic Common Ground Initiative, "Is Christ Divided? Dealing with Diversity and Disagreement," *Origins* 33/9 (July 17, 2003): 140-47; a fuller statement is in "Le valutazioni sulla *Gaudium et spes*: Chenu, Dossetti,

Ratzinger," in *Volti di fine Concilio: Studi di storia e teologia sulla conclusione del Vaticano II*, ed. Joseph Doré and Alberto Melloni (Bologna: Il Mulino, 2000), 115-53.

[25]David Tracy, "The Uneasy Alliance Reconceived: Catholic Theological Method, Modernity and Post-modernity," *Theological Studies* 50 (1989): 548-70.

[26]What follows draws heavily on my article, "Theologians in the Church," in *Church and Theology: Essays in Memory of Carl J. Peter* (Washington: The Catholic University of America Press, 1995), 63-87.

[27]"The only difference between the world as it was just after the event and the world as it had been just before is that the church was now in existence. A new kind of human community had emerged; a new society had come into being. There was absolutely nothing besides. This new community held and prized vivid memories of the event in which it had begun. It had a new faith; that is, it saw the nature of the world and of God in a new light. It found in its own life the grounds—indeed anticipatory fulfillments—of a magnificent hope. But the memory, the faith, and the hope were all its own; they had neither existence nor ground outside the community. Only the church really existed. Except for the church the event had not occurred"; John Knox, *The Early Church and the Coming Great Church* (London: Epworth Press, 1957), 45.

[28]Compare Thomas Aquinas on the new Law, *Summa theologica*, Ia-IIae, q. 106.

[29]For a description of Aquinas's effort to combine Aristotelian epistemology and Augustinian religious psychology, see M.-D. Chenu, "La psychologie de la foi dans la théologie du XIIe siècle: Genèse de la doctrine de saint Thomas, Somme théologique, IIa IIae, q. 2, a. 1," in *La parole de Dieu, I. La foi dans l'intelligence* (Paris: Cerf, 1964), 77-104.

[30]David Tracy, *The Analogical Imagination: Christian Theology and the Culture of Pluralism* (New York: Crossroad, 1981), esp. 3-98.

[31]See M.-D. Chenu, *Une école de théologie: le Saulchoir* (Paris: Cerf, 1985).

New Horizons in Moral Theology

Norbert Rigali

An important but generally unnoted fact about moral theology is that the term "moral theology" is no longer the univocal term that it was for centuries. While it originally named and referred exclusively to a specific science, in more recent times the term has come to be used generically. One example of its contemporary ambiguity appears in a recent work where moral theology is divided into seven historical periods: "1) patristics; 2) penitentials; 3) scholasticism; 4) confessional manuals; 5) casuistry; 6) moral manuals; and 7) contemporary moral theology."[1]

It is true, of course, that in these seven modes or eras moral matters have been addressed by Christians in one way or another. And there is nothing unusual about introducing a treatise or academic course on moral theology by noting the different stages of moral thought in church history. But designating these as phases of moral theology rather than as diverse kinds of moral reflection and, for the most part, historical antecedents of the science of moral theology has its drawbacks. First, it involves an anachronistic use of the term "moral theology," which originally appeared at the end of the sixteenth century to name a new discipline independent of dogmatic theology. And, second, it obscures the identity of this science by applying its name to a number of other kinds of Christian reflection on moral matters.

While I will return to the lately acquired ambiguity of this term, this preliminary observation is meant to clarify the perspective of the present essay, which focuses on the science of moral theology. To it I look back, and from it I look to the present and to what appears to lie ahead.

Moral Theology as a Science

In the manuals of moral theology with which this science was identified from its inception until the eve of the Second Vatican Council, theologians defined moral theology as the science of human acts inasmuch as these are to be ordered to God as the ultimate end.[2] Human acts constituted—in Aristotelian terms—the material object of the science, and its formal object was the prescribed ordering of these acts to God as ultimate end.

The science was a creature of its times. In the Counter-Reformation the Council of Trent had called for the establishing of seminaries for the spiritual formation and education of future priests and had also decreed that in the Sacrament of Penance the penitent was to confess each mortal sin according to its species and number. In the execution of these mandated reforms moral theology manuals came into existence. Developed as a means of preparing seminarians to be ministers of the Sacrament of Penance and of providing priests ongoing assistance in the carrying out of their sacramental ministry, the manuals presented a new moral science, separated from both dogmatic theology and ascetical theology.

Since the confessor's role in the sacrament had been understood at Trent as largely that of a judge, the new science immediately became what has been characterized as "a moral theology just for solutions of cases in the confessional."[3] Or to borrow the colorful language of Richard McCormick, moral theology was seminary-controlled, sin-centered, and confession-oriented.[4] And its long-term effect was, as J. Augustine DiNoia points out, the practically undisputed reign for nearly four hundred years of a legalism of Catholic life and sacramental practice in which morality was understood "not in terms of good and evil but of the permitted and the forbidden" and "moral norms were viewed more as laws to be enforced and obeyed than as principles for a good life, lived in view of God's invitation to ultimate communion."[5]

Although the long reign of the legalism of moral theology was practically undisputed and unchallenged, it was, nevertheless, not absolutely so. From time to time there were theologians who attempted to reform the discipline, among whom, in the nineteenth century, were John Michael Sailer and John Baptist Hirscher and, in the twentieth, Fritz Tillman and Gerard Gilleman.[6] But if the works of such theologians were signs of things to come, it was Bernard Häring who more than anyone else set in motion the transformation of moral theology that would eventually be sanctioned officially by the church at the Second Vatican Council.

The year in which Pope John XXIII first announced the Council, 1959, was also the year in which the fifth German edition of Häring's summa of Christian morality, *Das Gesetz Christi*, appeared. First published just five years earlier, this enormously popular work went through three printings in its first year and appeared in French the following year. It was soon rendered into thirteen other languages, with the English version, *The Law of Christ*, appearing in 1963, shortly after the beginning of the Council.[7]

An Early Attempt at Reform

Even the titling of Häring's monumental preconciliar work—*The Law of Christ: Moral Theology for Priests and Laity*—suggests that the term "moral theology" is being given quite a different meaning. The title reveals that the science now has a Christocentric focus, and the subtitle discloses what is already implicit in the title: moral theology is no longer a seminary science but a discipline for Christians in general. When early in the course of the book, then, a definition of moral theology is called for, the definition Häring presents is, as one might expect, far removed from any the authors of the moral theology manuals would have recognized. Moral theology has become "the doctrine of the imitation of Christ, as the life in, with, and through Christ."[8]

The Law of Christ constituted, to be sure, only a rudimentary phase in the transformation of moral theology. This limitation Häring himself would recognize when, a quarter of a century later, he published not a revised edition of the book but instead a new three-volume work, *Free and Faithful in Christ*. Nevertheless, *The Law of Christ* did bring about an all-important "Christocentric turn" for Catholic moral thought.

By the time the Second Vatican Council was preparing its "Decree on the Training of Priests," many Council Fathers had become so dissatisfied with the legalism of moral theology that they were hoping to have the Council prohibit the legalistic manuals. As a *peritus* of the Council at the time, Häring was consulted by the responsible commission. Not wanting the Council to act through condemnation, he drafted a brief statement about the reform of moral theology and suggested the Council use it instead.[9] His draft statement was accepted into the Council decree and became its often-cited passage about moral theology:

> Special care should be given to the perfecting of moral theology. Its scientific presentation should draw more fully on the teaching of holy Scripture and should throw light upon the exalted vocation of the faithful in Christ and their obligation to bring forth fruit in charity for the life of the world.[10]

Häring understood *The Law of Christ* as an effort to perfect the science of moral theology. He sought to conform his work to the pattern Vatican II would prescribe—at his suggestion—for priestly training. He seems not to have realized that he was not perfecting the Counter-Reformation science of moral theology, but in fact creating a new theological discipline centered on the Christian life. Even as he presented his essentially transformed definition of moral theology, he seemed unaware that he was moving into a new science. To redefine a science, nevertheless, is in fact to present a different science. A science is specified through its material and formal objects, and to change these is to move from one science into another. Whereas moral theology was previously seen as a science of human acts in relation to God as ultimate end, Häring was pursuing a science of Christian life as "life in, with, and through Christ."

Even if he failed to realize that his proposed science of Christian life as imitation of Christ would be a discipline distinct from traditional moral theology, Häring could not fail to recognize that he was attempting to do something theologically quite different from what his predecessors had done. Traditional moral theology treated individual human acts in relation to God as humans' ultimate end. Häring treated of human life in Christ. If the term "moral theology" could cover both these disciplines, then it could also be extended to cover diverse modes of reflection on morality. Häring introduced this generic use of "moral theology" in the opening chapter of *The Law of Christ*, "Historical Survey of Moral Theology." In sum, the term "moral theology" had three meanings in *The Law of Christ*: (1) it was the name of the Counter-Reformation science; (2) it referred to the theological reflection that Häring considered to be a perfecting of that science but was in fact material of another, nascent science of the

Christian life; and (3) the term was applied generically to both these things together with all the other modes of Christian reflection on moral matters throughout the history of the church.

Thus, into theological reflection on morality *The Law of Christ* introduced both Christocentrism and ambiguity. But introducing ambiguity undermines the stability of science. Hence, Häring's work opened the way not only to progress but also to some adverse consequences in moral theology.

Had he recognized that moral theology was a time-bound science whose time had run out, and had he correctly identified his own work as attempting to create a new theological discipline, Häring might have proposed to the Second Vatican Council a statement significantly different from the one that appeared in the conciliar "Decree on the Training of Priests." And if Vatican II had called theologians to create a new theological science of Christian life instead of summoning them to the perfecting of what was in fact an obsolete discipline, perhaps the course of much early post-Vatican II theology would have been quite different from what it actually was.

If they had been aware of the need to create a new science determining their postconciliar agenda, theologians concentrating on moral concerns might have found that their immediate task was to work toward a consensus in conceiving and defining the aborning science and in determining its methodology in general and relative to biblical scholarship in particular. While Häring's conception of a science of "the imitation of Christ, as the life in, with, and through Christ" might have served as a point of departure in the task, this definition of the discipline would have needed to be refined using concepts and terms more congenial to scientific inquiry. And from the start it would have been clear that many elements from moral theology—terms, concepts, principles, and so on—would eventually be reintroduced into the new science, but with necessarily transformed meanings and functions.

The situation in which post-Vatican II moral theology actually emerged, however, was one of identity confusion. Among moral theologians there was in fact no longer a consensus as to precisely what their science was and how it was to be defined and pursued. The term "moral theology" had lost its attachment to a specific science and become a generalized term. It was possible for theologians to go about their work without having to address or even to recognize the underlying lack of consensus.

Revisionist Moral Theology

Reflected in the work of theologians, of course, was the ambiguity that had been introduced into the discipline's identity. Some theologians perceived the task of reform as one of revising and updating the work of the past, and they produced studies that were aptly designated as revisionist moral theology. As the science of human acts in their prescribed orientation to God as last end, moral theology had conceived its central project to be the determining of norms that distinguish unlawful acts from what is morally permissible. Revisionist moral theology thus emerged as a project of revising such norms.

Giving considerable external impetus to moral theologians' concern with revising moral norms, moreover, were several events that happened around and during the time of Vatican II, events all related to one material moral norm in particular—the church's norm against so-called artificial birth control.[11] In 1960 the newly invented birth-control pill became available to the public, creating in the church a need to study its norm anew. By the time the Council commenced two years later, artificial birth control had become the subject of much debate within the church, as many Catholics argued for change in the official teaching. When Pope Paul VI assumed office in 1963, after the Council's first session, he withdrew the question about artificial birth control from the Council and reserved it to himself. His predecessor, John XXIII, had formed a small commission to research the question, and Paul VI extended considerably the commission's membership. Eventually the commission concluded its study with a great majority recommending, as is well known, that the official teaching be changed. Well known, too, is that the pope rejected the recommendation and reaffirmed in his 1968 encyclical, *Humanae Vitae*, the moral norm that "each and every marriage act (*quilibet matrimonii usus*) must remain open to the transmission of life."[12]

The papal reaffirmation of the norm prohibiting artificial birth control immediately intensified concern among theologians not only with this norm but with material moral norms in general. Just months after the encyclical was made public, Josef Fuchs, in a lecture entitled "Is There a Specifically Christian Morality?" maintained that the moral norm governing artificial birth control and indeed moral norms in general cannot be specifically Christian norms but must be universal norms, the same for all people. Arguing that in *Humanae*

Vitae "the Pope in no way intended to provide a specifically Christian solution for a universal human problem,"[13] Fuchs went on to distinguish between the intentionality and the material content of morality. Christian intentionality, he said, is what distinguishes Christian morality from other morality. But intentionality, he insisted, does not determine morality's material content. For Christian and non-Christian alike, the material content is the same, a universal "morality of genuine being-human."[14]

At about the same time that Fuchs's lecture was published in Germany, in this country Charles Curran published a similar response to the same question. "[T]here is no distinctively Christian ethic," wrote Curran, because "the Christian and the explicitly non-Christian can and do arrive at the same ethical conclusions and can and do share the same general ethical attitudes, dispositions and goals."[15] The essays of Fuchs and Curran thus introduced what was to become one of the widely debated themes of revisionist moral theology, the thesis that there is no specifically Christian morality.[16] As reworded by Richard McCormick, the issue for revisionist moral theology was: "Are there concrete moral demands in our lives which are in principle unavailable to human insight and reasoning, and which therefore can only be known by revelation or its authentic custodians?"[17]

Like the thesis that there is no specifically Christian morality, the other major subjects and themes of revisionist moral theology were so many continuations of moral theology's focus on the material norms of human acts. There were deliberations and debates about the principle of double effect, about the distinction between premoral or ontic evil and moral evil, about proportionalism and the theory of incommensurable goods, and about the extent of the competence of the magisterium in regard to material moral norms. And always not far in the background of these discussions was the controversy that had arisen over the norm about artificial birth control reaffirmed in *Humanae Vitae*.

Eventually, however, revisionist moral theology waned and virtually disappeared. Among a number of things contributing to this diminishment of preoccupation with revising material moral norms were two interrelated changes: change in Catholic attitudes and change in sacramental practice. After the Second Vatican Council there was a steady, sharp decline in the number of Catholics looking for the kind of legalistic moral norms that preconciliar moral theology had provided. Catholics increasingly came to expect moral guidance from the church not in the form of "laws to be enforced and obeyed" but as principles for a life of communion with God and neighbor. And liturgical reform transformed the sacrament of penance accordingly into a sacrament of reconciliation, in which the confessor's role appeared as primarily not that of judge but that of minister of divine mercy and forgiveness.

A Second Step in Reform

Even before the momentum of revisionist moral theology subsided, however, other theologians were creating what was in fact, even if not in name, a new discipline of the Christian life. And just as in the preconciliar years Häring had planted the seeds of a new discipline and had led the way to the Council's call for the reform of moral theology, so in the postconciliar period he was in the forefront of the progress beyond revisionist moral theology into a new, transformed science. Between 1978 and 1981, a quarter of a century after he had authored *The Law of Christ*, he published, as noted earlier, a second three-volume work, *Free and Faithful in Christ*. Now realizing that the reform of moral theology required a change much more radical than what he had envisioned in his earlier work, Häring opted not to revise that work but to produce instead a different kind of ethics.

Decades earlier, when writing *The Law of Christ*, Häring's concern had been that moral theology was cut off from the influence of dogmatic theology and spirituality. Thus he had conceived the reform of moral theology as a project of perfecting its ethics by reconstructing it within a scriptural, Christocentric context. What he would recognize only later, in *Free and Faithful in Christ*, was that, having been created as a confession-oriented ethics unaffected by dogmatic theology and spirituality, moral theology was from its inception an ethics incompatible with a scriptural context and Christocentrism. The legalistic ethics of moral theology was itself now seen as the problem; it needed to be replaced with an ethics created within a scriptural, Christocentric frame of reference.

Traditional moral theology, Häring had come to realize, with its focus on determining material moral norms, was an ethics of obedience and control: obedience of the laity and control through confes-

sors.[18] While revisionist moral theology diminished the element of
control, it nevertheless continued moral theology's preoccupation with
determining material moral norms of human acts. Thus, it was moral
theology's "static code morality" or "ethics of principles and norms
which could be well controlled" that Häring now sought to transform.[19] And the transformation would consist, of course, not in replacing old material moral norms with new ones but in creating a
different kind of ethics.

This new ethics was not centered on individual acts. Rather, it was
a systematic reflection on Christian life as the many and diverse responsible lives in Christ of creative freedom and fidelity to God.[20] If,
by its turn to Scripture, dogmatic theology, and spirituality, *The Law
of Christ* had sought to change moral theology into a Christocentric
understanding of morality, *Free and Faithful in Christ*, by replacing
the self-centered legalism of moral theology with the responsibility of
creative freedom and fidelity in Christ, now brought to theological
reflection on the Christian life a second and very different kind of
turn, an openness to the world.

It was not only its lack of relatedness to Scripture, dogmatic theology, and spirituality and its sin-centered, confession-oriented structure that limited the nature, scope, and content of moral theology.
Moral theology was also restricted in that it was only a personal
ethics and did not encompass social ethics. But even the distinction
here between personal and social ethics is anachronistic; for when
moral theology was created, the church had no social ethics and moral
theology was its only ethics. Although Francis Suarez's theological
work would soon deal with questions of international law and just
war, moral theology existed for three centuries before Pope Leo XIII's
Rerum Novarum introduced into the church what were the beginnings of social ethics and a living tradition of Catholic social thought.

An ethics cut off from social reality, of course, cannot give an
adequate account of the moral life or reflect properly and fully the
nature of the human person. In this respect, however, moral theology
is again seen as a creature very much of its time and place. In end-of-
the-sixteenth-century Europe the ordinary person's awareness of social responsibility was essentially different from and much more restricted than the experience of social obligation in an age of established
democracies and worldwide interdependence. Thus, in its turn to the
world, Häring's *Free and Faithful in Christ* reflected on a host of
matters not even mentioned in his earlier work: health delivery and

health policy, science and technocracy, global development, vested interests, socio-economic problems, the megalopolis, the urban ghetto, ecology, the heritage of colonialism, world peace, and world order—to name but a small sample.

His *Free and Faithful in Christ* completed the change that Häring had initiated in *The Law of Christ*. It indeed presented a new discipline, one only remotely related to moral theology as the science of human acts inasmuch as they are to be ordered to God as ultimate end. Having as its subject the lives of Christians as lives of discipleship, the new discipline replaced moral theology's constricted field of individual human acts with the wide-open horizon of Christian life throughout the world.

As part of the reform it mandated for moral theology, the Second Vatican Council had in fact called for this opening to the world. It had said that moral theology, imbued with the teaching of Scripture, should illuminate the obligation of the faithful in Christ "to bring forth fruit in charity for the life of the world." Moreover, in addition to this explicit mandate and even more important in promoting the needed transformation of moral theology was the example itself of Vatican II: the spirit of openness to the world that characterized the Council and informed all its teachings, particularly its *Pastoral Constitution on the Church in the Modern World*.

Nevertheless, in a theological discipline about Christian life, an adequate and proper openness to the world is not something that an individual theologian achieves. This theological openness can exist only in the collective work of a community of theologians; for it entails comprehensiveness not only in the scope of the human matters reflected upon but also in the scope of the human experience that theologians bring to the reflection process. Before Vatican II moral theology lacked both dimensions of this openness. Besides being a personal ethics, it was also a science created by priests for men preparing to become priests. More specifically, it was created by European Catholic priests and was developed for nearly four centuries by them and, in the last half-century of that period, also by their North American counterparts. Moral theology's treatment of Christian life was thus directly rooted only in the human experience of European and North American Catholic male celibate priests. In a theology open to the world, in contrast, the treatment of Christian life needs to reflect the human experience of the people of God as a whole.

External Sources of Change

Even as the reforms of Häring and other theologians were bringing down the walls of legalistic moral theology from within, a number of external happenings also were contributing to the creation of a transformed discipline. Of these outside influences six are noteworthy here.

1. The Second Vatican Council's recovery of the dignity of the lay person's vocation and role in the church

While the conciliar teaching on the laity has influenced and continues to influence theology in innumerable ways, the most fundamental change it brought about for theology has been the transformation of the theological community itself. Since the Council a great number of lay persons have become theologians, thereby converting the community of theologians from the society almost exclusively of priests that it had been for most of its history into a community of clergy and laity alike. Indeed, the postconciliar theological community has been steadily moving toward becoming a predominantly lay community. Thus, in recent decades theological reflection has taken root in the experience of clergy and laity together, that is, in experience much more representative of the church community as a whole.

For no other theological discipline were the consequences of this change as extreme as they were for moral theology; for the change meant that the discipline that had been created centuries earlier as a science for confessors was now a thing of the past. No longer was it possible to confine the theological discussion of morality within the constricted context of what priests were supposed to know in order to be ministers of the Sacrament of Penance. From a community whose human experience and concerns were more directly those of the church as a whole there now came forth, naturally and inevitably, a more comprehensive theological discussion of Christian living.

2. The Council's teaching on the unity of Catholics and their "separated brethren," that is, on the unity of all Christians

The ecumenical spirit and teaching of Vatican II inspired and encouraged Catholic theologians to enter into ongoing dialogue with other Christian theologians and thus to understand and appreciate more deeply their work. Moral theology was, of course, a uniquely Catholic discipline, but among other Christian theologians there were those whose field of specialization was Christian ethics. The work of mainstream Christian ethicists was generally marked by both more attention to Scripture and less concern with determining absolute material moral norms than was moral theology. Thus, through the encounters between moral theologians and Christian ethicists a new discipline was in fact taking shape in an unprecedented ecumenical dialogue about Christian life.

3. The birth of liberation theology

Shortly after the council Gustavo Gutiérrez and other Latin American theologians became the creators and pioneers of liberation theology, whose spirit soon inspired the work of fellow theologians in other cultures and continents. These liberation theologians were dogmatic or systematic theologians concerned with the unjust, oppressive conditions in which their compatriots were living and with the praxis through which Christians could respond to these situations.

In two ways, then, liberation theology was forming the new discipline of the Christian life that was replacing moral theology. First, whereas moral theology presented a classicist view of human life and a "static code morality," liberation theology emerged in historical consciousness and viewed contemporary societies in light of their unjust social elements and their openings to divine grace. Christian reflection on morality was no longer a merely theoretical, deductive task; it had become prophetic, calling forth creative responses in the service of justice and peace.

Second, whereas moral theology had been a science separated from dogmatic theology and allied with canon law, liberation theology was created within a scriptural and theological context, independent of canon law, and free of the proclivity to legalism. Thus, liberation theology recovered within historical consciousness and in an analogical mode the unity of doctrinal theology and reflection on the Christian life that is found in the theological summa of St. Thomas Aquinas. Liberation theology shaped the theology of Christian life, then, into two things that moral theology was not: a truly theological discipline[21] and indeed a theological discipline from which prophetic teaching flows.

4. The rise of feminism

While the accessibility of the theologian's vocation to lay persons after Vatican II was of supreme importance in bringing about change in theology, it would have had little significance if only men had become lay theologians. In that case the change would have been merely from one imbalance to another. Among the first persons in the postconciliar period to become lay theologians, however, were women—married, single, and religious women. And, fortunately, a considerable number of them concentrated their theological interest on the Christian life, the subject in which it was particularly important that theology be rooted in the experience of both women and men.

The experience that women brought to theological reflection on Christian life included, of course, the experience underlying contemporary feminism: the intense and widely shared consciousness of the discrimination against women embodied in the structures and institutions of patriarchal society. Incorporated into theology, feminism disclosed this bias not only in civil society but also within the church and within theology itself, and it went on to counteract ways in which this prejudice distorts the understanding and living of the Christian life.[22] The insight feminism offers and the gender egalitarianism promoted by it constitute, thus, indispensable components of the new theology of Christian life that replaces moral theology.

5. The return to virtue ethics

Bringing back into philosophy the Aristotelian-Thomistic tradition's appreciation of the role of virtue in moral living, Alasdair MacIntyre's *After Virtue*[23] served as yet another catalyst in creating a theology of Christian life. This influential work awakened among theologians the need to recover and develop the virtue ethics so fundamental in Thomas Aquinas's understanding of Christian life but so sorely eclipsed in the manuals of moral theology.

The movement of theology after Vatican II away from legalistic moral theology was, to be sure, only the reverse, negative side of a positive development. The positive aspect of the process was the creating of a personalist theology in which all human activity is to be morally evaluated—in the words of an official Vatican II commentary—"insofar as it refers to the human person integrally and adequately considered."[24] For theology to consider the human person integrally and adequately, however, entails, among other things, taking into account the role of moral character in Christian living. And attending to character involves in turn appreciating the importance and the roles of the theological and moral virtues in Christian life.

Thus, the restoration and development of virtue ethics was an indispensable part of the transformative process that was creating the personalist theology of Christian life, just as virtue ethics is an essential component of that theology itself.

6. The globalization of the church

Vatican II, as has been often remarked, brought the church into its third age, changing it from a Eurocentric into a world church. Although the world church is still in its early development, it is already taking shape as a living symbol of the unity-in-diversity of Christian life. In the world church one sees that both Christian faith and Christian living exist only in particular and varied forms of inculturation. A theology of Christian life in a world church accordingly reveals that just as the substance of faith needs to be expressed in different formulations according to faith's time and place, Christian moral principles, too, must find diverse expressions in the life of the church. While the focal point of moral theology was uniformity in universal material moral norms, the theology of the Christian life recognizes and values, beyond uniformity, the unity of transcendent Christian principles in different cultural embodiments.[25]

Conclusion: The New Horizons in Moral Theology

Theology of the Christian life, then, must deal with life in all its complexity in today's world. Thus, the discipline cannot have the simplicity that characterized moral theology, whose content was discrete human acts and whose method was deduction. Whereas the proper literary genre of moral theology was the ethical summa authored by an individual moralist, theology of the Christian life can be expressed adequately only in the harmony of a chorus of theological voices representative of the church community throughout the world. Nor can the theology of Christian life be confined within the kind of sharply and absolutely defined boundaries of sciences set in the past; for, together with moral theology itself, the modern age's rationalistic understanding of theology that divided morality off from Scripture, dogma, and spirituality in the first place has passed into history.

The story of moral theology concludes, then, with moral theology having come to an end, with the foundations for a transformed theological discipline solidly established and in place, and with a new theology of the Christian life rising promisingly on those foundations into the church's third millennium.

Notes

[1]Daniel J. Harrington and James F. Keenan, *Jesus and Virtue Ethics: Building Bridges between New Testament Studies and Moral Theology* (Lanham, Md.: Sheed & Ward, 2002), 1-2.

[2]See, for instance, Heribert Jone, *Moral Theology*, 15th ed., trans. Urban Adelman (Westminster, Md.: Newman Press, 1956), 1: "the scientific exposition of human conduct so far as it is directed by reason and faith to the attainment of our supernatural final end"; F. Hürth and P. M. Abellán, *De Principiis—De Virtutibus et Praeceptis* (Rome: Pontifical Gregorian University, 1948), 7: "the theological science of deliberate human acts inasmuch as they are in relation to the ultimate supernatural end to be obtained through those acts themselves and through the means of salvation"; H. Noldin, A. Schmitt, and G. Heinzel, *Summa Theologiae Moralis*, 30th ed. (Innsbruck: F. Rauch, 1952), I:1: "the science of human activity as oriented to God, the ultimate supernatural end." Latin-text translations are the present writer's.

[3]Bernard Häring, *Free and Faithful in Christ: Moral Theology for Clergy and Laity* (New York: Seabury Press, 1978-1981), I:46.

[4]Richard A. McCormick, "Moral Theology 1940-1989: An Overview," in *The Historical Development of Fundamental Moral Theology in the United States; Readings in Moral Theology 11*, ed. Charles E. Curran and Richard A. McCormick (New York: Paulist Press, 1999), 47.

[5]J. A. DiNoia, "*Veritatis Splendor*: Moral Life as Transfigured Life," in *Veritatis Splendor and the Renewal of Moral Theology*, ed. J. A. DiNoia and Romanus Cessario (Princeton, N.J.: Scepter Publishers, 1999), 3-4.

[6]For a discussion of the work of these and other reform-minded theologians, see Bernard Häring, *The Law of Christ: Moral Theology for Priests and Laity*, trans. Edwin G. Kaiser (Cork, Ireland: Mercier Press, 1963-1967), I:22-33.

[7]Volumes I and II of *The Law of Christ* appeared in 1963, the third volume in 1967.

[8]Häring, *The Law of Christ*, I:61.

[9]Bernard Häring, *My Witness for the Church*, trans. Leonard Swidler (New York: Paulist Press, 1992), 60.

[10]"Decree on the Training of Priests," in *Vatican Council II: The Conciliar and the Postconciliar Documents*, ed. Austin Flannery (Collegeville, Minn.: Liturgical Press, 1980), no. 16, 720.

[11]On the ambiguous character of the terms *artificial birth control* and *contraception* in ethical discussion see Norbert Rigali, "Words and Contraception," *America* 183 (2000): 8-11.

[12]Pope Paul VI, *On the Regulation of Birth (Humanae Vitae)* (Vatican

City: Vatican Press, 1968), no. 11, 16.

[13]Josef Fuchs, "Is There a Specifically Christian Morality?" in *The Distinctiveness of Christian Ethics: Readings in Moral Theology 2*, ed. Charles E. Curran and Richard A. McCormick (New York, Paulist Press, 1980), 3.

[14]Ibid., 8.

[15]Charles E. Curran, "Is There a Distinctively Christian Social Ethic?" in *Metropolis: Christian Presence and Responsibility*, ed. Philip D. Morris (Notre Dame, Ind.: Fides Publishers, 1970), 114-15.

[16]For a detailed account of the debate see Vincent MacNamara, *Faith and Ethics: Recent Roman Catholicism* (Washington, D.C.: Georgetown University Press, 1985).

[17]Richard A. McCormick, *Notes on Moral Theology 1965 through 1980* (Washington, D.C.: University Press of America, 1981), 814.

[18]Häring, *Free and Faithful in Christ*, I:46.

[19]Ibid., 23.

[20]Ibid., 59.

[21]Even in the scholarly apparatus of a typical moral theology manual the non-theological character of moral theology is apparent. In the fifty-six pages of detailed tables of contents and indices for the 1,585-page text of the Noldin-Schmitt-Heinzel *Summa Theologiae Moralis*, for example, the words *Jesus* and *Christ* are not to be found.

[22]For an example of how feminist theology exposes and counteracts male-biased understandings of Christian life, see Anne E. Patrick, *Liberating Conscience: Feminist Explorations in Catholic Moral Theology* (New York: Continuum, 1996).

[23]Alasdair C. MacIntyre, *After Virtue: A Study in Moral Theory*, 2nd ed. (Notre Dame, Ind.: University of Notre Dame Press, 1984).

[24]*Schema constitutionis pastoralis de ecclesia in mundo huius temporis: Expensio modorum partis secundae* (Vatican City: Vatican Press, 1965), 37-38; cited in Richard A. McCormick, *Notes on Moral Theology 1981 through 1984* (Lanham, Md.: University Press of America, 1984), 49.

[25]For an example of what the understanding of world church brings to the theology of Christian life, see Eugene Hillman, *Toward an African Christianity: Inculturation Applied* (New York: Paulist Press, 1993).

New Horizons for Mysticism and Politics

How the Agenda Has Shifted

J. Matthew Ashley

The Mysticism and Politics Section of the College Theology Society was started on an experimental basis in 1994 and has continued ever since.[1] To show how we can map an agenda for the future, I first want to consider the origins of the pairing of terms that define the section—mysticism and politics. This takes us to the work of two figures who, if they by no means exhaust the list of pioneers of this correlation, do provide paradigmatic instances—Gustavo Gutiérrez and Johann Baptist Metz. What I will hope to show, briefly, is that both the reason why and the way in which liberation theologians and political theologians evoke a "mystical-political" correlation must be understood in terms of their context. Thinking about how our contexts are changing will make it possible to consider new horizons for our work.

The Mystical-Political Correlation in Latin American Liberation Theology

In his first major work Gustavo Gutiérrez announced that one of the most pressing challenges for liberation theology was to identify and develop further an incipient spirituality of liberation in the life and labors of those Christians committed to transforming society on behalf of the poor: "There is a great need for a spirituality of liberation; yet in Latin America those who have opted to participate in the process of liberation as we have outlined it above, comprise, in a manner of speaking, a first Christian generation. In many areas of their life they are without a theological and spiritual tradition. They are creating their own."[2]

Gutiérrez later co-edited the volume in the international journal *Concilium* that gives this section its name. In that volume, he wrote: "Commitment to the process of liberation, with all its political demands, means taking on the world of the poor and the oppressed in a real and effective manner. This sets up a new spiritual requirement at the very heart of the liberating praxis. I mean the matrix of a new theological reflection, of an intellection of the Word, of the free gift of God, breaking into human existence and transforming it."[3]

In *A Theology of Liberation* Gutiérrez connected this "spiritual requirement" with a crisis among Christian believers in Latin America.[4] Segundo Galilea, another prominent early proponent of a spirituality of liberation, described the crisis in this way: "as soon as the traditional Christian commits himself to the liberation of the workers or the peasants in tasks of an educational or political nature, he finds himself in a way exiled. The categories of his faith—sin, salvation, charity, prayer, and so forth—do not inspire or illuminate sufficiently his commitments. Hence the crisis."[5]

Three points are central to understanding the origins of liberation theology. First, liberation theologians understand theology as *always* an *actus secundus*, as Gutiérrez frequently asserts. More precisely, it is reflection on praxis in the light of the gospel.[6] Praxis is first; it is prior to theological reflection. Second, praxis means Christian praxis. This is a feature of liberation theology that is often overlooked by critics who attack its option for praxis as insufficiently critical. The praxis on which liberation theology reflects is a praxis that is already configured by a certain way of committing oneself to be a follower of Jesus, a response to the prevenient grace of God's love empowered by the Spirit. Looked at in this light, this praxis constitutes or at least entails a spirituality, a concrete way of making real and living out one's relationship to God. Third, by the middle of the twentieth century Christian praxis, or spirituality, had largely come to be understood as encompassing only personal or interpersonal (in the sense of the "I-thou" relationship) ethical behavior, on the one hand, and one's private relationship with God (call it "devotion"), on the other. Both the way that spirituality was thematically articulated by nineteenth- and twentieth-century spiritual teachers and theologians, and the way that theology as a conceptual (largely academic) enterprise was worked out, were intimately connected with this quite modern (post-Enlightenment) way of being a Christian. Christians in Latin America learned this spirituality and this theology, but were con-

fronted with a radically different context within which they had to
utilize and apply them.

In the 1960s and 1970s, the context was defined by what Gutiérrez
has called "the irruption of the poor" as the principal sign of the
times. For a variety of reasons, poverty as a massive, dehumanizing,
scandalous phenomenon moved to the center of Christian consciousness in Latin America. Moreover, developments in the social sciences
made poverty appear not as an arbitrary fate, and certainly not as
God's will, but as a social product with historical causes and, conse-
quently, social and historical remedies. The Second Vatican Council,
particularly *Gaudium et Spes*, inspired many Christians to confront
and heal this reality as an integral part of their Christian vocation, an
inspiration that was continued and intensified by the Latin American
bishops at Medellín in 1968. But when Christians responded to this
ecclesial prompting, they experienced disorientation and confusion
because the spiritualities and theologies that had grown up around
depoliticized post-Enlightenment Christian praxis simply failed to
inspire or illuminate the new context and the Christian commitments
it required. The old road maps no longer corresponded to the new
terrain.

The crisis that both Gutiérrez and Galilea described sent them
back to the tradition in search of new resources or new ways of
reading tried and true ones. Just as Job refused to accept the narrow
theology and spirituality of his counselors when and because it failed
to make sense of his experience, Christians committed to the praxis
of liberation refused to accept the narrowly defined spirituality and
theology of post-Enlightenment European theology and spirituality.[7]
As a result, Christian liberation movements and liberation theology
are marked by the creative appropriation of the larger Christian tradition and an innovative continuation of it, striving for new models
of spirituality to identify, thematize, and nurture "contemplation in
the action for liberation."[8] What must be stressed is that this was not
a matter of attaching politics of one sort or another to pre-existing
unpolitical Christian praxis or of "spiritualizing" a politics; rather, it
was a matter of expressing the incipient spirituality already present
in Christian struggle for liberation, using (*mutatis mutandis*) models
from Christian spirituality and theology in, say, the Franciscan, Jesuit, or Carmelite traditions, to name just a few.[9]

When liberation theologians used the adjective "mystical," then,
they were not referring so much to an unmediated encounter with

God as to that transcendent presence of God that is the enlivening heart of any Christian life, that qualifies it as Christian, and that, when it becomes the point of reference for describing that life as a whole and organizing its different elements, warrants denoting it as a "spirituality." When they used the adjective "political," they were not referring in the first instance to specific elements of intra- or international governance. Rather, they were alluding to a certain modern view of history that understands history to be a human project. To be "political" on this reading is to commit oneself to this project of taking charge of history, whether that be through political activity in the narrower sense of the term, or by embracing other forms of human action (economic, educational, artistic, and so on) with this broader sense of significance.[10] To argue for and from "the mystical and political dimension of Christianity" is to assert that one can, and perhaps must, find God's presence in the midst of struggling for shaping a history more worthy of human beings, especially of those human beings marginalized and condemned to an early death by history as it currently runs its course.

Johann Baptist Metz and the Mystical-Political Dimension of Christian Faith

While Gustavo Gutiérrez's German friend and contemporary, Johann Baptist Metz, has shown great concern for the scandalous presence of poverty and suffering in the world, his particular route to the assertion of the essential and integral mystical-political configuration of Christian faith grew from different contextual soil. For Metz, the Central European reality of the secularization of Christian faith brought the church to a different kind of crisis, a crisis which, however, also required a renewed articulation of the connection between the mystical element of Christian faith and its political dimension. To understand this crisis we need to go back to Metz's teacher, friend, and, as Metz calls him, "father in faith," Karl Rahner. In particular, we need to exegete Rahner's well-known assertion that "the Christian of the future will be a mystic or will not exist."[11]

Rahner argued that the context of Christian faith in Europe had changed dramatically due to the processes of the Enlightenment. In past ages Christians grew up in a more or less homogeneous Christian social and cultural milieu that formed in them a basic conviction that Christian doctrines made sense and *mattered* for them, *before* they came to learn and study those doctrines in greater depth.[12] This milieu has disappeared, and its reappearance does not seem likely in the immediate future (if ever). Now Christians have to *choose* to have this happen, in a way that was not true during the Middle Ages or even during the post-Tridentine Catholic Church. The resulting crisis is that even when Christians learn what the church teaches and practices what it prescribes, they also have a deeply rooted uneasiness, a disorienting sense that none of it really makes sense in modern life or *of* modern life. Hence, Christians must become "mystics" in the sense that, far more than Christians of past centuries, they must themselves foster and rely on a personal experience of God revealed in Jesus Christ that grows out of and nourishes a mutually illuminating relationship between the substance of the tradition and the events of their own lives.[13] Christian catechesis and theology must serve this work. They must be "mystagogy," a work of initiating Christians more and more into the mysteries of the faith that are "encoded" in doctrines and practices in order to give a profound and satisfying interpretation and orientation within the mysteries (both positive and negative) of one's own life.[14] This defines a central task, then, of theological discourse in a modern secularized context such as nineteenth- and twentieth-century Europe.

Metz picked up on this fundamental feature of Rahner's thought. According to Metz, in Rahner's theology doctrines become the "alphabet" in which one "spells out" the history of one's life as the history of an unfolding relationship with God, incarnated in the most mundane details of one's life.[15] This can and must involve a certain kind of apologetics, or "fundamental theology." However, in place of proofs of God's existence or reference to miracles, the credibility of faith is shown in reference to the still-unresolved problems (or "limit-questions") that plague the modern person, all the advances of modernity notwithstanding: human finitude, guilt, and one's always-impinging death. These three conditions threaten the project of being and becoming a subject in the modern sense. Rahner's claim is not that Christian faith offers pat solutions to these problems, but that it allows persons to live creatively, faithfully, hopefully, and honestly with respect to them. Metz agrees with the basic approach. Yet, whereas Rahner has taken the endangered identity of the subject as an individual to be the arena within which to demonstrate the truth and relevance of Christian faith, Metz argues that the arena must be expanded to include the individual's constitutive social-political embeddedness:

> In the entire approach of a practical fundamental theology it
> would be necessary to open this [Rahner's] biographical way
> of conceiving dogmatic theology to that theological biogra-
> phy of Christianity in which the dual mystical-political consti-
> tution of Christian faith—that is to say, its socially responsible
> form—would be taken even more seriously and become the
> motive force for theological reflection.[16]

In summary, Rahner conceives of the field within which theological
discourse can find some purchase as mapped out by the "mystical-
existential" character of human being. Doctrine and theology can be
grounded and justified by showing how they can make sense of and
empower human existence at the level of this mystical-existential
circumincessio, and thus at a deeper level than straightforward empirical accounts of human existence.[17] Metz agrees, but insists that
the existential-biographical framing of human existence is too narrow. It needs to be complemented, corrected, or even subsumed by a
political account that stresses more radically the ways we are consti-
tutively related to one another, not just in "I-thou" relationships but
in and through ambivalent historical traditions and conflict-ridden
social institutions (now on a global scale).

In Rahner's work the question raised of one's own guilt, suffering,
and eventual death threaten one's project of becoming an authentic
subject. In Metz's work, however, one's becoming and remaining a
subject in society and in the project of history are threatened both by
the guilt and uneasiness that come from involvement in ambiguous
histories in which "every document of civilization is also a document
of barbarism,"[18] and by the death of *the other*. The kind of spirituality that most corresponds to this is "a mysticism of open eyes," pain-
fully open to suffering in the world, a *Leiden an Gott*: a suffering
that turns us toward God, full of anguish and questioning, like Job
or like Jesus on the cross in the Matthean and Marcan accounts.
Thus, "mystical" in Metz tends to emphasize a relationship to God
that entails a painful sense of God's absence.[19] It energizes an apocalyptic sense of hopeful expectation of a renewed (or newly sensed in
unexpected places), interruptive presence of God that disrupts
modernity's increasingly "realistic," pared-back projections of what
might be possible in human history, particularly for the world's poor.
This in turn inspires and underwrites a more radical engagement in
history on their behalf. When Metz talks about politics he is in sub-

stantive agreement with Gutiérrez and other liberation theologians. Thus, his approach tends to converge with that of Latin American liberation theologians, but the difference in starting points is important to note.

The Future: Continuity and New Complexity

An agenda for future work can be derived, then, from a consideration of how the mystical element of Christianity appears differently today, as opposed to forty years ago; how the political element has changed; and how the underlying context has changed.[20] In all of this, of course, my acknowledging my particular social location—that of a white, middle-class North American academic—should make it clear that the list of issues I see as emergent is by no means intended as an exhaustive one. I do hope, however, that it provides a framework for subsequent discussions.

The Mystical

There are two changes that I would group under the rubric of the "mystical" dimension of Christianity that bear on the work of this section. First is the academic one. As a result of an explosion of scholarly work in the last twenty years we know far more than we used to about the history of Christian spirituality and mysticism.[21] This means first of all that we have many more historical prototypes that demonstrate that Christian spirituality has always correlated with some kind of positioning with respect to society and history, even if the latter have not been understood and experienced in the same way as they are today. These prototypes can provide inspiration for how this positioning is (or can be) present for us today. We have only just begun the work of exploring these resources.

In addition, we now have decades of lived experience on the part of Christian communities that have been trying to live out these sorts of commitments: from base Christian communities in Latin America to Catholic Worker houses in North America. These experiments in living out a new and vital correlation of the mystical-political dimension of Christian faith bear close examination. This examination should, moreover, be interdisciplinary. What difference, in fact, has the conscious appropriation of one or another model of contemplation in action made in the social and political features of the struggle for human rights? Has it had the leavening effect that proponents such as Gustavo Gutiérrez, Jon Sobrino, and Segundo Galilea, claim?[22]

An ongoing challenge that faces the attempt to elaborate and promote a "mystical-political" correlation in Christianity in North America is the continuing privatization of Christian spirituality. As authors such as Robert Wuthnow have noted, the privatization of spirituality, delinking it from social and institutional contexts, is if anything more marked than it was forty years ago.[23] The commonplace nature of the assertion, "I'm not religious but I consider myself a very spiritual person," ought to alert us to a very real danger. For the original advocates of forging a stronger link between spirituality and political commitment, "spirituality" still involved a strong institutional context and a certain stable and indispensable core, even if it was one that had been cut off from social-political dimensions of life.[24] Spirituality means something far more ephemeral now, which raises new issues for thinking about the promotion of a mystical-political correlation. If, as many modern commentators note, we are in age of "mix and match," build-it-yourself, and consumerist spiritualities,[25] then, while it is certainly true that some will include an element of the political in their spirituality, the danger is that the renewed emphasis on individual piety and devotion as the exclusive realm of spirituality in the United States will more and more militate against that possibility. However, given the present disenchantment, one might even say disgust, for the institutional Catholic Church in the United States, it is not easy to see how this trend can be reversed.

The Political

The correlation between the mystical and the political in Latin American liberation theology started with what Gutiérrez called "the challenge of the non-person." Although European political theology started from the crisis posed by secularization, it moved toward the same focal challenge in the 1970s and 1980s. It increasingly emphasized the challenge posed by modernity's ambiguous histories as the only adequate arena within which to confront secularization and the crisis of meaning for Christianity. In this sense, then, the way one sees the political side of the mystical-political will depend on how one construes the other whose personhood is threatened. In the early days of liberation theology this other was identified primarily in terms of economic poverty, but almost immediately other forms of political analysis began to emerge that highlighted other forms of oppression on the basis of gender, of race, and of ethnicity.[26] This led to other important variants of liberation theology, as well as to difficult problems of how to interrelate these different kinds of social and political marginalization and the kind of spiritualities appropriate to struggling against them. This problem has not yet been resolved.

Another new development is the growing force of globalization, which has interwoven all the different dimensions of marginalization in complex ways. Looked at in terms of the globalization of information-exchange and of the media, presenting the very real danger of the "McDonaldization" of the world's different cultures, globalization may well raise a different kind of crisis for Christians, particularly in relation to the need for both relative autonomy, on the one hand, and effective solidarity, on the other, between different regional churches of the globe. Globalization does offer new possibilities for real solidarity across national and cultural boundaries, but it would be a disaster if this solidarity was bought at the price of surrendering the cultural diversity, which is as essential to the world's "social ecology" as genetic diversity is to its biological ecology. How the power of free markets and new information technologies can be the substance and base of new kinds of spiritual practices at the service of the evangelization of now globalized cultures demands further research.

Third, the political dimension of Christian faith is ineluctably affected by the political matrix, in the narrower sense of the intra- and international deployment of resources and power, within which Christians live. For those of us in the United States, we now find ourselves living in the world's only superpower, a superpower recently stricken with anxiety over its starkly manifest vulnerability. We urgently need to consider in greater depth the kind of spirituality appropriate to confronting the politics and ideology of empire and "preemptive wars." This task is, for us, tied to the earlier issue of identifying and addressing the social marginalization of large groups of persons. We will not adequately grapple with the violence we perpetrate *ad extra* unless we begin coming to terms with the violence inscribed *ad intra* in our history. This leads me to suspect that the topic of reconciliation will become increasingly important in the coming years.

The Context

I argued above that the nature of the context and the crisis that it brought about for Christian believers had a great deal to do with the particular path to a mystical-political correlation in Christian faith and theology: in Europe that context was primarily one of secularization, whereas in Latin America it was primarily dehumanizing (even murderous) injustice. These contexts still obtain and are still important; however, I would close these reflections by pointing to two different contexts that require a further rethinking of the mystical-political dimension of Christian faith and theology. The first is the postmodern context of radical pluralism and the second has to do with our current environmental predicament.

Radical pluralism is now endemic to U.S. culture. How can Christians sustain and advocate the sort of robust political engagement, often by appeal to religious language and symbols, that inspired, say, the Civil Rights movement, once this utopian discourse has lost its power to move people to action and has been exposed to the withering critique of the so-called "masters of suspicion," modern and postmodern? How can we learn from the insights of postmodern thinkers, their ability to deconstruct and destabilize the taken-for-granted character of late modern capitalism with its truncated renderings of human fulfillment and ideals, cutting them back to fit "within the limits of (technical-manipulative) reason alone"?[27] "Postmodernity" is with us to stay and we need to identify both its pitfalls and its resources.

Our current environmental practices are unsustainable and our values confused. This crisis is a threat not just to the meaningfulness of Christian doctrines and practices, or to human survival, but to the survival of a great number, if not the majority, of species with which we share this planet. It requires its own politics and its own spirituality. It is not at all clear how we can respond to this context in a way that properly integrates the other crises mentioned above. Although important work has been done, the tensions and contrasts between different approaches—from a traditional stewardship approach to ecojustice approaches, deep ecology and ecofeminism, to name a few—make it clear that we are just in the beginnings of this important work. Here the continuing privatization and decontextualization of spirituality in the U.S. context, noted above, make the challenge more pressing. For while it is true that at least some scientists have been turning or returning to religion and spirituality, the religion they espouse is often ahistorical and apolitical.[28]

Conclusion

A lengthy and important agenda faces us theologians, particularly those of us involved in questions of mysticism and politics, as we look ahead to the next fifty years. The "discovery" of the mystical-political dimension of the Christian faith occurred in two primary contexts: on the one hand, dehumanizing poverty and injustice, and on the other, secularization of modern culture, connected with a new appreciation of history as a human project for which we are responsible, whether we choose to accept that responsibility or not. This new appreciation of the political dimension of human life made it possible, even requisite, that Christian faith and practice be rethought, which required in turn a re-envisioning of Christian spirituality. One way of mapping an agenda for the future starts by observing how the context has become more complex to the extent that it now includes the challenge of radical pluralism and environmental degradation. We have a richer knowledge of the diverse strands of the history of Christian spirituality as well as new conceptual tools for analyzing human political action and its consequences. There is a decades-long history of attempts to live out the mystical-political correlation in a creative, efficacious way that bears close examination.

Finally, the problem of the privatization and de-politicization of Christian spirituality has not been solved, but rather is in some senses even worse than in the 1960s and 1970s. Looking at this list of significant issues, it occurs to me that the general category under which this section belongs is "fundamental theology," that part of that theology that attempts "to give an account to those who ask it of the hope that is in us." From a recent trip to El Salvador, and from my involvement in planning a conference on the environment at Notre Dame, I am ever more cognizant of the hope that is still present and life-giving in so many Christian communities that, on the surface, would seem to have no reason to hope. It is our task as theologians to seek to understand this faith and this hope in order to encourage and nurture them into the next generation. I can think of no more exciting or fulfilling work.

Notes

[1] I thank the members of the College Theology Society who attended the session of the Mysticism and Politics Section at which I delivered this paper. Their comments and suggestions strengthened this final version. I also thank in particular Anne Clifford of Duquesne University who responded to my presentation. While I will cite her contribution at specific points in what follows, her commentary helped sharpen the whole essay. None of this, of course, ought to be taken to displace responsibility for errors of fact or argument, for which I still carry full responsibility.

[2] Gustavo Gutiérrez, *A Theology of Liberation: History, Politics, Salvation*, rev. ed. (Maryknoll, N.Y.: Orbis Books, 1988), 74.

[3] Gustavo Gutiérrez, "Liberation, Theology and Proclamation," in *The Mystical and Political Dimension of the Christian Faith*, ed. Gustavo Gutiérrez and Claude Geffre, *Concilium 96* (New York: Herder & Herder, 1974): 64.

[4] Gutiérrez, *A Theology of Liberation*, 74.

[5] Segundo Galilea, "Liberation as an Encounter with Politics and Contemplation," in *The Mystical and Political Dimension of the Christian Faith*, 20.

[6] Gutiérrez, *A Theology of Liberation*, 5-12.

[7] In light of my earlier, second claim, however, it is important to note that Job's "experience" was already theologically informed: it was informed by the covenantal theologies that had been so severely shaken by the events leading to the collapse of Judah in 586 B.C.E. Gutiérrez makes this point well. See Gustavo Gutiérrez, *On Job: God-talk and the Suffering of the Innocent* (Maryknoll, N.Y.: Orbis Books, 1987).

[8] For an exploration of this spirituality, see Ignacio Ellacuría and Jon Sobrino, *Fe y Justicia* (Bilbao: Descleé de Brouwer, 1999).

[9] For the appropriation of Franciscan models, see the work of Leonardo Boff; see Ignacio Ellacuría and Jon Sobrino for creative uses of the Jesuit tradition; on the Carmelite tradition, see Gustavo Gutiérrez's interpretation of John of the Cross.

[10] In fact, since the major impediment to the progress of Latin American peoples, particularly the poor, appeared to lie in the stranglehold that the wealthy had on the state, which in turn controlled the economies, many liberation theologians did understand the kind of commitment to be a political one in the narrower sense, but this was a strategic or tactical discernment on their part and not an unchangeable foundational one. See, for example, Galilea, "Liberation as an Encounter with Politics and Contemplation," 19.

[11] This statement is often repeated. See, for example, "The Spirituality of the Church in the Future," *Theological Investigations*, vol. XX, trans. Edward Quinn (New York: Crossroad, 1986), 149, and *Karl Rahner in*

Dialogue: Conversations and Interviews, 1965-1982 (New York: Crossroad, 1986), 176.

[12]See "The Spirituality of the Future," 148f., "The Intellectual Formation of Future Priests," in *Theological Investigations*, vol. VI (New York: Crossroad, 1982), 113-38, and *Foundations of Christian Faith: An Introduction to the Idea of Christianity* (New York: Crossroad, 1984), 5-6, 8-10.

[13]Rahner found in Ignatian spirituality a set of practices that was formed precisely for this purpose. For a discussion of Rahner's appropriation of Ignatian spirituality, see Philip Endean, *Karl Rahner and Ignatian Spirituality*, Oxford Theological Monographs (Oxford: Oxford University Press, 2001).

[14]See Rahner's introduction to James Bacik, *Apologetics and the Eclipse of Mystery: Mystagogy According to Karl Rahner* (Notre Dame, Ind.: Univ. of Notre Dame Press, 1980), ix-x.

[15]See the excursus to Chapter 12 ("Narrative") in Metz's *Faith in History and Society*. The original German title is revealing: "Karl Rahner—ein theologisches Leben: theologie als mystische Biographie eines Christenmensch heute" (Karl Rahner—a theological life: theology as the mystical biography of a Christian man or woman today), in *Stimmen der Zeit* (May 1974).

[16]Johann Baptist Metz, *Faith in History and Society* (New York: Crossroad, 1980), 224, translation emended.

[17]See, for example, Karl Rahner, "The Theological Dimension of the Question about Man," *Theological Investigations*, vol. XVII, 53-70.

[18]In Walter Benjamin's gripping formulation, "Theses on the Philosophy of History," in *Illuminations: Essays and Reflections*, ed. Hannah Arendt (New York: Shocken, 1968), 256.

[19]In this Metz is very much in line with the Christian mystical tradition. Bernard McGinn notes that "if the modern consciousness of God is often of an absent God (absent though not forgotten for the religious person), many mystics seem almost to have been prophets of this in their intense realization that the 'real God' becomes a possibility only when the many false gods (even the God of religion) have vanished and the frightening abyss of total nothingness is confronted" (*The Foundations of Mysticism: Origins to the Fifth Century* [New York: Crossroad, 1992], xviii). For Metz this abyss opens up when we consider the histories of suffering in which we are ineluctably indicted, especially the history of the Shoah.

[20]Since these three are intimately related to one another the division below is in some ways, of course, a matter of convenience. One could, for instance, describe our deepening knowledge of the history of Christian spirituality as a change in the academic context of Christian theology.

[21]As two examples, think of the Paulist Press series on the Classics of Christian Spirituality or Bernard McGinn's on-going five-volume magnum opus on the history of Christian mysticism.

[22]See, for example, the claims that Galilea makes in "Politics and Contem-

plation," 22f., or Jon Sobrino in *Spirituality of Liberation: Toward Political Holiness* (Maryknoll, N.Y.: Orbis Books, 1988), throughout but inter alia, see 9-10, 147-48.

[23]Robert Wuthnow, *After Heaven: Spirituality in America since the 1950's* (Berkeley: University of California Press, 1998).

[24]It is interesting to note that many of these advocates had strong associations with traditional schools of Catholic spirituality: Jon Sobrino and Johann Baptist Metz to Jesuit spirituality (even though Metz is not a Jesuit); Leonardo Boff to Franciscan spirituality; Gustavo Gutiérrez to Dominican spirituality (although he only entered the Order of Preachers a few years ago, his early training in France exposed him to such figures as M.-D. Chenu and Yves Congar). These religious orders were themselves in the process (mandated by Vatican II) of re-establishing a more vital connection with their historical roots. This led in the Jesuits, for instance, to the dramatic claim by their thirty-second General Congregation that the promotion of justice was an integral part of their spirituality.

[25]See Meredith B. McGuire, "Mapping Contemporary American Spirituality: A Sociological Perspective," *Christian Spirituality Bulletin* 5/1 (Spring 1997): 1-8.

[26]See Gutiérrez's introduction to the second revised edition of *A Theology of Liberation.*

[27]Vincent Miller's recent work, *Consuming Religion: Christian Faith and Practice in a Consumer Culture* (New York: Continuum, 2004), is a good example of mining the insights of postmodern cultural critique and critical theory in order to frame a chastened, but still substantive, commitment to Enlightenment ideals of solidarity and justice.

[28]Anne Clifford made this point with clarity and force in her response to my presentation: "In recent years, science and religion/spirituality conferences have been sponsored by organizations such as the Center for Theology and the Natural Sciences, thanks to funding from the John Templeton Foundation. At such conferences scientists reflect on the spiritual dimension of their vocation as scientists. At times the spirituality is connected with specifically religious commitments, while at other times the affirmation is of a science-based and religionless natural spirituality (e.g., Ursula Goodenough). At such conferences it is not unusual for scientists to give testimony about the dynamic of the analytical observer becoming enamored by the wonder of the universe and its processes. Such testimony reflects an apolitical spirituality that fails to give attention to important elements of doing science, such as who funds what and why. How science may be related to economic globalization and its victimization of the poor and destruction of eco-systems are not addressed" (Anne Clifford, "Response," unpublished presentation, Annual Meeting of the College Theology Society, Washington, D.C., June 6, 2004).

Part II

EXPANDING THE HORIZON

Teshuva and *Torah*

Jewish-Christian Partnership as a New Horizon for Biblical Interpretation[1]

Elizabeth T. Groppe

Within the lifetime of the College Theology Society, there has been a dramatic change in the manner in which the Catholic Church and other Christian communions understand our relation to the Jewish people. For nearly two thousand years, Christian-Jewish relations have been shaped by accusations of deicide and supercessionist theologies that denied the ongoing validity of God's covenant with the Jewish people, creating the context for the ostracism and persecution that Jews experienced throughout Christian Europe.[2] Just forty years ago, in the shadow of the Shoah, the Second Vatican Council repudiated the deicide charge and affirmed, with St. Paul, that "the Jews, because of their ancestors, still remain very dear to God, whose gifts and calling are irrevocable (Rom 11:29)."[3]

Subsequent papal and episcopal statements have affirmed that God's covenant with the Jewish people is eternally valid.[4] Pope John Paul II has called the Catholic Church to *teshuva* (Hebrew for "repentance"), and the transformation of Catholic theology has been carried forward by pioneering scholars in the field of Jewish-Christian relations, such as Mary Boys, Philip Cunningham, Eugene Fisher, John Merkle, and John Pawlikowski.[5] "*Dabru Emet* [To Speak the Truth]: A Jewish Statement on Christians and Christianity," published in the *New York Times* in 2000, is a response to these changes in Christian theology and manifests the gracious willingness of some leaders in the Jewish community to begin a new era of Jewish-Christian partnership.[6]

In an age of increasing religious fundamentalism, and in an era in which appeals to religion are used to legitimate hatred and violence, the emergence of a new Jewish-Christian partnership is a harbinger of hope. Both the willingness of some Christians to admit historical wrongdoing and to commit the church to *teshuva*, and the openness of some members of the Jewish community to dialogue and partnership with Christians, despite all that the Jewish people have suffered at Christian hands, offer a promising portent in our religiously fractious world, a sign that another future is possible.

This is not to say that the establishment of a new partnership will be easy. The transformation of Christianity's relation to Judaism takes us into waters uncharted in Christianity's two thousand-year history. As Eugene Fisher has noted, the documents of Vatican II were replete with footnotes referencing patristic theologians, papal statements, and texts of previous councils, while the short section on the Jewish people in *Nostra Aetate* has no footnotes at all, because there is little precedent in the pages of Christian history for the affirmation that the Jews remain the beloved of God.[7] "Without saying it so explicitly," John Pawlikowski observes, "the 2,221 Council members who voted for *Nostra Aetate* were in fact stating that everything that had been said about the Christian-Jewish relationship since Paul moved in a direction they could no longer support."[8]

Christianity's new-found conviction that God's covenant with the Jewish people is enduring presents us with many challenging questions, to which there are as of yet no definitive answers. Is there, for example, one covenant, in which both Jews and Christians share, or two covenants, one Jewish and one Christian?[9] How can the Christian conviction that Christ is universal savior co-exist with the Jewish conviction that Jesus of Nazareth did not usher in the messianic era?

The questions we face concern not only matters appropriate to the forums of interreligious dialogue, but also matters foundational to Christianity itself. Christianity's formative period was characterized by a polemic against Judaism in which Christians defined their own identity in counter-distinction to a false caricature of the Jewish faith: Judaism was the religion of law, and Christianity the religion of love; Judaism was the religion of the material, and Christianity the religion of the spiritual; and so forth.[10] As we desist from polemic rivalry and begin to understand Judaism on its own terms, there has been a growing realization that our denigration of Judaism was detrimental to the development of Christianity itself. When Christianity divorced itself from its Jewish roots, John Howard Yoder argued, we lost the concrete moral tradition of *halakha*, a decentralized system of governance, and the wisdom of how to live as a faithful people without imperial power.[11] Scott Bader-Saye maintained that we lost the ethos of a communitarian covenantal politics that can resist both voluntarism and violence, while R. Kendall Soulen claimed that our supercessionist approach to Judaism and the Old Testament distorted our reading of the economy of salvation, obscured the public and political character of God's engagement with humanity, and encouraged a flight from history.[12] In the assessment of John Pawlikowski, we have much to learn from the Jewish tradition about the communal character of salvation, covenantal responsibility, theological anthropology, and the contribution of Torah to the concretization of freedom in social life.[13] Today's transformation in Jewish-Christian relations presents us with the opportunity to renew dimensions of our heritage that we have repudiated or undervalued. Indeed, Christianity's reconceptualization of its relation to Judaism is of such significance that it has been called a "Copernican Revolution."[14] It is a new horizon that has implications for all areas of the theological discipline, not least of which is the interpretation of scripture.

This essay focuses on Christian interpretation of the Old Testament, or, as some now prefer to say, seeking a nomenclature free of connotations of obsolescence, the "Shared Testament," "First Testament," or "Hebrew Scriptures."[15] From today's new horizon, how are Christians to read and interpret Leviticus or Deuteronomy or Isaiah? The 2001 statement of the Pontifical Biblical Commission (PBC), *The Jewish People and Their Sacred Scriptures in the Christian Bible*, offers some guidelines in this regard.[16] After a brief discussion of the PBC statement, this essay offers some reflections on the dietary laws in Leviticus 11 as one concrete illustration of what it might mean to read the Christian Old Testament in a new dialogical relationship with the Jewish tradition of interpretation of the *Tanach*.[17]

The PBC's *The Jewish People and Their Sacred Scriptures in the Christian Bible*

The PBC's central contribution to contemporary Jewish-Christian relations is the affirmation of the validity of the Jewish exegetical tradition. Historically, Christian readings of the Old Testament have interpreted prophetic texts as a foretelling of the Christ event and applied typological and allegorical methods to the broader Old Testament canon, enabling theologians such as Origen to find referents to Jesus Christ even in the wood Moses used to sweeten bitter waters (Ex 15:22-25) and the scarlet thread of Rahab (Jos 2:18) (§20). Christians have faulted Jews for their blind failure to understand their own sacred texts.

"It cannot be said," the PBC emphasizes, to the contrary, "that Jews do not see what is proclaimed in the text." Prophetic words were not intended as specific predictions of future events (§21), and Christian allegorical readings of the Old Testament risk a detachment of these texts from their original contexts and an arbitrary superimposition of an extraneous layer of meaning (preface; §20). The PBC acknowledges that it is appropriate for Christians to read the Old Testament through the lens of the Christ event. In doing so, however, we must recognize that this reading goes beyond the historical and literal parameters of the text (§21), a recognition that opens the door to other possible interpretations. Whereas Christians once derided Jewish exegesis as an obstinate refusal to see Christ in the testimonies of their own prophets and sages, the PBC now maintains, remarkably, that *"the Jewish reading of the Bible is a possible one*, in continuity with the Jewish Sacred Scriptures from the Second Temple period, a reading analogous to the Christian reading which developed in parallel fashion."[18]

This, indeed, marks a significant new horizon in Catholic biblical interpretation. Rabbi Alberto Piatelli, a leader of the Jewish community in Rome, commented that this "changes the whole exegesis of biblical studies and restores our biblical passages to their original meaning."[19]

The PBC statement is not without its limitations and critics.[20] Yet whatever the shortcomings of the document, it is crystal clear in one significant affirmation: the Jewish reading of the Bible is a legitimate one. Jewish biblical interpretation merits our respect rather than our derision, and there is much that Christians can learn from the Jewish tradition (§22). The PBC document endorses what some Christians have begun to do: study the scriptures together with Jews in a partnership in which our readings of these texts can be inspired, informed, challenged, or held in tension with the traditions of rabbinic exegesis.[21] The PBC, in sum, officially established respect for the Jewish exegetical tradition as a new horizon in Catholic biblical interpretation.

New Horizons in Practice: Revisiting Leviticus 11

The practice of hermeneutics, according to Gadamer, requires the building of a bridge between a text that is unfamiliar or obscure and our present cultural consciousness. Somehow, he writes, "something *distant* has to be brought close, a certain strangeness overcome" through a process he describes as a "fusion of horizons" (*Horizontverschmelzung*).[22] The horizons of any given text, however, are not limited to those of past reality and present consciousness. Given the PBC's affirmation of the validity of the Jewish exegetical tradition, Catholics might approach a text that we share in common with Judaism from a multiplicity of horizons: our own present consciousness, the historical and literary context of the text as reconstructed through biblical scholarship, and the Jewish exegetical tradition. No complete "fusion" of these horizons may be possible or desirable, given the fundamental differences between the Christian and Jewish traditions. Nonetheless, including Jewish exegesis as an additional horizon of interpretation can lead to constructive new readings of texts common to both Christian and Jewish canons. A reading of Leviticus 11:1-23, 41-46, a text concerning dietary law, exemplifies this.[23] While a comprehensive analysis of this material is not possible within the confines of this essay, I will identify some of the features of the various horizons through which we can approach this text and offer some concluding reflections on its significance.

Leviticus 11 recounts God's instruction to Moses: the people of Israel may eat, among the quadrupeds of the land, only those that have cloven hooves and that chew their cud. The camel, the rock badger, the hare, and the pig are explicitly proscribed (2-8). Among aquatic creatures, Israel may eat only those that have both scales and fins (i.e., not crustaceans, mollusks, or sea creatures such as sharks) (9-12); among the birds of the air, twenty species are expressly prohibited (the eagle, the vulture, the osprey, the buzzard, the kite, the raven, the ostrich, the nighthawk, the sea gull, the hawk, the little owl, the cormorant, the great owl, the water hen, the desert owl, the carrion vulture, the stork, the heron, the hoopoe, and the bat) (13-19); and, finally, among amphibians and insects, winged leaping insects with jointed legs are permitted (i.e., the locust, the bald locust, the cricket, and the grasshopper), but all other winged insects with four feet are prohibited, as are creatures that crawl on their bellies, swarming creatures, creatures that move on all fours, and creatures with many feet (20-23, 41-43). The reason some animals are proscribed, God tells Moses, is that they are *tamei* (unclean or impure): "For I am the Lord your God. Sanctify yourselves, therefore, and be holy, for I am holy" (Lev 11:44).

The Horizon of Contemporary American Christian Consciousness

A Christian reads Leviticus 11 with a consciousness shaped by the gospel narratives, the Pauline epistles, and centuries of tradition. Most Christians have long assumed that Jesus himself, followed by Paul, abrogated the Jewish dietary laws, including the proscriptions limiting animal consumption in Leviticus 11. For most of Christian history, accordingly, this text has had no practical bearing on agricultural and dietary practice. The second century Epistle of Barnabus maintained that the biblical prohibition against eating pork means simply that one should not associate with people who are of the character of swine. The Jews did not grasp this, but we, "having rightly understood the commandments, explain them as the Lord intended."[24] In the medieval period, Thomas Aquinas used figurative exegesis to find a spiritual significance in Leviticus 11. The animal with the cleft hoof, he explained, is clean because the two parts of the hoof are a figure of the two testaments, or the two natures of Christ, or the Father and the Son, or the distinction of good and evil.[25] In our own day, Leviticus 11 and its parallel in Deuteronomy 14:2-21 are not part of the current Roman Catholic lectionary and garner little attention among theologians.

At the same time, however, there is a growing concern about dietary issues in the American Christian community. This, too, is a dimension of the consciousness with which we approach this biblical text. The National Catholic Rural Life Conference (NCRLC) has been engaged in a campaign to raise awareness among the urban Catholic populace that "Eating Is a Moral Act."[26] The NCRLC has attempted to educate Catholics about practices now standard in agribusiness that exploit farm laborers and animals, erode the soil and exhaust its fertility, contaminate rivers and groundwaters with toxic chemicals, and threaten biodiversity and the survival of family farms.[27] Its campaign addresses these issues from the foundation of a Catholic ethic that emphasizes human dignity, solidarity, the common good, the option for the poor, and the integrity of creation.

While the NCRLC has struggled to make its voice of conscience heard, Christian diet literature is now a flourishing industry, with popular titles such as Joan Cavanaugh's *More of Jesus, Less of Me*, Patricia Kreml's *Slim for Him*, and Terry Dorian's *Health Begins in Him*. Despite the common presumption that Jesus critiqued Jewish dietary practice as a mere external observance with no inherent spiritual meaning, Christian diet groups have flourished, including the Tennessee-based "Weigh Down Workshop," offered in ten thousand churches, and the program "Jesus Is the Weigh."[28] According to Gwen Shamblin of the Weigh Down Workshop, "God is too smart to let somebody like Weight Watchers or Jane Fonda be your savior and get all the credit" and so "will not let other diets work."[29] We may chortle at this kind of theology, comments R. Marie Griffith in her analysis of this phenomenon, but "hundreds of thousands of down-hearted dieters look to this kind of devotional advice for redemption as assiduously as they have ever listened to Sunday sermons, and often with a great deal more desperation."[30] This cultural horizon conditions us who read scripture.

The Horizon of Contemporary Historical Critical Biblical Scholarship

Jacob Milgrom has written a comprehensive commentary on the book of Leviticus. He identifies Leviticus 11 as the work of the first Priestly school (P), which places the text in the period of the first Temple with a *terminus ad quem* circa 750 B.C.E., after which time the second Priestly school (II) carries the tradition.[31] To the untrained eye, Milgrom explains, Leviticus can appear to be an esoteric and arbitrary compendium of cultic and legal material. In fact, it contains a coherent theology, expressed not through discursive pronouncements but embedded in ritual acts that are pregnant with meaning.[32] The dietary proscriptions of Leviticus 11 can only be properly understood in the context of the overarching theology of the Priestly school, which, in turn, must be read in contrast to the religious worldviews of the cultures that surrounded ancient Israel.

In other cultures of the Ancient Near East, Milgrom explains, the cosmos is embroiled in a conflict of good and evil demons, a contest between chthonic deities and the forces of life. In ancient Israel, in contrast, there is one supreme God, the God of life, challenged only by God's creatures who may choose a path of life or death.[33] Dietary practice is one of the fundamental ways in which this choice confronts us. All of creation, according to the Priestly account of cosmic origins in Genesis 1, is good, and designed in such a way that creatures do not kill one another, even for food. Humans are herbivorous, permitted to eat of "every plant yielding seed that is upon the face of the earth, and every tree with seed in its fruit" (Gen 1:29). Beasts, birds, and creeping things, in like vein, may eat of "every green plant" (Gen 1:30).

Following the transgression of Adam and Eve and Cain's murder of Abel, however, creation is beset by violence (*chāmās*) (Gen 6:11).[34] According to the Genesis account, God releases the waters of the great flood, and, in the Noachide covenant that follows as the flood waters subside, God renews troth with creation, yet stipulates that every human or animal life that is taken must be requited (Gen 9:5). As a concession to the human character, God does allow the consumption of animal flesh, but only under the condition that the blood of the animal (believed to be its life) is returned to God (Gen 9:1-4).[35] This proscription against consumption of a slain animal's blood, Milgrom emphasizes, is not a primitive taboo that has infiltrated ancient Israel; there is no evidence of this practice in any other culture of the Ancient Near East.[36] Rather, this is an intentional innovation rooted in a fundamental theological principle: "the human being must never lose sight of the fundamental tenet for a viable human society. Life is inviolable; it may not be treated lightly. [Human]kind has a right to nourishment, not to life."[37] The Priestly narrative "declares its fundamental premise that human beings can curb their violent nature through ritual means, specifically a dietary discipline that will necessarily drive home the point that all life (*nepesh*), shared also by animals, is inviolable, except—in the case of meat—when conceded by God."[38]

The stipulations of the Noachide covenant, including the ban on the consumption of animal blood, are binding on all humanity. The covenant of Sinai, which includes the dietary prescriptions of Leviticus 11, holds the people of Israel to an even higher standard of comportment. Milgrom enumerates and critiques the various theories that have been advanced in the attempt to explain these dietary laws.[39] In the end, he insists that we must take our interpretive cue from the text itself, which designates holiness as the rationale for the dietary proscriptions: "For I am the Lord your God; sanctify yourselves therefore, and be holy, for I am holy" (Lev 11: 44; cf. Lev 11:45).[40] Milgrom illuminates this passage through a broad analysis of the meaning of the term "holy" (*qadosh*) in the Priestly theology. Holiness is an attribute of God—and the antonym of *tāmē* (impure), a term associated with the forces of death.[41] *Qadosh* refers to the forces of life, to the God of life, and Israel's task as an elect nation "is to be holy, to seek life, for its God is holy; he is the source of life."[42]

In this context, the function of the dietary laws in Leviticus 11 is to restrict severely the forms of animal life that Israel can consume, for animals share in the covenant with God, and, like humans, they have the divine gift of *nepesh* (life).[43] Milgrom examines the forms of animal life that populate the region Israel inhabited during the period of the first Priestly school, and he concludes that observance of the dietary guidelines in Leviticus would leave Israel with the following limited inventory of animals permitted for human consumption: cattle, sheep, goats, several kinds of fish, pigeons, turtledoves, several other nonraptorial birds, and locusts.[44] Cattle, sheep, and goats are domestic animals needed for milk and wool, and would likely be slaughtered only on special occasions so as not to unduly deplete the herds, a practical reality further complicated by the fact that Israel is required to ritually slaughter all animals on an altar so as to return their blood to God (Lev 17:11).[45] The requisite travel to a sanctuary would severely limit the occasions on which Israel consumed animal flesh. In sum, Milgrom writes, the purpose of the Priestly dietary laws is "to teach the Israelite reverence for life by (1) reducing his choice of flesh to a few animals; (2) limiting the slaughter of even these few permitted animals to the most humane way;[46] and (3) prohibiting the ingestion of blood and mandating its disposal upon the altar or by burial as acknowledgment that bringing death to living things is a concession to God's grace and not a privilege to man's whim."[47]

The Horizon of the Jewish Tradition

Historically, the Jewish community has been so committed to the various dietary observances of their tradition, including Leviticus' injunction against eating proscribed animals, that they have often made heroic sacrifices in order to be faithful to this observance.[48] Orthodox Jews still consider the dietary laws binding. Reform Judaism dispensed with the dietary observances in the Pittsburgh Platform of 1885, but there has been a revival of *kashrut* observance even among some in the Reform tradition, with varying degrees of rigor of practice.[49]

The Jewish tradition offers various interpretations of Leviticus 11. Philo of Alexandria (20 B.C.E.- 50 C.E.) read these dietary laws as allegories of human vices and virtues. Maimonides (c.1135-1204 C.E.) sought a rational explanation for the tradition, and others have maintained that the dietary laws belong to the category of *chukkim*, religious observances divinely commanded for which there is no possible explanation in human terms other than sheer fidelity to God. Dayan Grunfeld explains that the various interpretive approaches of the Jewish tradition are not mutually exclusive; the laws have simultaneously an ethical, mystical, and symbolic significance.[50]

While a comprehensive account of Jewish interpretations of Leviticus 11 is not possible here, I will highlight one dimension of this tradition: the emphasis on dietary observance as an act of reverence for life. The Jewish community's horizon of interpretation of Leviticus 11 is the broader biblical narrative of the *Tanach*, beginning with Genesis 1, an account of cosmic origins in which (as Milgrom emphasized) neither human nor beast killed one another for food. "The first man," the Talmud states, "had not been allowed to eat meat."[51] This interpretation of Genesis is reiterated by Rashi (1040-1105), Rabbi Abraham Ibn Ezra (1092-1167), Maimonides (1135-1204), Nachmanides (1194-1270), Rabbi Joseph Albo (d. 1444), Rabbi Moses Umberto Cassuto (1883-1951), and other important commentators in the rabbinic tradition.[52]

According to this interpretive tradition, God allowed for the eating of animal flesh in the aftermath of the great flood only as a concession to the human condition, an accommodation accompanied by the proviso that "you shall not eat flesh with its life, that is, its blood" (Gen 9:4).[53] God recognized, explains Samuel Dresner in *The Jewish Dietary Laws*, that human lust for flesh could not be extinguished, and so attempted to discipline our lust by requiring reverence for any animal life that was taken.[54] The blood, the life force of an animal, is not to be consumed. The Mosaic covenant that weds the Hebrew people to God calls them to an even more exacting standard. Some Jewish interpreters of Leviticus 11 emphasize that the laws distinguishing pure and impure animals, if strictly observed, will prevent humans from eating animals that are themselves carnivorous.[55] This not only protects the people of Israel from eating the flesh of animals that have eaten the blood of other animals, precluding an indirect violation of the proscription against eating blood, but, according to Grunfeld, this also mitigates the transference of animal instincts and passions to humans.[56] The body is an instrument of the spirit, writes Samson Raphael Hirsch, and vegetable foods, or the flesh of herbivorous animals, are more appropriate for human consumption than the flesh of carnivorous beasts, which may make us indifferent to loftier, moral impulses.[57] Rabbi Abraham Isaac Kook interprets the restrictions on animal consumption in Leviticus as pedagogical measures cultivating a reverence for life that will ultimately lead Israel away from all flesh consumption.[58] Dresner, in similar vein, describes the messianic era as a return to the idyllic conditions of Eden in which even animals will cease to kill one another for food. "The lion and lamb," Isaiah prophesied, "will live together, and the leopard lie down with the kid" (Is 11:6-9; cf. 65:25). "If the carnivorous animal will disappear at the end of time," Dresner comments, "how much more so the carnivorous man?"[59] In the interim, observance of the dietary laws is a witness to the nations of the living God and a dimension of the people of Israel's vocation to holiness.[60]

Converging Horizons: A Contemporary Christian Reading of Leviticus 11

We have now seen, albeit in a cursory fashion, three different horizons for interpretation of Leviticus 11. There is a striking convergence between dimensions of the Jewish tradition of interpretation and Milgrom's analysis of the original Priestly theology.[61] The great obstacle to any Gadamerian "fusion" of the three horizons outlined above is the Christian tradition, which has long assumed that Jesus and Paul abrogated the Jewish dietary laws, which no longer have any practical significance and retain meaning, if at all, only in an allegorical sense. This position is virtually impossible to reconcile with Milgrom's analysis of the theology of the Priestly school and with those strands of the Jewish tradition that emphasize that it is precisely in the *practice* of limiting our consumption of animal flesh that we exercise the reverence for life that is enjoined by God in Leviticus 11.

Perhaps we must simply conclude that no convergence of horizons is possible, and that Jews and Christians will inevitably read texts such as Leviticus 11 in ways that are mutually exclusive and irreconcilable. After all, the Pontifical Biblical Commission affirms only that "the Jewish reading of the Bible is a possible one," not that Jewish and Christian readings can be harmonized. Before we conclude that there is no way to bridge the distance between these divergent readings of Leviticus, however, there are other dimensions of the interpretive horizon to consider.

First, biblical scholars Jesper Svartik and Peter Tomson have questioned traditional interpretations of New Testament passages that Christians have typically read as an abrogation of Jewish dietary law.[62] Svartik argues in *Mark and Mission* that Jesus' statement "there is nothing outside a person that by going in can defile, but the things that come out are what defile" (Mk 7:15/Mt 15:11) is not in fact, as has long been assumed, an abrogation of dietary observance, but a warning about the perils of impure speech.[63] Tomson maintains that Christian exegetes, unattuned to the fine lines of difference between Jewish dietary laws, laws of ritual purity, and laws concerning idolatry, have read texts such as Mark 7:2-23, Galatians 2:11-14, and Romans 14:1-15:13 as annulments of dietary law, when in fact these texts concern either ritual purity or idolatry.[64]

Second, whatever the ultimate verdict of New Testament specialists on these new interpretations of Mark and Paul, the fact remains that pastoral reality indicates a need for attention to dietary practice in the Christian community. The popularity of Christian diet programs and the efforts of the National Catholic Rural Life Conference to raise awareness that "Eating Is a Moral Act" are evidence of this pastoral exigency.[65]

What, then, might Leviticus 11 mean to a contemporary Christian community? I do not pretend to do justice here to all the complex issues involved in a re-reading of this text—issues of Jesus and Paul and the law, the sociology of the Christian-Jewish schism, and so forth. I will, however, venture one proposal for a reinterpretation of Leviticus 11, read through the multiple horizons of Christian faith and pastoral needs, Milgrom's analysis of Priestly theology, and the Jewish history of interpretation. From the vista of the original Priestly theology and the Jewish tradition, Leviticus 11 limits Israel's killing and consumption of animals in order that Israel might cultivate a reverence for life and witness to the holiness of God. The dietary proscriptions in Leviticus anticipate the advent of the messianic era, envisioned by the prophet Isaiah as an age in which the conditions of Eden will return and neither humans nor beasts will kill one another

for food. The Jewish community still awaits the Messiah, an expectation, notably, that the Pontifical Biblical Commission affirms as a
valid stance.[66] Christians, however, profess that the messianic age
has already begun in Jesus Christ, and, as the PBC document emphasizes, we read the Old Testament from the presumption that in Christ
there is a "new creation" (§21).[67] If Leviticus 11 is indeed an ethic for
the interim between Eden and the messianic age, as Rabbi Abraham
Isaac Kook maintains, and if Christians truly believe that Jesus Christ
has inaugurated this new era, then Christians can read Leviticus 11
as a challenge to desist from eating animal flesh altogether. All creation does still live in a state of anticipation and eager longing for the
promised redemption (Rom 8:18-23); the messianic age has been inaugurated, not consummated. Nonetheless, the horizons of interpretation of Leviticus 11 explored here suggest that it would be appropriate, at a minimum, for Christians to abstain from animal flesh on
Sunday, the feast of resurrection that marks the inbreaking of the
messianic time.[68]

This observance would not be an act of penitence, as was the
Friday abstinence from meat practiced in the Catholic Church before
Vatican II, but rather an act of celebration of the inauguration of the
peaceable kingdom that Isaiah promised.[69] Witness to God's peaceable kingdom is particularly important in a context in which the vast
majority of animals in this country are not bred on small bucolic
family farms or on the open range, but in so-called "factory farms"
that inflict tremendous suffering on animals and employ methods of
production that take a devastating toll on the environment.[70] In the
analysis of Francis Moore Lappé, moreover, the earth's limited soils
and waters can never provide adequate food for the billions of mal-
nourished members of our human family unless there is a reduction
in meat consumption among the affluent; grains and legumes feed up
to 40 times more people if consumed directly by humans rather than
used as fodder for feedlot animals bred for human consumption.[71] At
the messianic banquet that we anticipate in our Sunday observances,
there is abundance for all at the table, and no one is turned away
hungry.[72]

Milgrom emphasizes that the Priestly theology of reverence for
life is not just an ideal or an abstraction to "which humans may pay
lip service."[73] It is, rather, a theology embedded in ritual, and this is
key to its effectiveness. The establishment of some form of a Catholic
ritual dietary observance intended to cultivate a reverence for life

could make an important contribution to the NCRLC's effort to raise awareness that "Eating Is a Moral Act." In addition, it would establish a context that can serve as an important corrective to those Christian diet programs that are focused primarily on weight loss. Such programs embrace our commercial culture's ideal body type at the expense of those persons for whom it is metabolically impossible to become "Slim for Him." Moreover, these programs may distract us from the deeper meaning of a religious dietary observance. Something much more important is at stake in dietary practice, writes Jewish scholar George Robinson, than the "'how many calories, how many grams of fat' of the compulsive dieter."[74] Ultimately at issue, according to the Priestly writers, is nothing less than the holiness of the God of life.

Conclusion

The cathedral in Strasbourg, France, is one of many churches in Europe with a statue of "Ecclesia and Synagoga," a stone image that personifies Ecclesia as a woman triumphant and upright, and Synagoga as a woman with blindfolded eyes and a book of Torah slipping to the ground. This image communicates to all who enter or stroll past the cathedral that Judaism is a woman broken and blind, unable to read properly even her own scriptures. Today, the Pontifical Biblical Commission has rescinded the long-standing accusation of Jewish blindness and affirmed the validity of Judaism's own reading of its sacred texts. This presents the opportunity for Christians and Jews to engage together in the reading of scripture as partners rather than polemical opponents, a partnership expressed in a new version of the "Ecclesia and Synagoga" image commissioned by Mary Boys. In this image, two woman stand together, Synagoga with Torah scrolls held firmly in her hands.[75] The potential partnership of church and synagogue symbolized by this image is an important new horizon in theology. It affords Christians the opportunity to disabuse ourselves of the false caricatures of Judaism that we have inherited, and to reinvigorate our own tradition through conversation and dialogue with the Jewish people. We can now add a new horizon to our interpretation of the biblical texts we share in common with Judaism: the horizon of the Jewish exegetical tradition. This essay has offered one example of the potential fruitfulness of a re-reading of scripture from this perspective. In a context in which pastoral reality suggests a need for some form of dietary guidelines in the Christian community, Jewish readings of Leviticus 11 can stimulate reflection on the importance of corporate dietary observances that cultivate a reverence for life and testify to the holiness of God in anticipation of the messianic age.

Notes

[1]This essay originated in a joint session of the Contemporary Theologies and Scripture sections at the June, 2004, College Theology Society convention. It has been considerably enhanced and improved by critique and constructive suggestions from my scripture colleagues Carol J. Dempsey (University of Portland) and Sarah Melcher (Xavier University). My experience confirms the importance of collaboration between scripture scholars and systematicians. The position taken in the essay and the limitations of the analysis are, of course, my own.

[2]See Edward Flannery, *The Anguish of the Jews: Twenty-Three Centuries of Anti-Semitism*, 2nd ed. (Mahwah, N.J.: Paulist Press, 1999). The introduction notes that this reprinting is necessary because the publication's objective—to acquaint Christians with the sufferings of Jews throughout the Christian era—has not yet been realized: "The vast majority of Christians, even well educated, are all but totally ignorant of what happened to Jews in history and of the culpable involvement of the Church," which makes understanding and communication between Jews and Christians almost impossible (1). This year's enthusiastic reception of Mel Gibson's film *The Passion of the Christ*, despite the film's use of classic anti-Jewish motifs such as the association of Jews and the devil, illustrates how far we remain from realizing Flannery's educational objective. For commentary on Gibson's film from the perspective of Jewish-Christian relations, see *Pondering the Passion: What's at Stake for Christians and Jews?*, ed. Philip A. Cunningham (Lanham, Md.: Rowman & Littlefield, 2004.)

[3]*Nostra Aetate*, 4. *Shoah* is the Hebrew word for "catastrophe." It is preferred by many to the term "Holocaust," which literally means "sacrifice," as a designation for the genocide of the Jews of Europe.

[4]See, for example, Pope John Paul II, "Address to the Jewish Community on the Occasion of a Pastoral Visit to Australia," in *Spiritual Pilgrimage: Texts on Jews and Judaism 1979-1995*, ed. Eugene J. Fisher and Leon Klenicki (New York: Crossroad, 1996), 83. A selective list of statements on Jewish-Christian relations from a variety of denominations has been compiled by Mary Boys in *Has God Only One Blessing? Judaism as a Source of Christian Self-Understanding* (Mahwah, N.J.: Paulist Press, 2000), 252-53. Many of these statements are available on the internet at http://www.jcrelations.net. Other sources include Helga Croner, ed., *Stepping Stones to Further Jewish-Christian Relations: An Unabridged Collection of*

Christian Documents (New York: Paulist Press, 1977); Croner, ed., *More Stepping Stones to Jewish-Christian Relations: An Unabridged Collection of Christian Documents 1975-1983* (New York: Paulist Press, 1985); Allan Brockway, Paul van Buren, Rolf Rendtorff and Simon Schoon, eds., *The Theology of the Churches and the Jewish People: Statements by the World Council of Churches and Its Member Churches* (Geneva: WCC Publications, 1987); K. Hannah Holtschneider, *The 1980 Statement of the Rhineland Synod: A Landmark in Christian-Jewish Relations in Germany* (Cambridge, England: OJCR Press, 2002). An excellent resource for educators is the new film *Walking God's Paths: Christians and Jews in Candid Conversation*, produced by the Catholic Communication Campaign and the National Council of Synagogues, available from USCCB Publishing at 1-800-594-5617.

[5]Several of these scholars describe their engagement with Judaism in *Faith Transformed: Christian Encounters with Jews and Judaism*, ed. John C. Merkle (Collegeville, Minn.: Liturgical Press, 2003).

[6]*"Dabru Emet*: A Jewish Statement on Christians and Christianity" was co-authored by Michael A. Signer, Tikva Frymer-Kensky, David Novak, and Peter Ochs and signed by numerous Jewish scholars and religious leaders. The text is reprinted in Frymer-Kensky, Novak, Ochs, David Fox Sandmel, and Signer, eds., *Christianity in Jewish Terms* (Boulder, Colo.: Westview Press, 2000), xvii-xx. It is also available on-line at http://www.icjs.org/what/njsp/dabruemet.html. The statement "A Sacred Obligation: Rethinking Christian Faith in Relation to Judaism and the Jewish People" was promulgated by the ecumenical Christian Scholars Group on Christian-Jewish Relations, in part as a response to *Dabru Emet*. It is available on-line from the Center for Christian-Jewish Learning at Boston College at http://www.bc.edu/bc_org/research/cjl/Christian_Scholars_Group/Sacred_Obligation.htm. *Seeing Judaism Anew: Christianity's Sacred Obligation*, a book edited by Mary Boys that expands on this statement, is forthcoming.

[7]Lecture by Eugene Fisher at the University of Notre Dame, Spring 2001.

[8]John Pawlikowski, O.S.M., "Reflections on Covenant and Mission," in *Themes in Jewish-Christian Relations*, ed. Edward Kessler and Melanie Wright (Cambridge: Orchard Academic, 2004).

[9]See, for example, Michael A. Signer, "One Covenant or Two? Can We Sing a New Song?" in *Reinterpreting Revelation and Tradition: Jews and Christians in Conversation*, ed. John T. Pawlikowski, O.S.M. and Hayim Goren Perelmuter (Franklin, Wis.: Sheed & Ward, 2000), 3-23; John T. Pawlikowski, "The Search for a New Paradigm for the Christian-Jewish Relationship: A Response to Michael Signer," in *Reinterpreting Revelation and Tradition*, 25-48. For a survey of views on single-covenant, double-covenant, and multi-covenant perspectives, see John Pawlikowski, *Jesus and the Theology of Israel* (Wilmington, Del.: Michael Glazier, 1989), 15-47.

[10]See, for example, Justin Martyr, "Dialogue with Trypho," in *Saint Justin*

Martyr, Fathers of the Church, vol. 6, ed. Thomas Falls (Washington, D.C.: Catholic University Press, 1977), 11, 40, 41.

[11]John Howard Yoder, *The Jewish-Christian Schism Revisited*, ed. Michael G. Cartright and Peter Ochs (Grand Rapids: Eerdmans, 2003).

[12]Scott Bader-Saye, *Church and Israel after Christendom* (Boulder, Colo.: Westview Press, 1999); R. Kendall Soulen, *The God of Israel and Christian Theology* (Minneapolis, Minn.: Fortress Press, 1996).

[13]Pawlikowski, *Jesus and the Theology of Israel*, 88-95.

[14]Gilbert G. Rosenthal, "Introduction" to special symposium issue of *Midstream: A Monthly Jewish Review* 49 (January 2003): 2.

[15]For a critique of these alternative nomenclatures, see Amy-Jill Levine, "A Particular Problem: Jewish Perspectives on Christian Bible Study," in *Theology and Sacred Scripture*, ed. Carol J. Dempsey, O.P., and William P. Loewe, CTS Annual Volume, no. 47 (Maryknoll, N.Y.: Orbis Books, 2001), 15-18. On the debate about terminology, see also Roger Brooks and John J. Collins, eds., *Hebrew Bible or Old Testament?* (Notre Dame: University of Notre Dame Press, 1990).

[16]The Pontifical Biblical Commission, *The Jewish People and Their Sacred Scriptures in the Christian Bible*, trans. Maurice Hogan (Vatican City: Editrice Vaticana, 2002). The original French edition was published in 2001.

[17]*TaNaKh* is a common name for the thirty-nine books that compose the Jewish scriptures. It is an acronym for the three primary parts of the Jewish canon: Torah (Law), Nevi'im (Prophets), and Ketuvim (Writings).

[18]The Pontifical Bible Commission, *The Jewish People and Their Sacred Scriptures in the Christian Bible*, §22, my emphasis. As Elena Procario-Foley observed in the discussion that followed the presentation of this paper at the convention, this approach to the Hebrew scriptures advances Jewish-Christian dialogue in a more fundamental manner than the approach to Old Testament interpretation of both the 1985 Vatican Commission for Religious Relations with the Jews' statement "Notes on the Correct Way to Present Jews and Judaism in Preaching and Catechesis in the Roman Catholic Church," and the 1992 *Catechism of the Catholic Church*.

[19]Cited in John R. Donahue, S.J., "Joined by Word and Covenant: Reflections on a Recent Vatican Document on Jewish-Christian Relations," Msgr. George A. Denizer Lecture, Immaculate Conception Seminary, Huntington, Long Island, March 16, 2003. Available online at http://www.bc.edu/research/cjl/meta-elements/texts/articles/Donahue.htm.

[20]For both appreciative commentary and critique, see Donahue, "Joined by Word and Covenant"; Philip A. Cunningham, "The Pontifical Biblical Commission's 2001 Study on *The Jewish People and Their Sacred Scriptures in the Christian Bible*: Selected Important Quotations with Comments," posted online April 24, 2002 at http://www.bc.edu/research/cjl/meta-elements/texts/articles/PBC_2001_Summary.htm; Donald Senior, "Rome Has Spoken: A New Catholic Approach to Judaism," *Commonweal* 130 (January

31, 2003): 20-23; Markus Bockmuehl, "The Jewish People and Their Sacred Scriptures in the Christian Bible: First Response," *Scripture Bulletin* 23 (2003): 15-28; Edward Kessler, "The Jewish People and Their Sacred Scriptures in the Christian Bible: Second Response," *Scripture Bulletin* 23 (2003): 29-44; Oxford Bible Collective, "The Jewish People and Their Sacred Scriptures in the Christian Bible: Third Response," *Scripture Bulletin* 23 (2003): 46-52; Roland E. Murphy, "The Biblical Commission, the Jews, and Scriptures," *Biblical Theological Bulletin* 32 (2002): 145-49.

[21]On reading scripture in the context of Jewish-Christian dialogue, see Michael A. Signer, "The Rift That Binds: Hermeneutical Approaches to the Jewish-Christian Relationship," in *Ecumenism: Present Realities and Future Prospects*, ed. Lawrence Cunningham (Notre Dame: University of Notre Dame Press, 1998), 95-115; "Scripture," in *Christian-Jewish Dialogue: A Reader*, ed. Helen P. Fry (Exeter, England: University of Exeter Press, 1996), 163-92; Jonathon Magonet, "When I See What Christians Make of the 'Hebrew' Bible," in his *Talking to the Other: Jewish Interfaith Dialogue with Christians and Muslims* (New York: I.B. Tauras, 2003), 134-46; Gregory Mobley, "Protestant and Jewish Approaches to the Scripture (Or What I Learned . . . from Inter-faith Bible Study)," presentation to the May 19, 2004, meeting of Jewish-Christian Dialogue in Newton, Massachusetts, available online at http://www.bc.edu/research/cjl/meta-elements/texts/articles/ mobley.htm.

[22]Hans-Georg Gadamer, "On the Scope and Function of Hermeneutical Reflection," trans. G. B. Hess and R. E. Palmer, in *Philosophical Hermeneutics*, ed. David E. Linge (Berkeley: University of California Press, 1976), 22-23; Hans-Georg Gadamer, *Truth and Method* (London: Sheed & Ward, 1975), 273. See also Anthony C. Thiselton, *The Two Horizons: New Testament Hermeneutics and Philosophical Description* (Grand Rapids: Eerdmans, 1980).

[23]Given the length restrictions of this essay, I am omitting discussion of vv. 24-40, which identify those impure animals whose carcasses must not be touched. On the insertion of these verses into a previous block of text on dietary proscriptions, see Jacob Milgrom, *Leviticus 1-16: A New Translation with Introduction and Commentary*, Anchor Bible, vol. 3 (New York: Doubleday, 1991), 692-95. On the relationship between Leviticus 11 and the parallel text in Deuteronomy 14:4-21, see pp. 8-10, 698-704. My summary and paraphrase of Leviticus 11 is based on the NRSV translation in the Oxford Annotated Bible and Milgrom's translation in *Leviticus 1-16*, 643-45.

[24]"Epistle of Barnabas," in *The Apostolic Fathers*, 2nd ed., ed. Michael W. Holmes (Grand Rapids: Baker Books, 1992), 13.2.

[25]Thomas Aquinas, *Summa Theologiae*, Ia-IIae, q. 102, a. 6, r. 1. In q. 102, Aquinas offers a sophisticated synthesis of the various levels of meaning of the dietary laws. The discussion reflects his knowledge of the work of the medieval Jewish scholar Maimonides.

[26]For more information, see the NCRLC's website: http://www.ncrlc.com/.

[27]For further discussion of these issues, see Andrew Kimbrell, ed., *Fatal Harvest: The Tragedy of Industrial Agriculture* (Washington, D.C.: Island Press, 2002). For an alternative agricultural vision, see Dana L. Jackson and Laura L. Jackson, *The Farm as Natural Habitat: Reconnecting Food Systems with Ecosystems* (Washington, D.C.: Island Press, 2002).

[28]See R. Marie Griffith, "The Promised Land of Weight Loss: Law and Gospel in Christian Dieting," *The Christian Century* 114 (May 7, 1997): 449.

[29]Cited in Griffith, "The Promised Land of Weight Loss," 449.

[30]Ibid.

[31]Milgrom, *Leviticus 1-16*, 28. On the relation and distinction of P and H, see pp. 1-41.

[32]Ibid., 42, 45.

[33]Ibid., 42-43, 47.

[34]Ibid., 26, 48.

[35]On the allowance of consumption of animal flesh as a concession, see Milgrom, *Leviticus 1-16*, 705-706. On blood as life, see p. 46. On the requirement to return the blood to God, see pp. 704-706. On the killing of an animal as equivalent to murder if not expiated by the dashing of the animal's blood on God's altar, see p. 49.

[36]Ibid., 706.

[37]Ibid., 713.

[38]Ibid., 48. On the commonality of *nepesh* to both animals and human-kind, see Genesis 9:9-10; Leviticus 11:10, 46 and 24:18. For commentary, see Milgrom, *Leviticus 1-16*, 72, 712, and 720.

[39]Ibid., 718-29.

[40]Ibid., 46, 694, 729.

[41]Examining the various forms of ritual impurity in Leviticus 11-15, Milgrom concludes that the common denominator is "the association with death" (686; see also 45-46, 731-32).

[42]Ibid., 686. The theology of holiness as being "set apart" must be seen in the context of a theology of the holy as the life of God (724-25).

[43]On animals as participants in God's covenant, see Milgrom, *Leviticus 1-16*, 720. On Leviticus 11 as a restriction and limitation on Israel's access to the animal world, see pp. 652 and 661.

[44]Among quadrupeds of the land, there are technically a few forms of wild animals permissible to Israel given the criteria in Leviticus 11, but these were so rare as to be virtually inaccessible. The primary forms of aquatic life available in the region inhabited by Israel during the era of the Priestly school were mollusks and crustaceans, disqualified for consumption. See Milgrom, *Leviticus 1-16*, 652, 661, 735-36.

[45]On the prohibitive economic cost of slaughtering livestock, see Milgrom, *Leviticus 1-16*, 735. On the requirement to slaughter on an altar, see pp. 710-11.

[46]On the requirements of ritual slaughter, which include strict procedural guidelines intended to ensure a death that is as quick and painless as possible, see Milgrom, *Leviticus 1-16*, 713-78.

[47]Ibid., 735.

[48]Samuel H. Dresner, *The Jewish Dietary Laws: Their Meaning for Our Time* (New York: Burning Bush Press, 1966), 47-49.

[49]See Peter S. Knobel, "Reform Judaism and *Kashrut*," *Judaism* 39 (1990): 488-93. The term more familiar to us is *kosher*, a Yiddish form of the Hebrew word *kasher*, which means simply "fit" or "proper."

[50]Dayan I. Grunfeld, *The Jewish Dietary Laws*, 2 vols. (New York: Soncino Press, 1972), I:11-25.

[51]Sanhed. 59b.

[52]Cited in Richard Schwartz, *Judaism and Vegetarianism* (New York: Lantern Books, 2003), 1. On this point, see also James M. LeBeau, *The Jewish Dietary Laws: Sanctify Life* (New York: United Synagogue of America, 1983), 41-42.

[53]On the permission to eat meat as God's concession, see, for example, Umberto Cassuto, *A Commentary on the Book of Genesis*, 2 vols., trans. Israel Abrahams (Jerusalem: Magnes Press, 1961), 1:58; Isaac Klein, *A Guide to Jewish Religious Practice* (New York: Jewish Theological Seminary of America, 1979), 309; Abraham Yitzhak Hacohen Cook, "A Vision of Vegetarianism and Peace," in "None Shall Hurt or Destroy: A Translation of 'A Vision of Vegetarianism and Peace' with Introduction and Commentary," by Jonathan L. Rubenstein (Rabbinic Thesis, Hebrew Union College—Jewish Institute of Religion, 1986), 65-66; Dresner, *The Jewish Dietary Laws*, 21-27.

[54]Dresner, *The Jewish Dietary Laws*, 26-27. In a similar vein, see also LeBeau, *Jewish Dietary Laws*, 74.

[55]The limitation of edible land animals to those that chew the cud restricts edible mammals to herbivores, and, as the rabbis have noted, all the birds expressly proscribed in Leviticus are predators. See Milgrom, *Leviticus 1-16*, 661. On this point from an anthropologist's perspective, see also Mary Douglas, "The Forbidden Animals in Leviticus," *Journal for the Study of the Old Testament* 59 (1993): 3-23.

[56]Grunfeld, *Jewish Dietary Laws*, 1:8-9, 1:213.

[57]Samson Raphael Hirsch, *Horeb: A Philosophy of Jewish Laws and Observances*, trans. I. Grunfeld (London: Soncino Press, 1962), 317-18.

[58]Abraham Isaac Kook, "Fragments of Light: A View as to the Reasons for the Commandments," in Kook, *The Lights of Penitence, The Moral Principles, Lights of Holiness, Essays, Letters, and Poems*, trans. Ben Zion Bokser (New York: Paulist Press, 1978), 317-23; Kook, "A Vision of Vegetarianism and Peace," 67-119. On dietary observance as a means to progress from an imperfect to more perfect condition, see also Yitzhak Damiel, "Letter and Spirit," *Judaism* 21 (1953): 110-16.

[59]Dresner, *Jewish Dietary Laws*, 24. On this point see also Milgrom, *Leviticus 1-16*, 720. For an analysis of Isaiah's vision from the perspective of a Catholic biblical scholar, see Robert Murray, *The Cosmic Covenant* (London: Sheed & Ward, 1992), 103-12. Some Jews do practice complete vegetarianism, and one of the reasons some give for this discipline is the Jewish principle that one should act in such a way as to advance the coming of the messianic age. On vegetarianism in contemporary Judaism, see Louis Berman, *Vegetarianism and the Jewish Tradition* (New York: KTAV, 1982); Roberta Kalechofsky, ed., *Rabbis and Vegetarianism: An Evolving Tradition* (Marblehead, Mass.: Micah Publications, 1995); Roberta Kalechofsky, *Vegetarian Judaism* (Marblehead, Mass.: Micah Publications, 1998); Richard Schwartz, *Judaism and Vegetarianism* (New York: Lantern Books, 2003).

[60]On *kashrut* observance and holiness, see, for example, J. H. Hertz, ed., *The Pentateuch and Haftorahs* (London: Soncino Press, 1958), 448; LeBeau, *Jewish Dietary Laws*, 31-36; Dresner, *The Jewish Dietary Laws*, 12-21, 44-47, 52-53.

[61]This may be due in part to the fact that Milgrom himself is a Jewish scholar who acknowledges his debt to the Rabbinic tradition, even as he is also a master of modern historical critical method. See Milgrom, *Leviticus 1-16*, 63-67.

[62]See also Jiri Moskala, *The Laws of Clean and Unclean Animals of Leviticus 11: Their Nature, Theology and Rationale (An Intertextual Study)*, Adventist Theological Society Dissertation Series no. 4 (Berrien Springs, Mich.: Adventist Theological Society, 2000). I was not able to access a copy of this dissertation, but according to a review it argues that "the rationale and theology behind the Pentateuchal dietary laws seems to be valid also in the New Testament economy because the cross of Jesus does not abrogate the theology and rationale behind this specific kind of uncleanness." See Ralph K. Hawkins, Review of Moskala, *The Laws of Clean and Unclean Animals*, in *The Catholic Biblical Quarterly* 65 (2003): 12-13. The citation is from Moskala, p. 373. Hawkins notes that Moskala's work is a contribution to the field, but questions some of his conclusions, which, in his assessment, do not account for Acts 15:20.

[63]Jesper Svartik, *Mark and Mission: Mark 7:1-23 in Its Narrative and Historical Contexts*, Coniectanea Biblica New Testament Series no. 32 (Stockholm, Sweden: Almquist & Wiksell International, 2000). In Mark 7:15, Svartik argues, Jesus challenges the practice of the Pharisees on the basis of the higher authority of biblical law, and it is thus most implausible that his teaching on defilement is an abrogation of the dietary observances in Leviticus or Deuteronomy. Svartik's position that Jesus' statement is a warning of the perils of evil speech is supported by an analysis of comparable parabolic sayings in the Jewish tradition.

[64]Peter J. Tomson, "Jewish Food Laws in Early Christian Community Discourse," *Semeia* 86 (2001): 193-211. Tomson argues that there was no

outright rejection of dietary law among the early Christian communities until the Bar Kochba war (132-135 C.E.), when social tensions precipitated a deepening of the Christian/Jewish schism and mutual exclusion on both sides of the divide.

[65]In a recent survey conducted by *U.S. Catholic* magazine, 96 percent of the respondents indicated that the issue of making ethical food choices had never been addressed in their parishes ("Feedback," *U.S. Catholic* 69 [March 2004]: 22).

[66]The Pontifical Biblical Commission, *The Jewish People and Their Sacred Scriptures in the Christian Bible*, §21.

[67]For reflection on the meaning of this affirmation in dialogue with contemporary scientific developments, see Carol J. Dempsey, "Creation, Evolution, Revelation, and Redemption: Connections and Intersections," in *Earth, Wind, & Fire: Biblical and Theological Perspectives on Creation*, ed. Carol J. Dempsey and Mary Margaret Pazdan (Collegeville, Minn.: Liturgical Press, 2004), 1-23.

[68]A comparable ethical argument has been made for a theology of Christian marriage. Jesus' position against divorce in Matthew 5:31, it has been said, is an eschatological sign of the inbreaking of God's reign that restores the pristine state of creation in which male and female were united as one flesh. See Kenneth R. Himes, O.F.M. and James A. Coriden, "The Indissolubility of Marriage: Reasons to Reconsider," *Theological Studies* 65 (2004): 467.

[69]My argument for Sunday abstinence from meat as an act of celebration rather than a penitential observance is not intended to negate the importance of penitential practices. In the context described above, however, abstinence from meat can be seen as a joyous act. The establishment of this form of corporate dietary observance, moreover, could fill a void that Eamon Duffy finds in the post-Vatican II Catholic Church. The discontinuation of Friday abstinence from meat, he writes, has resulted in the loss of an important mark of Catholic identity, a prophetic communal stand of solidarity with the poor and hungry, and he upholds Judaism as a counter example of a religious tradition in which dietary observances have contributed so much to corporate identity and witness. The 1983 Code of Canon Law actually does require abstinence from meat on Fridays, but the U.S. Catholic bishops and other national conferences allow for the substitution of another unspecified sacrifice. "What had been a corporate mark of identity," Duffy laments, has become "another individual consumer choice, like going on a diet." Eamon Duffy, "Fasting—Our Lost Rite," *The Tablet* 258 (January 31, 2004): 6. Duffy's position may appear, in my rendering, one of pure nostalgia for the past, but it is clear from the context of his article that his motivation is a much deeper concern for an authentic living of the gospel and a preservation of the corporate and symbolic character of Catholicism.

[70]On the conditions in factory farms, see C. David Coats, *Old MacDonald's*

Factory Farm (New York: Continuum, 1989); Jim Mason and Peter Singer, *Animal Factories*, rev. ed. (New York: Harmony Books, 1990). Rabbi David Rosen believes that traditional Jewish dietary observances are inadequate in our contemporary context, in which the tremendous suffering that animals experience in factory farms defeats one of the primary purposes of the laws of ritual slaughter: the minimizing of animal suffering and pain (David Rosen, "Vegetarianism: An Orthodox Jewish Perspective," in Kalechofsky, *Rabbis and Vegetarianism*, 53-55). For the NCRLC's position on the treatment of farm animals, see http://www.ncrlc.com/card03backtext.html. On the devastating environmental consequences of modern methods of meat production, see, for example, "Choices for a Healthy Environment" and "Once Upon a Planet," in John Robbins, *The Food Revolution* (Berkeley, Calif.: Conari Press, 2001), 231-52 and 253-82; Ed Ayres and Thomas Prugh, "Meat: Now, It's Not Personal!" *World Watch* 17 (July/August 2004): 12-19. The problem is evident in the following statistics: a hamburger yielding about 400 calories of food energy requires 8,000 calories of fossil-fuel energy to produce (not including transportation, cooling, and cooking) and, in addition, 600 gallons of fresh water. According to one estimate, each quarter-pound hamburger made from Central American beef destroys 55 square feet of rainforest (cleared for grazing), while a quarter-pound of U.S. feedlot beef results in the erosion and loss of about 9 pounds of topsoil ("The Humble Hamburger," *World Watch* 17 [July/August 2004], cover page).

[71]The grain used to produce an 8-ounce steak, she notes, would fill the empty bowls of 40 hungry people. This is the most extreme example, as cattle are the most inefficient feedlot animals. It takes 16 pounds of grain and soy to produce 1 pound of beef. The corresponding ratio for pork is 6.1, for turkey, 4:1, and for chicken, 3:1. See Frances Moore Lappé, *Diet for a Small Planet*, rev. ed. (New York: Ballantine Books, 1982), 61, 69-71. Lappé recommends that those of us privileged with multiple dietary options eat lower on the food chain, but she also emphasizes that solutions to world hunger will require structural changes in patterns of the production and distribution of food. On the relationship between diets high in meat consumption and world hunger, see also John Robbins, *May All Be Fed: Diet for a New World* (New York: William Morrow, 1992); Francis Moore Lappé and Anna Lappé, *Hope's Edge: The New Diet for a Small Planet* (New York: Tarcher, 2002); Mark Gold, *The Global Benefits of Eating Less Meat* (Hampshire, England: Compassion in World Farming Trust, 2004).

[72]On the connection between eucharistic celebration and the alleviation of world hunger, see Monika Hellwig's classic *The Eucharist and the Hunger of the World*, 2nd rev. ed. (Kansas City: Sheed & Ward, 1992).

[73]Milgrom, *Leviticus 1-16*, 736.

[74]George Robinson, *Essential Judaism: A Complete Guide to Beliefs, Customs, and Rituals* (New York: Simon & Shuster, 2000), 253.

[75]Mary C. Boys, *Has God Only One Blessing?*, 32 and 246.

Science and the Soul

Keeping the Essentials

Michael Horace Barnes

The human soul can be defined in a very general way as whatever it is about us humans that enables us to have self-reflective consciousness and choice, to have intellect and free will in standard language. It is what Karl Rahner refers to simply as "spirit" or as the power of self-transcendence.[1] The soul has also traditionally been defined more specifically as a spiritual reality in the sense of being non-material or non-physical, each soul in fact requiring a special act of creation by God. This definition goes a step beyond merely asserting that humans have intellect and will to asserting that only a non-material reality could be the source of intellection and choice. That elaboration has provided a basis for saying that science cannot study the soul, because the object of science is material reality.

Nonetheless, current neurological studies, especially in concert with studies in paleontology, anthropology, evolutionary and developmental psychology, and information sciences are pushing outward the horizons of our understanding of the origin and nature of human mental processes. The cumulative effect of the work of these sciences makes it plausible to claim that the modern human power of thought and conscious choice emerged gradually over millions of years through the material process of evolution, and that even the most complex thought processes, including the power of reflective self-transcendence, are produced entirely by the human brain (and the cultural history that provides cognitive tools for that brain to use).[2]

As a result, a number of Christians have proposed an *emergentist* and *physicalist* interpretation of the soul. These interpretations, on the face of it, seem decidedly contrary to the standard Christian doctrine of a non-material soul created specially by God, and they even challenge the use of the word "soul." The first part of this essay briefly reviews current speculations about the soul along with some background information that leads to that speculation. The second part addresses three additional issues relevant to continued reflections about the soul. The conclusion is that contemporary theological reflection on these scientific developments offers a new horizon: the soul as physical and emergent, and yet fitting with many of the central concerns articulated in traditional doctrines of the soul

Some Contemporary New Understandings of the Soul

Work by theologians on the topic of the soul in the light of modern brain science is in process. Warren S. Brown, Nancey Murphy, and H. Newton Maloney, along with six other contributors to their book *Whatever Happened to the Soul*, many of them professors at the somewhat conservative Fuller Theological Seminary, have perused the relevant scientific literature. They identify the soul with the mind, and they are persuaded that what we call the mind or soul has *emerged* from the material process of evolution. As a result they now proclaim their support for what they call a "non-reductive physicalism."[3] The word "physicalism" signifies that mind/soul arises from activities of the physical brain. The word "non-reductive" indicates that mind/soul is nonetheless distinct from the brain, though not separate from it. These authors claim the emergent mind/soul is then in a position of supervenience—of "top down" causality—in relation to the brain.[4] This is intended to preserve the notion of human free choice; the mind is not fully determined by the activities of the brain.

There are in fact a variety of physicalist or emergentist positions on the soul.[5] Keith Ward agrees that the soul emerges from the evolution of matter. He supports a "soft materialism," as he calls it, which takes seriously that what emerges from matter might be yet more than material.[6] Richard Swinburne also concludes that the soul is a product of the material evolution of the universe, but he claims that soul has become so distinct from matter that only a new sort of body-mind dualism adequately describes the nature of this evolved soul.[7] Christian philosopher William Hasker proposes that the human mind is a "soul-field" generated by the brain, analogous to a magnetic field generated by a magnet—both fields real and distinct from, but not separate from, what generates them. He too is concerned to assert that this "soul-field" can exert "downward causation" in order to escape determinism.[8]

Fortunately, we do not have to decide now among these and other speculations. Scientific explorations of the evolution, development, and functioning of human consciousness are impressive, but a great deal of work still lies ahead. This is evident, for example, in heated debates among philosophers of consciousness who are knowledgeable about the state of neurophysiological studies and yet cannot agree on the nature of subjectivity or self-awareness. Duke University philosopher Owen J. Flanagan coined the name "mysterians" to label those who argue that human consciousness is far too complex and strangely different to be analyzed using neurophysiological categories alone. Two of the best-known mysterians are David Chalmers of the University of Washington and Colin McGinn of Rutgers. A common retort is the sort offered by Thomas Metzinger, who says we think we are selves because we have formed a "self-model." This model is transparent—we do not see it, rather we use it to see ourselves. Metzinger is in general agreement with the influential philosopher Daniel Dennett.[9] The number of books on the topic keeps expanding.[10] For brevity's sake I will not review the various arguments here.

Instead, I will focus more narrowly on the question of what is essential in the traditional Catholic doctrine of the soul and what is legitimately open to the sort of change modern neurophysiology suggests. The first part below articulates in a general way which notions associated with belief in a spiritual soul are probably essential to a Christian understanding of the person. The second surveys briefly some early history of notions of the soul, to see to what extent these notions were indeed part of ancient science. The third locates and comments on authoritative church declarations about the soul that might place limits on speculation. The fourth recaps the place of "spirit" in the evolutionary history of the universe according to Karl Rahner.

What Is Essential in the Catholic Doctrine of the Soul?

Pope John Paul II offers a starting point. In a recent statement on evolution, the pope rejects a kind of emergentism: "[T]heories of evolution which, in accordance with the philosophies inspiring them, consider the spirit as emerging from the forces of living matter or as a mere epiphenomenon of this matter, are incompatible with the truth about man. Nor are they able to ground the dignity of the person." The pope asserts that the empirical sciences cannot deal adequately with the kinds of inner experiences "of metaphysical knowledge, of self-awareness and self-reflection, of moral conscience, freedom, or again, of aesthetic and religious experience." He refers to an "onto-logical discontinuity" between nature and these spiritual activities or experiences. Because of the power of reason and choice, the human person is "called to enter into a relationship of knowledge and love with God himself, a relationship which will find its complete fulfill-ment beyond time, in eternity."[11] Therefore, he continues, the church must maintain that the soul is not a product of material evolution. Rather we must hold to the belief, as Pius XII said in *Humani Generis*, that each soul is specially created by God.

The pope's concerns could be summed up in Rahner's concern for preserving the "transcendentality" of the person.[12] The power of self-transcendence includes self-awareness as a metaphysical openness to the infinite; it includes the ability to reason and choose; it is the basis for hope or belief in an eternal relation with God; it is the foundation of a special human dignity. The question, then, in its simplest form, is whether the power of self-transcendence could come only from a non-physical soul, as tradition and John Paul II have it, or whether this power could be attributed entirely to the processes of the ex-traordinarily complex human brain.

A Brief History of the Soul: Some Options from the Past

The history of Christian belief about the soul is complex. It is probably safe to say that the earliest Christian belief in salvation was not based on belief in a Platonist sort of purely immaterial and there-fore naturally immortal soul. It was based on belief in God's power and promise to raise the dead to a new life. John Cooper argues persuasively that it was common for Jews of Jesus' time to believe that a ghostlike self (*psyche*) did survive death, but its fate was a dreary Hades-like existence. Jewish and Christian apocalyptic thought instead offered a glorious risen life of the whole person into the won-derful kingdom of God.[13]

In antiquity a number of theories of human nature contended with each other. The Stoics argued that a divine Logos was at work in the universe and that every person's rational and animating principle was a spark of that Logos.[14] Here cosmology and anthropology merged. The Stoics, however, believed that at death the person's inner rational self was dissolved back into the Logos, so Christians could not adopt a Stoic anthropology. Various forms of Platonism argued that the universe emanated from an ultimate One. Following one or more of Plato's leads, Platonists claimed that the inner powers of abstract thought indicated that each person had an immaterial soul whose natural mode of existence was other than the concrete conditions of materiality. Since the Platonist desire to escape materiality conflicted entirely with Christian belief in a physical resurrection, Christianity could not accept an unqualified Platonism.

It was apparently not long until most Christians arrived at their own modified Platonic anthropology of the sort one finds in the works of Augustine. His work *The Literal Meaning of Genesis*, for example, testifies to the still uncertain notions of the soul and how it relates to the body. Augustine's main problem concerning the soul in this work is where souls come from. Are they pre-existent and sent to their bodies at the appropriate time, as Origen might have thought? Or do they exist in the "causal reasons" that God planted in the universe at the beginning, out of which the many later kinds of things in the world eventually emerge? Or did God specially create the very first soul in Adam, out of which subsequent souls are passed on through reproduction (or in Eve's case by a kind of divine cloning)? Or does God create every new soul individually, as needed?[15] To some of these questions Augustine could not provide firm answers, though he favored special creation of each soul by God.

Much of this theological speculation has its roots in ancient science. Aristotelian science, for example, explained plant life by vegetative souls, animal life by sensitive souls, and human life and thought by intellective souls. Modern biology addresses the same questions about life activities, but uses a different explanation to account for them. In the cosmology of the Neoplatonists, the hierarchy of being from the One, then the Nous and World Soul, through gods (some of them planetary souls), humans, animate beings, down to dirt, explained the order of the universe. Modern science explains order by the story of cosmic evolution, from the Big Bang to the appearance and evolution of life, including eventually human life. In Neoplatonic physics and biology (though the latter term had not yet been coined), soul-power emanating from the One, given certain categorical order by the Nous and passed on by the World Soul, provided the motive power and the goal-orientation to the patterns of the cosmos and to the living beings within it. In modern science the DNA information code, developed over billions of years of variation and natural selection, now accounts for the life processes and their apparent goal-directed behavior. Early Christian understanding of the human person wrestled with ancient philosophies functioning as science, adapting them to fit basic belief in the freedom of the person to choose good or evil and the possibility of eternal life with God offered through Christ.

The question now is how far we might legitimately go to extricate key notions about the human spirit from these ancient frameworks. Modern science may not be at odds so much with traditional basic Christian doctrines of the person, as at odds with the ancient sciences (including philosophy) used to articulate that basic doctrine.

Authoritative Declarations on the Nature of the Soul: Limits to Speculations

Three major councils have spoken directly about the soul. Lateran IV in 1215 declared that God has created all things "visible and invisible, spiritual and corporeal" including the human person, "constituted by the union of spirit and body."[16] The council thereby affirmed that whatever exists, not just spiritual but also material, is created by the one God. About a century later the Council of Vienna in 1312 condemned as heretical the proposition that "the rational or intellective soul is not truly and of itself the form of the body."[17] The primary intent of Lateran IV and Vienna's statements was not to define what "soul" is, but to fight against Albigensian or Cathar notions that matter is evil or even that the soul by nature would ideally seek to be free of bodily existence.

In 1513 Lateran V condemned "all who assert that the intellective soul is mortal, or that there is a single soul in all humans" and reasserted Vienna's statement that this soul is "truly, of itself, and essentially the form of the human body."[18] We might read this as simply the use of a by-then-traditional idea about souls adopted from Hellenic thought, used in a context where the real purpose of the declaration is to affirm again the goodness of material creation (and also to exclude acceptance of Aristotle's notion of a single agent intellect in all humans). The Councils of Vienna and Lateran V both use

Aquinas's Aristotelian argument that the human soul is to be understood as truly and intrinsically the form of the body, intimately part of the single whole person (though Aquinas says the soul is able to subsist apart from the body).[19] This too could be read as a declaration in favor of the goodness of the material aspect of the person, rather than as a clear definition of the nature of the human soul. At least some of the emergentist and physicalist concepts of the soul noted above could accommodate these traditional claims.

The statement that the soul is naturally immortal may be more difficult to deal with in a physicalist interpretation. Yet, as Rahner argued, self-transcending consciousness of the person is open to the Infinite and able to make a salvific choice about its eternal relation to God, no matter how this consciousness arises. In this sense self-transcendence always implies a relation to eternity.[20] If indeed self-transcendence can arise from material operations of the brain, then a non-physical soul is not needed.

Catholic theologians have been enlarging the horizons of ideas about the soul for the last century and a half, at first because of the challenge from Darwin's theories. Darwin proposed that humans descended from ape-like ancestors, and he argued that as the intelligence of an ape has its origins in its primordial ancestors yet far exceeds that of these ancestors, so also human intelligence can exceed that of apes and yet have its origin in this earlier form of consciousness.

The first responses were mostly quite cautious. Catholics such as St. George Mivart were skeptical that even the human body might have evolved, and of course were sure that soul was immaterial, could not arise from matter, and in fact required a special and immediate creation by God.[21] Likewise, in the early twentieth century William Reany, in his clearly Catholic work, *The Creation of the Human Soul*, said that the body may have evolved, but defended the immediate creation of a naturally immortal soul for each person. Reany nonetheless claimed (in this work with an *imprimatur* and *nihil obstat*) that this was not dogma. "In this question there is no formal definition of the Church to which assent must be given by Divine Faith."[22]

Reany's analysis was bolder, however, than the dominant Catholic response of that time. That is better represented, perhaps, by Cardinal Ernesto Ruffini. He cited a multitude of theologians, not only from antiquity but from modern times, who insist that scripture is quite clear that God directly and immediately formed Adam's body from the dust of the earth. (Among Ruffini's many sources is a book by Achille Ratti, upholding this interpretation of scripture. Ratti, of course, became Pius XI[23]). Ruffini's biblical literalism has not held up well in Catholic theology. As theology has come to terms with the notion of the evolution of the human body, so also it might come to terms with the notion of the evolution of the soul.

At least some twentieth-century theology, however, pushed the horizon further outward. In 1966 the Jesuit Robert North published *Teilhard and the Creation of the Soul*.[24] North defended the emergentist views of Teilhard de Chardin and Karl Rahner, who said we might best conceive of the soul as a product of the evolution of the universe. Like Reany, North provided a critical review of the history of ideas about the soul, from scripture up through the patristic period, and through the few councils noted above that made statements on the nature of the soul. He responded to Pius XII's statement in *Humani Generis* that "The Catholic faith commands us to retain that souls are immediately created by God," by noting that this statement, included somewhat as an aside, does not seem to be based on any prior dogmatic formulations.[25]

Pope John Paul II nonetheless has asserted that a notion of the soul arising from matter cannot provide an adequate basis for these essentials. But whether this is the case is precisely the question raised by modern science, as the pope implicitly acknowledges by addressing the issue. Given what we have seen so far, the question is still whether it is possible to interpret "soul" (or "spirit") as a very high level of brain activity, a mode of activity that has been made possible by emergent evolution (as well as cultural evolution).

The Emergence of Spirit in the Evolution of Matter

Robert North is correct to point to Karl Rahner's reflections in *Hominisation* as a valuable guide for rethinking the Christian doctrine of the soul.[26] This has been spelled out well by North and elsewhere, so it is possible to be brief here.

Rahner began with the outline of cosmic history sketched by Teilhard: the universe has developed from raw energy to complex forms to planetary systems to cellular life to multi-celled life to sensate and conscious life and to human life. Even before there were humans around to raise the question of their inner spirit, matter was constantly becoming more than it had been. Matter had already become more than mere matter when even the simplest life appeared. For a Christian, all of this is part of the ongoing creative concursus of God. If the inner consciousness and freedom of the earliest humans (wherever we might locate this) emerged from the evolutionary process of the universe, this is God's creativity at work. The same is true of each new child conceived. That this universe can bring forth both rational thought and consciously chosen love could be a religiously comforting thought to those who claim that the evolving universe is truly God's creation.

Rahner also elaborated a metaphysical basis for the Teilhardian approach. For its continuing existence the universe is radically dependent on a continuing sustenance in being by God. God is "creating" the universe at every moment, by actively keeping it in being rather than allow it to collapse into nothingness. Were this a static universe, the concursus would simply sustain everything more or less as it is. But this has been an evolving universe, in which raw space-time/matter-energy has continued to achieve ever greater levels of complexly interrelated order and functioning, even ever greater levels of responsiveness and consciousness and, in us humans, reflective self-awareness. So God has been creating all things all the time—including that most significant of creations, human souls. As North points out, this perspective allows Rahner to say both that God creates every soul just as God is constantly creating everything, and also that the parents of a child are the parents of the whole person, including what we mean to identify when we speak of both body and soul. Here distinctively human thought and freedom may be a product of God's creativity exercised through the secondary causality of evolution.[27] In Rahner's analysis, because materiality, like all aspects of creation, comes from nothing except God's power, from the Infinite Spirit, then even matter is a kind of "frozen" spirit. He argues that "materiality itself must be understood as the lowest stage of spirit."[28]

Three Key Issues

This section addresses the questions of 1) the degree to which doctrine on the soul uses outmoded science, 2) whether a physicalist interpretation of the soul is a form of reductionism, and 3) whether a physicalist interpretation is deterministic and thereby eliminates free will. A common element in the comments offered here will be the role of *history*—of doctrine, of the overall evolutionary process including hominization, and of the individual and the culture that forms the individual.

Ancient Science in the Notion of the Soul

It has happened before in Catholic tradition that old science was mistaken for true doctrine: the condemnation of Galileo's Copernicanism by the Roman Inquisition. The Inquisitors said that the Copernican hypotheses "are contrary to the true sense and authority of Holy Scripture." This was not an aside. They repeated that heliocentrism "is absurd and false philosophically, and formally heretical because it is expressly contrary to the Holy Scripture."[29]

Ironically, the astronomy that the Inquisitors were defending was at least as much Ptolemaic as it was scriptural. Galileo had already made the point that the astronomy of the Bible was different from the Ptolemaic view that the Inquisitors defended.[30] In his now famous letter to the Grand Duchess Christina, he cited Augustine's attempt to reconcile the account of creation in the Hebrew scriptures with the Hellenistic science of his time. "What is it to me," Augustine asks, "whether heaven, like a sphere, surrounds the earth on all sides as a mass balanced in the center of the universe [as the Greek astronomers said], or whether like a dish it merely covers and overcasts the earth? [as Genesis 1 seems to say] (*De Genesi ad Literam*, ii.9)"[31] Galileo continued Augustine's discussion of whether the heaven is indeed a "firmament," as Genesis says, and if so how it is possible for heaven to rotate, carrying the fixed stars imbedded in it around and around the earth. Even though the flat earth of Genesis, covered with a solid dome that held back the surrounding waters, was not the geocentric multi-heavened world of Hellenistic natural philosophy, Christianity nonetheless came to adopt the Ptolemaic view and used it to interpret the scriptures.

The case of Copernicanism, however, differs in one very important way from Platonist or Aristotelian notions of the soul. Both the Ptolemaic view and the Copernican were proposals that could in principle be shown by empirical evidence to be false. There is no way, however, to provide empirical evidence against the existence of a nonmaterial soul. No matter how much mental activity can be tied directly to brain states or processes, it could nonetheless still be possible that there is an additional, invisibly operating, non-material soul lurking behind these material processes.

A more relevant comparison here is to nineteenth- and early twentieth-century vitalism and the effect that the theory of evolution and the discovery of genes and DNA had upon vitalism. Vitalism supporters argued that life activities could not be accounted for by materiality alone or by "mechanistic" processes. The amazing and orderly development of every embryo, the ability of animal bodies to heal wounds, the power of regeneration of limbs in some organisms could not possibly be the result of material processes alone. Some guiding and vital force, some goal-directed non-material agent had to be involved, the vitalists argued.[32] As in the case of the soul (or of miraculous interventions such as special creation of each soul) there is no way to disprove vitalism. Some such soul-like power might be at work in a hidden manner.

But developments in science have made vitalism unnecessary and implausible. Darwin's theory explained how complex life forms might arise, not through goal-directed forces like souls, but through a blind process of variation and natural selection. Darwin's theory gained a further foothold in the early twentieth century when it became clear that each organism had a complex body of genetic units that could be passed on in various combinations. A staunch vitalist could still argue, however, that perhaps each "gene" had its own goal-directed soul. In the middle of the twentieth century, of course, Watson and Crick described the basic structure of DNA, a highly coded structure that "directs" the production of various proteins and thereby accounts for reproduction, healing, and other life processes. Our devoted vitalist could argue that there still might be hidden non-material soul-like forces at work. But this hypothesis has become unnecessary; there is no longer any evidence to make it at all plausible.

The same has become increasingly true of the notion of a non-physical soul. As the relevant sciences continue their work on the brain, as they continue to be able to account for more and more aspects of human thought, a non-physical soul is increasingly becoming an unnecessary hypothesis. If neurological sciences do in fact turn out to be able to account well for human intellection, that will make it much more plausible that whatever the human soul is, it is part of the evolving natural world of space-time/matter-energy. It should not be surprising that modern empirical sciences have something to say about even the soul, just as ancient sciences once provided a different framework.

The Threat of Reductionism

To say that science can study the soul may still sound like a simplistic reductionism, whereby the enormous complexities and subtleties of the workings of the mind are reduced to the relative simplicity of neurological activity. It is important to say "relative" simplicity, because the countless billions of neural connections in the brain are staggeringly complex. In fact, it is often misleading for neurophysiologists to declare they are reductionists. In practice most of them simply mean that they think mind activities are entirely due to brain processes, rather than to the brain plus an additional spiritual agent.[33] A comparison to a different problem in science may be helpful.

In the part of physics that is concerned with working out mathematically such things as the effect of gravity on physical bodies, there has long been what is called the "three body problem." It is not horribly difficult to work out the mathematics of the gravitational interplay between the earth and the sun. Nor is it difficult to do this with Jupiter and the sun. But the interplay of the gravitational pull of both the sun and Jupiter on the earth is too complex to handle. In the eighteenth century, physicists armed with Newton's laws tried to figure out whether the pull of Jupiter upon the earth would eventually drag the earth from its orbit and set it adrift in the cosmos. Right through the nineteenth and twentieth centuries, they kept trying to get the math right, but the many factors involved made the problem intractable. A first major step toward a solution was to simplify, to pretend that certain parameters could be ignored. Modern supercomputers have brought physics closer to a solution, but still only through an artificially simplified model.[34]

The actual workings of the human brain are on a level of complexity that makes the three body problem as simple as 2 x 2 = 4. Neurophysiology will undoubtedly be able to tell us a lot about how the brain operates, about which parts are active when making choices or analyzing a problem. But no matter how complex the neurophysiological description becomes, it will remain only a severely simplified model of what is actually going on. Consider five words you are familiar with: "Tomorrow, and tomorrow, and tomorrow. . . ." Your minds may have already jumped ahead "to the last syllable of recorded time," perhaps even to the "sound and the fury, signifying nothing." Brain scans can identify which neural pathways are involved, which long- and short-term memory functions, which emotional centers, and so forth. Yet there are countless allusions, connections, implications, connotations already rumbling just beneath the surface in your mind. Perhaps you see Great Burnam Wood walking up high Dunsinane Hill. Perhaps you hear echoes of general human ambition, betrayal, and loss. Perhaps you are slipping into reveries about high school and the teacher who introduced you to *Macbeth*. On and on the mind reaches, crowded with personal stories built upon hundreds and thousands of years of human cultural development. Perhaps these words even remind you of the ever-receding horizon of mystery, within which all this memory and experience and thinking take place. The neurophysiologists may be correct that all this is what the brain does. But they mislead themselves when they think their science can get much beyond the relatively simpler "three body" stage of mind.

The realm of human thought and choice covered in the humanities in academia is something like a multibillion body problem. Freeman Dyson has called this the "complexity frontier" of science, or what we could describe as an ever-receding complexity horizon.[35] The neurophysiologists often forget this when they write about how much our understanding of the brain has increased. Theologians and philosophers and humanists in general can stand ready to remind scientists of the transcendental reach of human thought. The humanists will not have much of an audience among scientists, however, if they insist on retaining ancient science to explain that transcendentality.

Determinism and Free Will

If the brain is fully material, then it would seem to be restricted by the cause-and-effect determinism that rules nature. This determinism itself seems limited in nature in two instances. One is the "chaos" element. The famous image of a butterfly's wing setting in motion what will become a major storm on the other side of the world illustrates this element. But it would be more accurate to see this as another instance of the complexity frontier or horizon. Chaos theorists do not deny cause-and-effect determinism here; they only note that the variable effects of specific events are far too complex to predict.

The instance where strict determinism in fact does fail is on the quantum level, where only statistical probability and not deterministic cause-and-effect rules. Quantum indeterminacy gets rid of full determinism in favor of a degree of randomness. But if free will exists only as a function of a somewhat random quantum indeterminacy, then free will is not the reflectively conscious choosing that the idea of free will seeks to save.

Oddly, there is justification in Catholic tradition *not* to try to save the concept of free will. Thomistic scholasticism did quite well without it for centuries. Aquinas proposed that we do indeed make free *choices*. But the will is determined by its nature to seek whatever the intellect presents to it as the good. Choice lies with the intellect, as it reflects on things and determines where the good lies and where it does not.[36] The fallen intellect is not very good at this; hence the frequency of sin. But it is the responsibility of every person to seek to understand clearly what is good and what is not—to develop an informed conscience, in rather traditional language.

There is another problem that appears in attempts to save the concept of free will. Two alternatives dominate the discussions. One is the possibility favored by many theologians and philosophers that there is some non-determined causality exerted by the will in making a genuinely free choice. This possibility, however, posits a cause other than God that in some small way is like God—uncaused. This is a rather awkward position for Christian theology. The other alternative is that our choices are made by our brains, which are fully physical and therefore fully determined by the ordinary laws of cause and effect of all material reality. This might seem to eliminate freedom altogether.

There is a third way of thinking about freedom. This focuses on the historical reality of a person's life and choices.[37] Some have sought to save free will by the idea of a top-down influence, a "vertical" image of mental causality. It would be truer to the historical nature of existence to use a "horizontal" image, to represent the ongoing influence of sequences of past states of self-reflective consciousness on subsequent states of the brain. Every state of human self-consciousness is part of a stream of consciousness, a changing stream in which thoughts upstream *determine* something of the path of thoughts downstream.

The causal flow from past to present and future states of consciousness is highly complex. Most of what the mind does is not part of waking consciousness. The brain keeps the autonomic nervous system running, for example. This keeps our innards operating as they should, without our awareness (except when things go wrong).

Similarly, when we are prompted to identify ourselves by typing in our mother's "maiden" name, our brain somehow pulls that name up out of storage into consciousness without us knowing or even experiencing what the brain is doing to accomplish this. This is only one of thousands of acts of memory our brain performs for us, without us experiencing the actual neural activity as such. We also carry on oral arguments without being able to sense the operations of Broca's area, Warnicke's area, the relevant motor control areas of tongue, lips, and larynx, yet they are all highly involved in the process.

Interestingly, even much of what we think happens first in self-conscious choice and then is carried out by our brains seems to work the other way around. The neurophysiologists tell us that a non-conscious activity first takes place in the part of the brain whose activity signals decisions being made.[38] This non-conscious activity occurs as much as a half second *before* there is activity in the part of the brain where people *consciously* make decisions. Should we therefore conclude that non-conscious brain activity and not conscious choice determines what we do or think? We should conclude that, only if we forget that the non-conscious activity was itself preceded by prior conscious activity. Philosophical analyses of how a given decision takes place, whether from the top down or the bottom up, often commit a form of Whitehead's "fallacy of misplaced concreteness." It is not the single moment of reflection or choice that should be the object of attention; it should be the stream of states of reflective consciousness and unconsciousness that constitute the actual and concrete mental life of any person. Moments of self-reflective awareness might be only a small part of that stream. But those moments are the most important for the human, because those are the moments wherein lies the human ability to accept responsibility, to make choices that are deliberately moral. Those are the moments that make the whole stream of brain activity properly human.

It is all even much more complex than this "stream" image implies. Cultural development is part of this story also. If we can now choose to forego revenge against someone who has harmed close kin, it is because culture has educated and even habituated us to act contrary to our normal human tendencies. If we can extend kindness and compassion to those who are unlike us and who will not contribute to our well-being, it is because culture—perhaps a religious tradition—has educated and even habituated us to this. Ideas that become part of our conscious life partly determine non-conscious habits (perhaps even virtues or components of virtues?), which in their turn will determine what our next state of consciousness is like.

The linguist Derek Bickerton divides consciousness into two types, online and offline.[39] Online consciousness belongs to animals in general, including humans. This is the cat fascinated by the chirping of a fledgling, or the dog who marks its territory. It is immediate awareness. Offline consciousness seems to belong almost exclusively to us humans (chimpanzees may be a partial and very limited exception). This is the ability to create scenarios in our minds of past conditions or events, as well as of alternative possible present and future states. We get this ability partly just from being human. But we need society and culture to teach us how to do it well and usefully and morally. This ability is indeed *determined*—by our genetics, by our personal development, and by our social context and its history. But it is not therefore a loss of conscious choice. For in the ongoing flow of consciousness, we can set before ourselves with deliberate consciousness the alternative paths of action we can take, the possible outcomes of those actions, and the moral standards our life and education have given us to be able to evaluate those outcomes. This is the power of moral choice, with none of it requiring some uncaused cause activity by a non-physical soul.

Conclusion

The words "soul" or "spirit" still serve the important purpose of reminding us of our humanness, of our ability to come into even exquisite degrees of deliberative self-consciousness, influencing both non-conscious activities and online consciousness. The words remind us of the awesome complexity horizon within which we operate. They remind us of our dignity and our orientation toward the Infinite Mystery.

This short paper cannot encompass all the issues related to the soul. It has shown that emergentist and physicalist notions of the soul are congruent with modern science and are not subject to the critiques that such notions entail "reductionism" or "determinism."[40] But as ancient science did in the past, so the discoveries of neurophysiology are pressing on theology now. It is prudent to explore the implications of these new horizons.

Notes

[1]He speaks this way about the human spirit in a context relevant to the topic of this paper in Karl Rahner, *Theological Investigations*, vol. XXI, trans. Hugh M. Riley (New York: Crossroad, 1988), 43-46.

[2]Kenan Malik, *Man, Beast, and Zombie: What Science Can and Cannot Tell Us about Human Nature* (New Brunswick: Rutgers University Press, 2000) provides an excellent survey. Malik correctly insists that we humans have "extended" minds, meaning that it is social interaction that enables us to develop whatever innate powers of speech and thought we may have.

[3]Warren S. Brown, Nancey Murphy, and H. Newton Maloney, *Whatever Happened to the Soul: Scientific and Theological Portraits of Human Nature* (Minneapolis: Fortress Press, 1998).

[4]Jaegwon Kim has the most extensive set of essays on top-down causality. He claims that the early twentieth-century "emergentists" such as Samuel Alexander were the first "non-reductive physicalists." See his *Supervenience and Mind: Selected Philosophical Essays* (New York: Cambridge University Press, 1993), xi.

[5]The list of positions here is only suggestive of the range. For more, see Robert John Russell et al., eds., *Neuroscience and the Person: Scientific Perspectives on Divine Action* (Vatican City: Vatican Observatory Publications; and Berkeley: Center for Theology and the Natural Sciences, 1999).

[6]Keith Ward, *Religion and Human Nature* (New York: Oxford University Press, 1998), esp. 145-47.

[7]Richard Swinburne, *The Evolution of the Soul* (Oxford: Clarendon Press, 1986). This collection of two Gifford Lectures plus other previously published essays has a consistent theme.

[8]William Hasker, "Emergentism," *Religious Studies* 18, no. 4 (December 1982): 473-88, or his more recent *The Emergent Self* (Ithaca: Cornell University Press, 1999). For other recent speculations, see Kelly Nicholson, *Body and Soul: The Transcendence of Materialism* (Boulder: Westview Press, 1997) and A. G. Cairns-Smith, *Evolving the Mind: The Nature of Matter and the Origin of Consciousness* (New York: Cambridge University Press, 1996). Owen Flanagan's *The Problem of the Soul: Two Visions of Mind and How to Reconcile Them* (New York: Basic Books, 2002) is a semi-popular book showing how to get rid of the traditional idea of a non-physical soul. Some brief historical background on vitalism can be found in Michael H. Barnes, "The Evolution of the Soul from Matter and the Role of Science in Karl Rahner's Theology," *Horizons* 21, no. 1 (1994): 85-104.

[9]Owen J. Flanagan, *Consciousness Reconsidered* (Cambridge: MIT Press, 1992); Thomas Metzinger, *Being No One: The Self-Model Theory of Subjectivity* (Cambridge: MIT Press, 2003); Daniel C. Dennett, *Consciousness Explained* (Boston: Little, Brown and Co., 1991). A brief review of

Chalmers and McGinn is available in John Horgan, "Can Science Explain Consciousness?" *Scientific American* (July 1994): 88-94. For a thorough review of issues and relevant science, see the forty-nine articles in Ned Joel Block, Owen Flanagan, and Güven Güzeldere, eds., *The Nature of Consciousness: Philosophical Debates* (Cambridge: MIT Press, 1997). For more on the debate, see Jonathan Shear, ed., *Explaining Consciousness: The 'Hard Problem'* (Cambridge: MIT Press, 1995-97); this volume of only 422 pages contains twenty-eight articles representing differing opinions.

[10]Books favoring a physicalist view of the soul have flooded the market in recent years. In addition to books named in the previous two notes, see also William H. Calvin, *The Cerebral Code: Thinking a Thought in the Mosaics of the Mind* (Cambridge: MIT Press, 1996), with excellent drawings to illustrate various aspects of brain operations. George Lakoff and Mark Johnson, in *Philosophy in the Flesh: The Embodied Mind and Its Challenge to Western Thought* (New York: Basic Books, 1999), say a great deal through their three simple opening sentences, each a paragraph: "The mind is inherently embodied. Thought is mostly unconscious. Abstract concepts are largely metaphorical" (3). For a broad survey, see Steven Pinker, *How the Mind Works* (New York: W. W. Norton, 1997).

[11]Pope John Paul II, "Message to the Pontifical Academy of Science on Evolution," *Origins* 26, no. 22 (November 14, 1996): 350-52; quotations from 352. *The Quarterly Review of Biology* (72, no. 4, December 1997) carries both the French text and English translation, followed by commentaries by Edmund Pellegrino, Michael Ruse, Richard Dawkins, and Eugenie Scott. Pellegrino declares flatly that "For the soul to emerge from matter, as some evolutionary theories contend, is not, and never has been, an acceptable concept in Catholic teaching" (Pellegrino, "Theology and Evolution in Dialogue," op. cit., 385-89; quotation at 387).

[12]See again, Rahner, *Theological Investigations*, vol. XXI, 43-46, where he uses a word awkwardly translated as "transcendentality" precisely to name what must be preserved when discussing the nature and origin of the soul in an evolutionary context.

[13]John W. Cooper, *Body, Soul, and Life Everlasting: Biblical Anthropology and the Monism-Dualism Debate* (Grand Rapids: Eerdmans, 1989), as part of a larger analysis, reviews relevant biblical texts and common beliefs among Jews in the first century.

[14]See Marcia Colish, *The Stoic Tradition from Antiquity to the Early Middle Ages*, vol. I, *Stoicism in Classical Latin Literature* (Leiden: E. J. Brill, 1985).

[15]Saint Augustine, *The Literal Meaning of Genesis*, trans. John Hammond Taylor, S.J., Ancient Christian Writers Series 42 (Ramsey, N.J.: Newman Press, 1982). Book 7, 3-31, and 10, 96-132 chew over these possibilities at some length.

[16]"[Q]uasi communem ex spiritu et corpore constitutam." Henricus

Denzinger and Adolphus Schönmetzer, *Enchiridion Symbolorum, Definitionum, et Declarationum de Rebus Fidei et Morum,* 32nd ed. (Friburg: Herder, 1963), 259, #800.

[17]"[Q]uod substantia animae rationalis seu intellectivae vere ac per se humani corporis non sit forma . . . ." (Denzinger-Schönmetzer, *Enchiridion,* 284, #902).

[18]"[D]amnamus et reprobamus omnes asserentes, animam intellectivam mortalem esse, aut unicam in cunctis hominibus, et haec in dubium vertentes, cum illa non solum vere per se et essentialiter humani corporis forma exsistat, sicut in canone felicis recordationis Clementis papae V praedecessoris Nostri in *[generali]* Viennensi Consilio edito continetur . . . ." (Denzinger-Schönmetzer, *Enchiridion,* 353-54, #1440).

[19]The strongest official support for a Thomistic non-traducianist interpretation appears in the scheme *proposed* for Vatican I, that might have been adopted had the Council lasted longer. The schema asserts that the soul is "created from nothing, immaterial, incorruptible and immortal, gifted with intelligence and free will. . . ." See John F. Clarkson et al., *The Church Teaches: Documents of the Church in English Translation* (St. Louis: B. Herder, 1955), 150-51, for relevant passages. This proposed language does not appear in Denzinger-Schönmetzer.

[20]See Karl Rahner, "Ideas for a Theology of Death," *Theological Investigations,* vol. XIII, trans. David Bourke (New York: Crossroad, 1983). Rahner argues that eternal life is the finality of each person's "personal history of freedom" (174-75). Peter C. Phan, in *Eternity in Time: A Study of Karl Rahner's Eschatology* (Cranbury, N.J.: Associated University Presses, 1988), analyzes Rahner's thought on this.

[21]St. George Jackson Mivart, in *The Origin of Human Reason, Being an Examination of Recent Hypotheses Concerning It* (London: K. Paul, Trench, 1889), summarizes his own earlier position and responds to attacks on it by Romanes. The evolution of the human body was not officially accepted until Pius XII's *Humani Generis* in 1950 (Denzinger-Shönmetzer, *Enchiridion,* 779, #3896).

[22]William Reany, *The Creation of the Human Soul: A Clear and Concise Exposition, from Psychological, Theoretical, and Historical Aspects* (New York: Benziger, 1932), 46.

[23]Cardinal Ernesto Ruffini, *The Theory of Evolution Judged by Reason and Faith* ([Italian original, 1949] New York: Joseph B. Wagner, 1959). See chapter three for the sources supporting direct creation of Adam; p. 136 for Ratti.

[24]Robert North, S.J., *Teilhard and the Creation of the Soul* (Milwaukee: Bruce, 1966). He observes that Gregorian University teacher Fr. Flick-Alszeghy once assigned the theological note of "theologice certa" to the special creation of each soul, but later changed his mind and supported Rahner's position (221). Shortly thereafter Joseph F. Donceel, S.J., published

his *Philosophical Anthropology* (New York: Sheed & Ward, 1967). In this philosophical work, Donceel does not explore scriptural and conciliar sources. But he too strongly supports the Teilhard-Rahner notion of the emergence of the soul from biological evolution and the generation of the whole person, body and soul, by the parents, esp. 81-88. See also Benedict Ashley, O.P., *Theologies of the Body: Humanist and Christian* (Braintree, Mass.: Pope John XXIII Medical-Moral Research and Education Center, 1985). This work is only secondarily on the soul, but provides, nonetheless, an excellent review and analysis of it.

[25] "Animas enim a Deo immediate creari catholica fides nos retinere jubet" (Denzinger-Schönmetzer, *Enchiridion,* 779 #3896). In making excerpts from *Humani Generis,* Clarkson et al. in *The Church Teaches,* 154, made an interesting editorial and perhaps theological choice in their translation by putting this sentence in parentheses.

[26] Karl Rahner, *Hominisation: The Evolutionary Origin of Man as a Theological Problem,* trans. W. T. O'Hara (New York: Herder & Herder, 1965). Subsequently, Rahner made a few more points along the same lines; see "Natural Science and Reasonable Faith," *Theological Investigations,* vol. XXI, trans. Hugh M. Riley (New York: Crossroad, 1988), 16-55.

[27] In North, *Teilhard and the Creation of the Soul,* 239 (the prior chapter seven has a thorough review of previous doctrinal statements and theological opinions). In Rahner, "Natural Science and Reasonable Faith," 25.

[28] Karl Rahner, *Hominisation,* 165. Or see Karl Rahner, "The Unity of Spirit and Matter in the Christian Understanding of Faith," *Theological Investigations,* vol. VI, trans. Karl-H. and Boniface Kruger (Baltimore: Helicon, 1969), 177.

[29] Taken from a translation of the whole decree as it appears in Janelle Rohr, *Science and Religion: Opposing Viewpoints* (St. Paul: Greenhaven Press, 1988), 23-28, whose source for the decree was Karl Von Gebler, *Galileo Galilei and the Roman Curia* (Merrick, N.Y.: Richwood Publishing, 1879), no pages given.

[30] John Brooke and Geoffrey Cantor make this point in passing in *Reconstructing Nature: The Engagement of Science and Religion* (Edinburgh: T & T Clark, 1998), 110.

[31] Translation of Galileo's letter, including passages from Augustine, taken from *Discoveries and Opinions of Galileo,* trans. Stillman Drake (New York: Doubleday Anchor, 1957), 182-87.

[32] A particularly interesting perspective on vitalism is provided by Hans Driesch, *History and Theory of Vitalism,* trans. C. K. Ogden (London: Macmillan, 1914), who conceded that traditional belief in Aristotelian-type souls might no longer be plausible, even while he continued to defend his own "neovitalism." For a summary of its later fate, see Michael Horace Barnes, *Stages of Thought: The Co-Evolution of Religious Thought and Science* (New York: Oxford University Press, 2000), 163-68.

[33]Paul M. Churchland, for example, in his *The Engine of Reason, the Seat of the Soul: A Philosophical Journey into the Brain* (Cambridge: MIT Press, 1995), 208-13, provides what he calls a "reductionist" account, but in fact only means that it is a physicalist or naturalistic account, which "reduces" mind to brain activity.

[34]For a simple explanation of the three body problem, see the American Mathematical Society page: http://www.ams.org/new-in-math/cover/orbits1.html Or see http://www.physics.cornell.edu/sethna/teaching/sss/jupiter/jupiter.htm

[35]Freeman Dyson, "The World on a String," a review of Brian Green's *The Fabric of the Cosmos* in the *New York Review of Books* 51, no. 8 (May 13, 2004): 19.

[36]Thomas Aquinas, *Summa Theologica* (New York: Benziger, 1947), I-II. Q. 9, a. 1 "Whether the Will Is Moved by the Intellect" and I-II, Q. 13, a. 6 "Whether Man Chooses of Necessity or Freely."

[37]In his most recent work on free will, Daniel C. Dennett, *Freedom Evolves* (New York: Viking, 2003) sums up and expands ideas he has presented earlier. He emphasizes evolutionary development in a way that meshes well with the emphasis on the temporal process of learning to be a self and making responsible decisions. He does not directly call this the "historical" dimension of our thinking and choosing, however.

[38]Benjamin Libet's *Mind Time: The Temporal Factor in Consciousness* (Cambridge: Harvard University Press, 2004) is the product of one of the pioneers of this field of study. The book summarizes many studies on ways in which the brain "decides" or "acts" before there is conscious awareness or choice on the part of the person. Libet himself seeks to save free will (140-56). He proposes that his studies show the person has a free-will veto over decisions first made non-consciously, but has to consider whether the veto itself arises from some prior non-conscious process (145).

[39]Derek Bickerton, *Language and Human Behavior* (Seattle: University of Washington Press, 1995).

[40]The most important issue not considered here, perhaps, is the traditional idea of eternal life. However, it is not clear how emergentist and physicalist conceptions of the soul would have more problems with a Christian (not Platonist) understanding of eternal life than would a classic spiritual understanding of the soul. Specific issues such as ensoulment and abortion or the soul and purgatory also need to be and have been addressed more thoroughly. For some thoughts on ensoulment and abortion, see Joseph Culliton, "Rahner on the Origin of the Soul: Some Implications Regarding Abortion," in *Thought: A Review of Culture and Ideas* 53, no. 209 (June 1978): 202-14. For ideas about eternal life, purgatory, and such, see Peter C. Phan, *Eternity in Time.*

"Catholic Baptists" and the New Horizon of Tradition in Baptist Theology

Steven R. Harmon

In keeping with the theme of the 50th Annual Convention of the College Theology Society, and with apologies to Hans-Georg Gadamer,[1] I wish to call attention to an emerging trend in contemporary Baptist theology: the recognition of tradition as a horizon within which the doing of theology takes place. This is a new horizon for Baptist theology in the sense that much Baptist theology has proceeded on the basis of a radicalized *sola scriptura* hermeneutic that dichotomizes scripture and tradition. The result is that many Baptists reflexively regard any post-biblical theological development as superfluous, theologically suspect, and possessing no authority for Christian faith and practice. The emergence of Baptist theologians who give more positive attention to tradition may be a counterintuitive phenomenon for some observers. Within an ecclesial tradition that has a tradition of dispensing with tradition[2] and in the wake of Baptist denominational controversies in which selected traditional interpretations of scripture have become theological litmus tests,[3] several non-fundamentalist Baptist theologians are increasingly invoking tradition as a source of religious authority. They offer constructive proposals for a Baptist or Free Church retrieval of tradition. After placing this new horizon for Baptist theology in the larger context of the historical development of Baptist thought vis-à-vis the Enlightenment, this essay will offer an overview of notable contributions to this new horizon. It concludes with proposals of my own for a Baptist retrieval of tradition that is faithful both to the theological tradition of the church catholic and to the Baptist tradition of dissent.

Baptist Theology and the Horizon of Tradition

There is a sense in which tradition is not an entirely new horizon for the doing of Baptist theology. Seventeenth-century Baptists inherited from their forebears in the denominational traditions out of which they came or which influenced them theologically a horizon that stubbornly persisted despite conscious adherence to the *sola scriptura* hermeneutic of the Reformation. The framers of early Reformed and Anabaptist confessions of faith could not help but read the Bible through the lenses of the ancient *regula fidei* and its Niceno-Constantinpolitan and Chalcedonian clarifications, even as they privileged scripture as the source of this traditional horizon of interpretation. The earliest Baptist confessions demonstrate that seventeenth-century Baptists picked up the same reading glasses when they turned to the Bible as their authority for faith and practice.[4]

Baptist confessions issued during the seventeenth century are surprisingly rich with echoes of the patristic doctrinal tradition. Language and concepts of patristic origin appear primarily, but not exclusively, in trinitarian and christological statements of these confessions. For example, the *Orthodox Creed*, a 1678 English Baptist confession, echoes patristic trinitarian and christological language. It also refers to three of the four Niceno-Constantinopolitan *notae ecclesiae* in Article XXIX and reproduces and commends the Apostles', Nicene, and Athanasian creeds in Article XXXVIII.[5] Nevertheless, in the instance of the *Orthodox Creed* and other points of contact between the early Baptist confessions and the patristic tradition, these tend to be borrowed continuities. Some of this language was lifted wholesale from the Anglican *Thirty-Nine Articles* or the Reformed *Westminster Confession of Faith*.[6] These borrowings served an apologetic motive of establishing the Baptists' continuity with the larger Christian tradition as well as their distinctive place within it. They also demonstrate that the pre-Enlightenment genesis of Baptist theology took place within a horizon circumscribed by tradition. As Philip Thompson has argued, there is a "catholic spirit" to be discerned in the faith and practice of the earliest Baptists.[7]

Modern Baptists, however, drank deeply from the well of the Enlightenment's antagonism to tradition. The anti-traditional hermeneutic represented by the slogan "no creed but the Bible"[8] served well the theological agenda of both liberal and fundamentalist expressions of Baptist theology. Both types of responses to modernity claimed access to truth unmediated by any sort of interpretive horizon. In Gadamer's metaphor a tradition is a horizon; in consciously dispensing with the horizon of tradition, both liberal and fundamentalist modern Baptists traded the deeply textured and richly variegated horizon of the historic Christian tradition for the comparatively flat and monochrome modern horizon of supposedly traditionless reason, itself a tradition of sorts, albeit a very thin one.

The contemporary recovery of tradition as a horizon for Baptist theology may then be characterized as a constructive response to the postmodern milieu. This recovery both welcomes the postmodern critique of modern pretensions of traditionless rationality and embraces the traditioned rationality of the Christian mind. It is not merely coincidental that serious engagement of tradition in written expressions of Baptist systematic theology has been undertaken largely by Baptist theologians who are consciously doing theology in response to the postmodern situation and in sympathy with many of its criticisms of modernity. In an essay reviewing Terrence Tilley's *Inventing Catholic Tradition* from a Baptist perspective, Mark Medley surveys the place of tradition as a theological category in ten major Baptist systematic theologians from John L. Dagg (1794-1884) to Stanley J. Grenz (1950-), finding that among these only the living theologian Grenz and the late James Wm. McClendon, Jr. (1924-2000) enter into extensive and constructive considerations of tradition.[9] Millard J. Erickson (1932-), on the other hand, who has strongly criticized constructive engagement of postmodernity by evangelical theologians,[10] gives minimal attention to tradition in his major systematic theology text.[11] Openness to tradition in Baptist theology thus seems to flourish where there is also openness to postmodern perspectives and responsiveness to postmodern concerns.

The New Horizon of Tradition and the Emergence of "Catholic Baptist" Theologians

In the last five years Grenz and McClendon have been joined by a noteworthy number of Baptist theologians who urge their fellow Baptists to acknowledge the authority of tradition and to explore the implications of the catholic tradition for Baptist faith and practice. This is no less than an identifiable movement in Baptist theology. Taking my cue from a 1994 essay by Curtis Freeman calling Baptists to locate themselves within the tradition of the whole church, I suggest that we might identify such theologians as "catholic Baptists."[12] I will introduce these "catholic Baptist" theologians by enumerating what I perceive to be the identifying marks of their thought.

First, catholic Baptist theologians explicitly recognize tradition as a source of theological authority. In a journal article published in 2000, Philip Thompson urged Baptists "to discuss seriously the normativity of tradition," along with "the Baptist identity's relation to the Baptist, and the Christian, past."[13] That discussion is already well underway. Grenz includes tradition in a threefold pattern of authoritative sources for theology in which scripture is "theology's norming norm," tradition is "theology's hermeneutical trajectory," and culture is "theology's embedding context."[14] He understands tradition as "comprised of the historical attempts of the Christian community to explicate and translate faithfully the first-order language, symbols, and practices of the Christian faith, arising from the interaction among community, text, and culture, into the various social and cultural contexts in which that community has been situated."[15] For Grenz, "to understand the tradition of the church as providing a hermeneutical trajectory is to acknowledge the importance of tradition without elevating it to a position of final authority" in light of "the ongoing life of the church as it moves toward its eschatological consummation."[16] Medley echoes Thompson's concerns and reflects some of Grenz's proposals in recommending that Baptists enter into ecumenical conversation with those who have a tradition of employing tradition as a theological category. He urges Baptists to move beyond an understanding of tradition as a continuity of static doctrinal propositions to a more dynamic "retrospective" understanding of tradition. Tradition should be understood as a critical, open-ended "looking back" to the Christian past in configuring continuity for present contexts. Baptists can locate discussions of the authority of tradition not in the formal theological discourse of doctrinal statements but rather in Baptist communities at worship.[17] Baptist patristics specialist D. H. Williams has cogently argued that if Baptists and other Free Church Christians will move beyond the historiographical myth of the "Constantinian Fall" of the church, then they can constructively retrieve the patristic theological tradition as formative of their own tradition.[18]

Second, catholic Baptist theologians seek a place in Baptist ecclesial life for the ancient ecumenical creeds as key expressions of the larger

Christian tradition. It may seem counterintuitive that in the context of an enforced doctrinal rigidity in the Southern Baptist Convention, some among those who might be identified as "disenfranchised moderates" have proposed ways in which Baptists might reclaim the proper function of the creeds. Barry Harvey, for example, rejects the mantra that "Baptists have no creed but the Bible," contending that "our time and effort would be better served if we attended to the question, What are the proper and improper uses of the ancient creeds and confessions, in worship and in the pedagogical responsibilities of the church?"[19] Harvey highlights the potential value of the ancient creeds as instruments of Christian education that shape the narrative mind of the church. Among British Baptists, Paul Fiddes encourages the recitation of the creeds in Baptist worship, as "it enables those who say the creed to be drawn anew into God's story, and so into God's own fellowship of life."[20] Elsewhere I have drawn upon the work of Disciples of Christ historian Paul Blowers on the narrative character of the *regula fidei* in my suggestion that Baptists ought to think of the creeds as concise liturgical summaries of the story that is told at length and with rich particularity in the scriptures.[21] Curtis Freeman, Steven Harmon, Elizabeth Newman, and Philip Thompson have issued a call for Baptists to repeat in the centennial gathering of the Baptist World Alliance in Birmingham, England, in July 2005 their predecessors' recitation of the Apostles Creed at the inaugural meeting of the Baptist World Alliance in London in 1905. Participants at that inaugural meeting recited the creed as a demonstration of Baptist solidarity with the larger Christian communion. Freeman and his colleagues also recommend that Baptist congregations adopt the practice of reciting the ancient creeds in their weekly worship.[22] The vast majority of Baptist congregations in the United States now do not recite either the Apostles' Creed or the Niceno-Constantinopolitan Creed in their services of worship. Yet the most recent hymnal and service book produced for use in the churches of the Baptist Union of Great Britain (1991), which benefited from advisory input from British Baptist theologians, includes the text of the Apostles' Creed as a liturgical resource. A model covenant service published in 2000 by the same body prints the Apostles' Creed in its main text and the Niceno-Constantinopolitan Creed as a supplementary resource.[23]

Third, catholic Baptist theologians give attention to liturgy as the primary context in which Christians are traditioned. They recognize the validity of Prosper of Aquitaine's maxim *"lex supplicandi statuat legem credendi"*—"let the rule of praying establish the rule of believing."[24] The Baptist tendency to reject forms and practices of worship deemed to be without biblical precedent has resulted in the separation of much Baptist worship from the liturgically sited tradition of the larger Christian community to which Baptists belong. However, several recent and current Baptist projects in liturgical theology seek to incorporate the *lex orandi, lex credendi* principle into the life of Baptist communities at worship. Complementing the recommendation of Medley and Thompson that Baptists root discussions of the role of tradition in the first-order life of worshipping communities,[25] Anthony Cross, Philip Thompson, Christopher Ellis, and others are exploring various aspects of liturgy as a means through which Christians are formed by the Christian tradition.[26]

Fourth, catholic Baptist theologians locate the authority of tradition in the community and its formative practices. As Medley has noted, one of the most significant expressions of Baptist interest in a dynamic conception of tradition is the joint statement "Re-Envisioning Baptist Identity: A Manifesto for Baptist Communities in North America," co-authored by Mikael Broadway, Freeman, Harvey, McClendon, Newman, and Thompson.[27] The authors of this document, frequently referenced in Baptist circles simply as the "Baptist Manifesto," received their theological educations and became academic theologians themselves in the midst of the aforementioned theological controversies in the Southern Baptist Convention. They contend that both polarized parties in the conflict (variously labeled in the rhetoric of the controversy as fundamentalists and liberals, conservatives and moderates, or ultraconservatives and progressives) embraced conceptions of freedom and authority that have more to do with the modern milieu in which Baptist life flourished in the United States than with "the freedom graciously given by God in Jesus Christ." Drawing "from earlier sources of the Baptist heritage . . . that have resisted modern notions of freedom and have practiced a more communal discipleship," the authors make the following affirmations:

> (1) "We affirm Bible Study in reading communities rather than relying on private interpretation or supposed 'scientific' objectivity"; (2) "We affirm following Jesus as a call to shared discipleship rather than invoking a theory of soul competency";[28] (3) "We affirm a free common life in Christ in

gathered, reforming communities rather than withdrawn, self-chosen, or authoritarian ones"; (4) "We affirm baptism, preaching, and the Lord's table as powerful signs that seal God's faithfulness in Christ and express our response of awed gratitude rather than as mechanical rituals or mere symbols"; and (5) "We affirm freedom and renounce coercion as a distinct people under God rather than relying on political theories, powers, or authorities."[29]

Medley rightly suggests that the emphasis of the "Baptist Manifesto" on Baptist practices of Bible reading, witnessing, gathering, and worship may be restated as an ecclesiology of the church in its local and catholic expressions that is an actively traditioning community rather than a community that merely possesses a tradition.[30]

Fifth, catholic Baptist theologians advocate a sacramental theology. By "sacramental" I mean not only a more robust appreciation of the Lord's presence in baptism and the Eucharist than is the case with the symbolic reductionism typical of Baptist theologies of the ordinances influenced by the Zwinglian tradition, but a richer theology that understands the sacraments of baptism and the Eucharist as paradigmatic of the relation of God to the material order that is disclosed in the incarnation. Exemplars of this feature of a catholic Baptist theology include contributors to the volume of essays on *Baptist Sacramentalism* edited by Cross and Thompson.[31] Their proposals, though far from monolithic, share a common interest in retrieving from the larger Christian tradition this sacramental narration of the world that forms the Christian self. Especially noteworthy are Thompson's study of the political factors underlying the modern loss of an earlier Baptist sacramentality, Harvey's exploration of the political implications of a hoped-for recovery of Baptist sacramentalism, Freeman's essay reflecting on the Eucharist as divine nourishment, and Newman's Baptist proposal for a theory of real presence.[32] Beyond this collection of essays, a deeply sacramental theology rooted in a participatory understanding of the work of the Triune God figures prominently in recent books by Fiddes. Fowler has also engaged the recovery of baptismal sacramentalism by twentieth-century British Baptist theologians as a superior alternative to the symbolic reductionism of much Baptist baptismal theology. Medley has given attention to the self-forming efficacy of eucharistic celebration.[33]

Sixth, catholic Baptist theologians engage tradition as a resource for contemporary theological construction in a manner similar to the *ressourcement* agenda of the *"nouvelle théologie."* For example, Baptist theologians are increasingly becoming participants in the contemporary renaissance of trinitarian theology under the banner of social trinitarian thought. In retrieving a perichoretic understanding of the Trinity in the Cappadocian/Damascene tradition, Baptist theologians Fiddes, Medley, and Molly Marshall have discovered important resources that would never have been discovered in an a-traditional encounter of the individual theologian with the biblical text.[34] As in the *nouvelle théologie*, the task of *ressourcement*, "retrieval," is prerequisite for *aggiornamento*, "updating." Harvey's recovery of the patristic concept of the church as *altera civitas* for contemporary ecclesiology and the limited but significant Baptist engagements of patristic and Byzantine concepts of divinization by Fiddes, Grenz, and Clark Pinnock explored by Medley also exemplify this sort of constructive retrieval of the tradition.[35]

Seventh, catholic Baptist theologians are proponents of a thick ecumenism. A "thin" ecumenism seeks to overcome difference through a too facile identification of lowest common denominator agreements between denominations. In contrast, a "thick" ecumenism proceeds on the basis of a common commitment to deep exploration of both the ancient ecumenical tradition and the particularities of the respective denominational traditions.[36] This is the sort of ecumenism exemplified by the Center for Catholic and Evangelical Theology and its journal *Pro Ecclesia*. The thirteen volumes of *Pro Ecclesia* published to date contain articles by Tarmo Toom, Daniel Williams, Timothy George, Barry Harvey, Ralph Wood, Stephen Holmes, Philip Thompson, Scott Moore, and Roger Olson, all Baptist theologians committed in some manner to this thick ecumenism that characterizes a catholic Baptist theology operating within the horizon of tradition.[37] Fiddes has explored at length the implications for Baptist faith and practice of an ecumenism that "begins from the bottom up rather than top-down," has a "vision of 'full communion' rather than 'one world church,'" and is open to "the acceptance of diversity in the unity."[38]

Not all Baptist theologians mentioned in connection with these seven identifying marks of a catholic Baptist theology would identify themselves with all seven marks. Doubtless, other Baptist theologians unnamed herein would gladly concur with all seven marks. Of the Baptist theologians in the United States with whose work I am familiar, Freeman, Harvey, Medley, Newman, Thompson, Williams, and Wood most fully exemplify my description of catholic Baptist theologians (though some of them might wish to qualify such a categorization). Among British Baptists, one may easily discern all seven catholic Baptist marks in the writings of Fiddes.

I would identify myself with these catholic Baptist theologians so described and in the remainder of this essay propose some of my own prescriptions for a catholic Baptist appropriation of tradition, which in turn are indebted to the contributions of others mentioned herein.

A Postmodern Baptist Hermeneutic of the Catholic Tradition

I offer this proposal for a catholic Baptist retrieval of tradition in terms of a postmodern Baptist hermeneutic of tradition.[39] A hermeneutic of tradition that addresses the postmodern situation must have three characteristics. It must seek alternatives to static, propositional understandings of tradition. It must be open to premodern expressions of tradition as resources for the revitalization of contemporary faith and practice. It must give attention to the relationship between tradition and the community that has produced it and for which it has some normative function. A Baptist hermeneutic of tradition must also maintain a place for the ecclesial distinctiveness of Baptist communities while becoming more open to the traditional resources of the larger Christian community.[40] I submit this brief outline of a postmodern Baptist hermeneutic of tradition in the hope that it might fulfill these conditions and play some small role in fostering a constructive dialogue about tradition as a new horizon for Baptist theology.

First, I suggest that Baptists re-envision tradition as the authority of the community. While it is true that Christ and the scriptures that bear witness to him have always been the preeminent sources of authority for Baptist faith and practice, Baptists have also ascribed a derivative authority to the local church as a covenant community gathered around the proclamation of the Word of God under the lordship of Christ. The ancient Christian confession of belief in the *communio sanctorum* may suggest ways in which Baptists may extend this authority to the larger Christian community to which they belong, and thus to its tradition, without abandoning the distinctiveness or authority of their own communities. The *communio sanctorum* is a "fellowship with holy persons" in the sense of all believers, both living and deceased,[41] and thus includes Baptists along with all other

Christians of all ages in one real, living, and continuous community under the lordship of Christ.

Any Baptist who engages in theological reflection must do so first as a member of the communion of saints and then as a Baptist who is a member of the communion of saints. This communion possesses an authority under the lordship of Christ. It is the community that in every age has confessed its faith on the basis of the biblical story of God's saving acts and has retold this story in worship. That confession and worship have thus shaped, clarified, and applied the tradition in every age so that no Christian can read scripture except through lenses ground in earlier ages. This traditioning community is not limited to a superior class of recognized saints but includes all Christians from all ages. Hence, its authority is not limited to the writings of "doctors of the church" or the creeds and canons of ecumenical councils or any other body of orthodox propositions. Rather, its authority resides in the community as a whole and thus in every denominational branch thereof. The stories of all Christian traditions constitute the traditional resources available to postmodern Baptist communities. Therefore, Baptists will need to become more diligent students of church history and better observers of the contemporary church in all its wonderfully varied expressions in order to benefit from tradition thus conceived.

Second, I suggest that Baptists re-envision tradition as the story by which they are formed in worship. If tradition in this paradigm is the authority of the community composed of all the saints, how can the diversity this entails have some normative function? George Lindbeck's cultural-linguistic or regulative theory of doctrine is helpful at this point.[42] The "grammar" that makes certain ideas and practices identifiable and meaningful as Christian "language" is the traditional story of the communion of the saints. Since this story is told in rich particularity by the canonical scriptures, wherever the Bible is read, proclaimed, taught, and practiced in community, there the tradition of the community that formed and has been formed by these scriptures is made present. The community functions as a normative authority for the church, even when it fosters diversity in faith and practice. For many Baptists, the proclamation of the Word is the irreducible minimum of worship. Even if this were the exclusive focus of worship, the authority of the community of all the saints would be made present through this mode of telling its authoritative story. This normative function of communal tradition will be enhanced, however, if the story is also made present through the confession of the ancient creeds, the singing of hymns from the whole of the Christian tradition, and the tangible enactment of the story in water, bread, and wine. Baptists have traditionally prized the gospel story as declared in the Spirit-enabled preaching of the Word and personal testimony as the means by which people encounter the living Christ. The formation of Baptists may well be enhanced through the internalization and embodiment of the gospel story by also drawing upon the liturgical tradition of the larger Christian community in planning services of worship that maximize the community's exposure to the story that regulates its life.

Third, I suggest that Baptists re-envision tradition as an ongoing argument about the significance of the Christian story. As Baptists have a distinctive place in the history of the church as dissenters, a Baptist hermeneutic of tradition should allow for dissent within the tradition.[43] When I have had my divinity students read the "Baptist Manifesto," I have invariably heard questions in response along these lines: "Where would a Martin Luther have a place in this vision?" "Doesn't this ignore the Baptist tradition of dissent?" "What if the community studying the scriptures together is a fundamentalist one?" While the "Baptist Manifesto" does reject authoritarianism in the community, its case for the authority of the traditioning community could be strengthened by affirming the indispensability of the dissenter for the communal argument that constitutes, drives, and clarifies the tradition of the community. In other words, Baptists might re-envision tradition in terms of Alasdair MacIntyre's definition of "a living tradition" as "an historically extended, socially embodied argument, and an argument precisely in part about the goods which constitute that tradition." MacIntyre also observes that "when an institution . . . is a bearer of a tradition of practice or practices, its common life will be partly, but in a centrally important way, constituted by a continuous argument" regarding what the institution is and ought to be, because traditions and the institutions that carry them "when vital, embody continuities of conflict."[44] Baptists, and different types of Baptists, have their own distinctive contributions to make to the larger church's argument about the goods that constitute its tradition.

I hope that these observations and proposals regarding tradition as a new horizon for Baptist theology will further this vital argument.

Notes

[1] The concept of "horizons of interpretation" is developed in Hans-Georg Gadamer, *Wahrheit und Methode: Grundzüge einer philosophischen Hermeneutik*, 2d ed. (Tübingen: J. C. B. Mohr, 1965); ET, *Truth and Method*, 2d rev. ed., trans. Joel Weinsheimer and Donald G. Marshall (New York: Crossroad, 1989).

[2] My language here echoes the observation of Philip E. Thompson that "Baptists have come to make a tradition of rejecting tradition, Baptist or otherwise." Thompson, "Re-envisioning Baptist Identity: Historical, Theological, and Liturgical Analysis," *Perspectives in Religious Studies* 27, no. 3 (Fall 2000): 302.

[3] For historical and sociological studies of the recent controversy in the Southern Baptist Convention, the largest denominational expression of Baptist church life and largest Protestant denomination in North America, see Bill Leonard, *God's Last and Only Hope: The Fragmentation of the Southern Baptist Convention* (Grand Rapids: Eerdmans, 1990); Nancy Tatom Ammerman, *Baptist Battles: Social Change and Religious Conflict in the Southern Baptist Convention* (New Brunswick: Rutgers University Press, 1990); David T. Morgan, *The New Crusades, the New Holy Land: Conflict in the Southern Baptist Convention, 1969-1991* (Tuscaloosa: University of Alabama Press, 1996); Barry Hankins, *Uneasy in Babylon: Southern Baptist Conservatives and American Culture* (Tuscaloosa: University of Alabama Press, 2002).

[4] See Steven R. Harmon, "Baptist Confessions of Faith and the Patristic Tradition," *Perspectives in Religious Studies* 29, no. 4 (Winter 2002): 349-58.

[5] William L. Lumpkin, *Baptist Confessions of Faith*, rev. ed. (Valley Forge, Penn.: Judson Press, 1969), 297-334.

[6] Harmon, "Baptist Confessions of Faith and the Patristic Tradition," 352-53.

[7] Philip E. Thompson, "A New Question in Baptist History: Seeking a Catholic Spirit among Early Baptists," *Pro Ecclesia* 8, no. 1 (Winter 1999): 51-72.

[8] The slogan "no creed but the Bible" is actually not indigenous to the Baptist movement proper but rather seems to have originated in the Restorationist movement led by Barton W. Stone, Walter Scott, and Thomas and Alexander Campbell. A variant slogan, "no creed but Christ," emerged later in the movement (M. Eugene Boring, *Disciples and the Bible: A History of Disciples Biblical Interpretation in North America* [St. Louis: Chalice Press, 1997], 18; William Tabbernee, "Unfencing the Table: Creeds, Councils, Communion, and the Campbells," *Mid-Stream* 35, no. 6 [1966]: 417-32; and William Tabbernee, "Alexander Campbell and the Apostolic Tradition,"

in *The Free Church and the Early Church: Bridging the Historical and Theological Divide*, ed. D. H. Williams [Grand Rapids: Eerdmans, 2002], 163-80). In the latter essay, Tabbernee points out that Alexander Campbell's aversion was not to patristic creeds properly used but rather to the inappropriate use of post-Reformation confessions to exclude people from the fellowship of the church, and Campbell in fact frequently referenced the ancient creeds in order to defend orthodox trinitarian and Christological positions.

By the time of the formation of the Southern Baptist Convention in 1845, however, it had become such a common axiom in Baptist circles that William B. Johnson could declare, "We have constructed for our basis no new creed; acting in this manner upon a Baptist aversion to all creeds but the Bible" ("The Southern Baptist Convention, To the Brethren in the United States; To the Congregations Connected with the Respective Churches; and To All Candid Men," in *Proceedings of the Southern Baptist Convention in Augusta, Georgia, 8-12 May 1845* [Richmond: H. K. Ellyson, 1845], 17-20).

⁹Mark Medley, "Catholics, Baptists, and the Normativity of Tradition," *Perspectives in Religious Studies* 28, no. 2 (Summer 2001): 119-20, n. 2. Grenz's most extensive treatment of tradition appears in Stanley J. Grenz and John R. Franke, *Beyond Foundationalism: Shaping Theology in a Postmodern Context* (Louisville: Westminster John Knox, 2001), 93-129; McClendon's perspectives on tradition are summarized in James Wm. McClendon, Jr., *Systematic Theology*, vol. 2, *Doctrine* (Nashville: Abingdon, 1994), 468-72.

¹⁰Millard J. Erickson, *Postmodernizing the Faith: Evangelical Responses to the Challenge of Postmodernism* (Grand Rapids: Baker Books, 1998); see esp. chap. 3, "To Boldly Go Where No Evangelical Has Gone Before: Stanley Grenz" (83-102).

¹¹Millard J. Erickson, *Christian Theology* (Grand Rapids: Baker Books, 1985), 258. This brief three-paragraph treatment of the relationship of tradition to authority notes that all Christians are influenced by tradition and ascribes "positive value" to tradition as an aid in biblical interpretation, but then cautions that "we should consult them [the Fathers] as we do other commentaries."

¹²Curtis W. Freeman, "A Confession for Catholic Baptists," in *Ties That Bind: Life Together in the Baptist Vision*, ed. Gary Furr and Curtis W. Freeman (Macon, Ga.: Smyth & Helwys, 1994), 85: "I suggest that Baptists may more easily explore the vast resources of Christian spirituality and that other Christians may more readily receive the unique contributions of Baptist spirituality if we attempt to think of ourselves (at least experimentally) as (little c) catholic (little b) baptists." Freeman's spelling of "baptist" with a lower-case "b" in this context is derived from the usage of James Wm. McClendon, Jr., *Systematic Theology*, vol. 1, *Ethics* (Nashville: Abingdon Press, 1986), 17-35, in which McClendon makes his case for rooting his theological vision in a broad yet distinctive ecclesial tradition that includes

not only Baptists proper but also other denominations with roots in the Radical Reformation as well as various Pentecostal and evangelical bodies with comparable ecclesiologies. In my own usage herein I retain the lower-case "catholic" from Freeman's suggested self-understanding but neverthe-less capitalize "Baptist," as the theologians to whom I apply this categoriza-tion belong to the Baptist tradition proper.

[13]Thompson, "Re-envisioning Baptist Identity," 302.

[14]Grenz and Franke, *Beyond Foundationalism*, 57-166.

[15]Ibid., 118.

[16]Ibid., 126.

[17]Medley, "Catholics, Baptists, and the Normativity of Tradition," 121, 126-28.

[18]D. H. Williams, *Retrieving the Tradition and Renewing Evangelicalism: A Primer for Suspicious Protestants* (Grand Rapids: Eerdmans, 1999), 101-31.

[19]Barry Harvey, "Doctrinally Speaking: James McClendon on the Nature of Doctrine," *Perspectives in Religious Studies* 27, no. 1 (Spring 2000): 56-57, note 82; cf. Harvey, "Where, Then, Do We Stand? Baptists, History, and Authority," *Perspectives in Religious Studies* 29, no. 4 (Winter 2002): 359-80, esp. 371-79.

[20]Paul S. Fiddes, *Tracks and Traces: Baptist Identity in Church and Theology*, Studies in Baptist History and Thought, vol. 13 (Carlisle, Cumbria, U.K.: Paternoster Press, 2003), 217.

[21]Harmon, "Baptist Confessions of Faith and the Patristic Tradition," 356-57; Paul M. Blowers, "The *Regula Fidei* and the Narrative Character of Early Christian Faith," *Pro Ecclesia* 6, no. 2 (Spring 1997): 199-228.

[22]Curtis W. Freeman, Steven R. Harmon, Elizabeth Newman, and Philip E. Thompson, "Confessing the Faith," *Biblical Recorder* (July 8, 2004), available online at http://www.biblicalrecorder.org/content/opinion/2004/7_8_2004/gc080704confessing.shtml (accessed August 23, 2004). The fol-lowing paragraph quoted from the statement is representative of the document's critique of common Baptist attitudes toward the creeds: "The staunch anti-creedalism in Baptist life often leads to the faulty assumption that modern Christians can leapfrog from the primitive Christianity of the Bible to the contemporary situation with relative ease. This hermeneutical naiveté fails to offer any realistic means for present-day Bible readers to discern the central themes of Scripture that give a sense of its whole message as good news. Ironically, in the wake of the Baptist encounter with modernity those from both ends of the theological spectrum employed the slogan 'no creed but the Bible' in their theological arguments. Serious Bible readers will find much needed hermeneutical guidance by returning to the ancient creeds of the church."

[23]Psalms and Hymns Trust, *Baptist Praise and Worship*, ed. Alec Gilmore and others (Oxford: Oxford University Press, 1991); Baptist Union of Great

Britain, *Covenant 21: Covenant for a Gospel People* (London: Baptist Union, 2000), 14-15, cited in Fiddes, *Tracks and Traces*, 217, n. 81.

[24]Prosper of Aquitaine, *Praeteritorum Sedis Apostolicae episcoporum auctoritates, de gratia Dei et libero voluntatis arbitrio* 8; ET "Official Pronouncements of the Apostolic See on Divine Grace and Free Will," in *Defense of St. Augustine*, trans. P. de Letter, Ancient Christian Writers, no. 32 (Westminster, Md.: Newman Press, 1963), 183.

[25]Medley, "Catholics, Baptists, and the Normativity of Tradition," 127, approvingly citing Thompson, "Re-envisioning Baptist Identity," 290.

[26]Although there is presently no Baptist liturgical theology of the magnitude of Geoffrey Wainwright's *Doxology: The Praise of God in Worship, Doctrine, and Life. A Systematic Theology* (New York: Oxford University Press, 1980), several recent projects are making contributions to rectifying this deficiency: Thompson, "Re-envisioning Baptist Identity"; Barry Harvey, "The Eucharistic Idiom of the Gospel," *Pro Ecclesia* 9, no. 3 (Summer 2000): 297-318; Stanley K. Fowler, *More Than a Symbol: The British Baptist Recovery of Baptismal Sacramentalism*, Studies in Baptist History and Thought, vol. 2 (Carlisle, Cumbria, U.K.: Paternoster Press, 2002); Anthony R. Cross and Philip E. Thompson, eds., *Baptist Sacramentalism*, Studies in Baptist History and Thought, vol. 5 (Carlisle, Cumbria, U.K.: Paternoster Press, 2003); and the articles in *Review and Expositor* 100, no. 3 (Summer 2003), a thematic issue on "Baptists and Liturgy" edited by Philip E. Thompson. Three recent dissertations and theses on these themes are worthy of note: Christopher J. Ellis, "Baptist Worship: Liturgical Theology from a Free Church Perspective" (Ph.D. diss., University of Leeds, 2002); Steven B. O'Connor, "*Lex Orandi, Lex Credendi*: An Investigation into the Liturgy and Theology of New Zealand Baptists" (Th.M. thesis, University of Auckland, 2001); Nathan Charles Nettleton, "The Liturgical Expression of Baptist Identity" (Th.M. thesis, Melbourne College of Divinity, 2000). The studies cited in this note were foreshadowed by the contributions of Stephen Winward to the mid-twentieth-century liturgical renewal movement among British Baptists; see Stephen F. Winward, *The Reformation of Our Worship* (Richmond: John Knox Press, 1965).

[27]Mikael Broadway, Curtis Freeman, Barry Harvey, James Wm. McClendon, Jr., Elizabeth Newman, and Philip Thompson, "Re-envisioning Baptist Identity: A Manifesto for Baptist Communities in North America, published in *Baptists Today*" (June 26, 1997): 8-10, *Perspectives in Religious Studies* 24, no. 3 (Fall 1997): 303-10, and online at http://www.chowan.edu/acadp/Religion/pubs/manifesto.htm (accessed August 23, 2004).

[28] "Soul competency" refers to a principle articulated by Baptist theologian E. Y. Mullins (1860-1928) in *The Axioms of Religion: A New Interpretation of the Baptist Faith* (Philadelphia: American Baptist Publication Society, 1908), in which he develops a sustained argument for the notion that "religion is a personal matter between the [individual] soul and God" (54) as

"the sufficient statement of the historical significance of the Baptists" (53). The case that this is a reductionistic re-reading of the Baptist tradition through intellectual and political lenses ground in modern America is well argued by Curtis W. Freeman, "E. Y. Mullins and the Siren Songs of Modernity," *Review and Expositor* 96, no. 1 (Winter 1999): 23-42.

[29] The document develops each of these affirmations more fully and joins them with rejections of various Baptist perversions of these ecclesial principles. For critical responses to the "Baptist Manifesto" from Baptist historians and theologians, see Walter B. Shurden, "The Baptist Identity and the Baptist *Manifesto*," *Perspectives in Religious Studies* 25, no. 4 (Winter 1998): 321-40; Robert P. Jones, "Re-Visioning Baptist Identity from a Theocentric Perspective," *Perspectives in Religious Studies* 26, no. 1 (Spring 1999): 35-57. For additional reflections and counter-responses from co-authors of the "Baptist Manifesto," see Curtis W. Freeman, "Can Baptist Theology Be Revisioned?" *Perspectives in Religious Studies* 24, no. 3 (Fall 1997): 273-310; idem, "A New Perspective on Baptist Identity," *Perspectives in Religious Studies* 26, no. 1 (Spring 1999): 59-65; Thompson, "Re-envisioning Baptist Identity."

[30]Medley, "Catholics, Baptists, and the Normativity of Tradition," 126-27.

[31]Cross and Thompson, eds., *Baptist Sacramentalism*.

[32]Philip E. Thompson, "Sacraments and Religious Liberty: From Critical Practice to Rejected Infringement," in *Baptist Sacramentalism*, ed. Cross and Thompson, 36-54; Barry Harvey, "Re-Membering the Body: Baptism, Eucharist and the Politics of Disestablishment" (96-116); Curtis W. Freeman, " 'To Feed Upon by Faith': Nourishment from the Lord's Table" (194-210); Elizabeth Newman, "The Lord's Supper: Might Baptists Accept a Theory of Real Presence?" (211-27).

[33]Paul S. Fiddes, "The Incarnate God and the Sacramental Life," in *Participating in God: A Pastoral Doctrine of the Trinity* (Louisville: Westminster John Knox, 2000), 278-304; idem, *Tracks and Traces*, 107-92; Fowler, *More Than a Symbol*, see esp. 196-253; Mark S. Medley, " 'Do This': The Eucharist and Ecclesial Selfhood," *Review and Expositor* 100, no. 3 (Summer 2003): 383-401.

[34]Fiddes, *Participating in God*; Mark S. Medley, *Imago Trinitatis: Toward a Relational Understanding of Becoming Human* (Lanham, Md.: University Press of America, 2002); Molly T. Marshall, *Joining the Dance: A Theology of the Spirit* (Valley Forge, Pa.: Judson Press, 2003). In the cited works by Medley and Marshall, the retrieval of perichoretic trinitarianism is mediated by an engagement with feminist trinitarian theologians such as Patricia Wilson-Kastner and Catherine Mowry LaCugna who make much constructive use of patristic perichoretic thought.

[35]Barry Harvey, *Another City: An Ecclesiological Primer for a Post-Christian World* (Harrisburg, Pa.: Trinity Press International, 1999); Mark

S. Medley, "The Use of *Theosis* in Contemporary Baptist Theology" (paper presented to the annual meeting of the American Academy of Religion—Southeast Region, Atlanta, Georgia, March 5-7, 2004, and the joint annual meeting of the College Theology Society and National Association of Baptist Professors of Religion Region-at-Large, Washington, D.C., June 3-6, 2004).

[36]Tarmo Toom, an Estonian Baptist teaching theology in the United States, calls this a "diachronic ecumenism" that "takes a deep look into the shared past of Christianity and finds there the basis for mutual understanding and appreciation" (Tarmo Toom, "Baptists on Justification: Can We Join the *Joint Declaration on the Doctrine of Justification?*" *Pro Ecclesia* 13, no. 3 [Summer 2004]: 291, note 7).

[37]Toom, "Baptists on Justification," 289-306; Daniel H. Williams, "The Disintegration of Catholicism into Diffuse Inclusivism," *Pro Ecclesia* 12, no. 4 (Fall 2003): 389-93; Timothy George, "The Sacramentality of the Church: An Evangelical Baptist Perspective," *Pro Ecclesia* 12, no. 3 (Summer 2003): 309-23; idem, "An Evangelical Reflection on Scripture and Tradition," *Pro Ecclesia* 9, no. 2 (Spring 2000): 184-207; Barry Harvey, "Review Essay: Martin B. Copenhaver, Anthony B. Robinson, and William H. Willimon, *Good News in Exile*; Marva J. Dawn, *A Royal 'Waste' of Time*; Craig Van Gelder, ed., *Confident Witness-Changing World*; Jonathan R. Wilson, *Living Faithfully in a Fragmented World*," *Pro Ecclesia* 10, no. 4 (Fall 2001): 487-90; Stephen R. Holmes, "The Justice of Hell and the Display of God's Glory in the Thought of Jonathan Edwards," *Pro Ecclesia* 9, no. 4 (Fall 2000): 389-403; Ralph C. Wood, "Review Essay: David W. Fagerberg, *The Size of Chesterton's Catholicism*," *Pro Ecclesia* 9, no. 2 (Spring 2000): 236-40; Scott H. Moore, "The End of Convenient Stereotypes: How the *First Things* and Baxter Controversies Inaugurate Extraordinary Politics," *Pro Ecclesia* 7, no. 1 (Winter 1998), 17-47; Roger E. Olson, "Whales and Elephants: Both God's Creatures, but Can They Meet? Evangelicals and Liberals in Dialogue," *Pro Ecclesia* 4, no. 2 (Spring 1995): 165-89; as well as the previously cited articles by Harvey, "Eucharistic Idiom of the Gospel," and Thompson, "New Question in Baptist History."

[38]Paul S. Fiddes, "The Church's Ecumenical Calling: A Baptist Perspective," in *Tracks and Traces*, 193-227.

[39]This final section of the essay is a condensation and adaptation of portions of Steven R. Harmon, "The Authority of the Community (of All the Saints): Toward a Postmodern Baptist Hermeneutic of Tradition," *Review and Expositor* 100, no. 4 (Fall 2003): 587-621.

[40]The maintenance of Baptist ecclesial distinctiveness must not grow out of an erroneous conviction that Baptists have uniquely preserved Christian truth but rather out of an appreciation for the particular experiences that have uniquely shaped their own denominational trajectory of living the larger Christian story. Some aspects of this unique trajectory may need to be rethought or even abandoned in light of a re-appropriation of the larger

tradition (e.g., the autonomous individualism of modern Baptists in the United States or anti-Catholicism), while other Baptist ecclesial distinctives may be valued as Baptist contributions to the larger catholic tradition (e.g., religious liberty).

[41]The Latin phrase *communio sanctorum*, which originated in Gaul at the end of the fourth century and in the following century began appearing in the predecessors of the received text of the Apostles' Creed, is capable of multiple translations and interpretations: (1) with *sanctorum* taken as neuter, a sharing "of holy things," i.e., participation in the sacraments; or (2) with *sanctorum* as masculine, (a) a "fellowship [consisting] of holy persons," (b) a "fellowship with holy persons" in the sense of the martyrs and saints [distinguished from ordinary Christians], or (c) a "fellowship with holy persons" in the sense of all believers, both living and deceased. J. N. D. Kelly, *Early Christian Creeds*, 2nd ed. (New York: David McKay, 1960), 388-91.

[42]George A. Lindbeck, *The Nature of Doctrine: Religion and Theology in a Postliberal Age* (Louisville: Westminster John Knox, 1984), esp. 15-29 and 73-90.

[43]"Dissent" within the community must always be understood as a state of affairs that reflects the current failures of the church to embody the unity that is an eschatological mark of the church. Dissent can be a step toward unity only if pursued as a conversation that requires contestation because of the present fallenness of the church en route to the eschatological realization of its unity.

[44]Alasdair MacIntyre, *After Virtue: A Study in Moral Theory*, 2d ed. (Notre Dame: University of Notre Dame Press, 1984), 222.

Globalization at Large

Approaching the Ecclesial Question of Tradition in the Twenty-first Century

Colleen M. Mallon

There are few theological horizons more important or more urgent than the contemporary context of globalization. In an address to the worldwide Dominican Order, Robert Schreiter spoke of the "responsibility . . . to probe as deeply as we can into the movements and currents of our own time in order to live faithfully the commitments to preach the Gospel which are incumbent upon us."[1] Globalization needs to be addressed from dual perspectives: "the emerging forms of global discourse and the proliferating forms of local discourse."[2] Attending to the global-local relationship and their respective discourses focuses renewed attention on the significance of traditions, cultural-social identities, and the human endeavor to construe both meaningful and viable lives.

Today as in the past, the question of tradition arises in a context marked by profound shifts in social, political and economic life. Theologically speaking, the ambiguous character of religious traditions and the social identities they are said to fashion offer a fertile field of inquiry. If globalization is the context from which all theology today is done, what can theologians interested in tradition learn from social theorists currently assessing the emerging world (dis)order?[3] What bearing might these insights have on the emerging theologies of tradition?[4]

In this essay I explore the work of social scientists Roland Robertson, Arjun Appadurai, and Saskia Sassen in order to tease out strands of significance (using a metaphor that fits these reflections better than "new horizons") impacting the ecclesiological question of religious traditions in a globalized world. By exploring the contemporary context within which religious identity questions are emerging, this essay is the first part of a larger study devoted to the question of refiguring the notion of tradition in Roman Catholicism. In a globalized context, what happens to the very notion of cultural traditions and the social identities that these symbol systems fund? What do theologians need to pay attention to? Among the multiple contributors to globalization discourse, the works of Robertson, Appadurai, and Sassen are at once thoughtful and contrastive in their perspectives. While each shares an interest in how we currently conceive of the world as a whole, they also attend to cultural questions arising from the tensive relationship between the local and the global. In this essay I introduce their perspectives by discussing the imaginative frameworks that Robertson, Appadurai, and Sassen use to organize and analyze the data of globalization. Following this, I reflect on these juxtaposed pictures of the global reality and point towards strands of significance which provide important material for further theological reflection. It is important, however, to first address the question of defining globalization.

Defining Globalization: A Work in Progress

Defining globalization is a work in progress. Since the middle of the 1980s, social theorists have attempted to describe the peculiar contemporary phenomena of economic, socio-cultural and political forces fashioning a new sense of the world as a whole. Numerous events and trends contribute to a burgeoning, unprecedented consciousness of "world as a whole": networked and intrinsically related. Some of these are the growth of multinational corporations and the subsequent trade agreements that forged a new era of global capital; the rise of brutal ethnic conflicts and the destabilization of geographic borders often in the name of self-determination; the ecological crisis, issues of nuclear proliferation, ozone depletion, coupled with the pernicious worldwide threat of hunger and the AIDS epidemic.

There remains a lack of consensus regarding both the causes and defining features of globalization.[5] While many concur that globalization involves both compression and expansion, (the compression of space and the expansion of modernities), they vary in their assessment of these and other significant factors.[6] In a recent article Arjun Appadurai points to the increasing disparity within the discourse of globalization and notes the growing chasm between academics and policy makers and "the everyday understanding of global forces by the poor."[7]

No one stands outside of globalization; how each of us participates in and is affected by this process shapes our observations of it. The context of our specific epistemic communities informs each of our viewpoints. More will be said about this, but it is important to point out that any definition of globalization is very much a work in progress.

Robert Schreiter's work in globalization remains a seminal work in Christian reflection on our present global predicament. Schreiter identifies three factors that characterize contemporary globalized contexts: they are deterritorialized, hyperdifferentiated, and hybridized.[8] Deterritorialization highlights the magnitude of the flow of persons across the planet. Another way to express this might be to say that hypermobility is the flip side of deterritorialization. The displacement of peoples occurs for a variety of reasons and purposes. War, famine, and fear of repression represent one end of the continuum of human desire drawing peoples across borders into new and unfamiliar places. Pleasure, intellectual curiosity, and business opportunities comprise a whole different set of motivations that spur peoples into new spaces.

The propinquity of multiple forms of life in what Saskia Sassen calls "global cities" fuels the need for diverse peoples to express the distinctness of their cultural lives. Hyperdifferentiation flows from collective expressions of difference. Where geographical boundaries can no longer delineate the distinctiveness of ethnicities, boundaries of difference serve to both separate and integrate. Borders once monitored by state regulations are culturally maintained by migrating peoples in their new contexts. Here "imagined communities" of sameness and of shared heritage function to provide wayfarers with a continuing sense of social identity. Traditions serve to bind people to communities, families and cultural institutions, no matter the distance. Recreating these traditions, however, in new spaces where materials and the overall social climate may lack significant elements, often forces migrating peoples to rethink and adapt their customs to the present circumstances. Moreover, in a global city where the mix of populations is inevitable, new relationships evolve into new social networks. Cultural flow between strangers (who are proximate neighbors in global cities) occurs as new multi-cultural communities emerge from the joint effort to create a livable space for themselves and their families. The exchanges often result in the hybridization of once insular cultural traditions.

Going Deeper: Analyzing and Interpreting a Global World

Schreiter's three descriptors offer a helpful entry to the current phenomena of globalization and raise numerous questions regarding how to proceed with appropriate analysis and interpretation. The social sciences, themselves a product of the globalizing forces functioning at the turn of the twentieth century, can be particularly helpful to theologians assessing the complexities of our global "signs of the times." The increasing concern for contextualizing theology makes the work of sociologists and anthropologists ever more significant for theology. As Kathryn Tanner has pointed out, the shift in understanding from modern notions of culture to postmodern notions of culture raises important questions: the universal-particular dilemma, the issue of continuity-over-time, the meaning of diversity, and the function of power in the production of culture.[9] What are the consequences of hypermobility and deterritorialization? How are social identities and commitments changing? Is hybridization a gloss for a kind of global homogenizing process? What commitments inform the various narrations of the global-human condition available today? How might a careful study of diverse sociological perspectives on globalization aid theologians towards assessing the contemporary "historical processes of exchange and interconnection"?[10]

Roland Robertson: Mapping the Global Field

Roland Robertson of the University of Aberdeen is a pioneer in the area of globalization research.[11] Robertson contends that global thinking has two intrinsic components. Global thinking is an awareness of worldwide interdependence even as it is also a conception of what that interdependence looks like.[12] To speak of "the world" is to already have an imaginative construct of what is in the world and how these entities are related. Convinced that global systems analysis is still possible, Robertson argues for a multidimensional model of globalization that resists flattening complex global forces into market dynamics. Robertson's own approach, mapping what he calls "global fields," attempts to be comprehensive without being totalizing.[13] His goal is "to make analytical and interpretative sense of how quotidian actors, collective and individual, go about the business of conceiving of the world, including attempts to *deny* that the world is one."[14]

Conceptions of the world as a whole are not recent phenomena. However, how the world is "world" today, both conceptually and functionally, is admittedly more complex. Forms of life, juxtaposed and often contentious, face off more regularly and more rapidly than ever before. To reduce these conjunctions and collisions to either economics or to the workings of Western modernity fails to get at the global complexities constantly informing social actors, communally and individually. Robertson maps what he calls "global fields" by focusing on "the most general features of *life* in relatively recent history."[15] Robertson proposes four reference points which are by themselves empirically measurable, yet are inherently interdependent: national societies, individual selves, the world system of societies, and humankind (as species). These four reference points represent "the empirical constituents of the world of relatively recent times."[16] According to Robertson, the conceptual framework of global fields, first, attends to how the four reference points operate as "constraining" elemental components and, second, function as an analytical tool for examining globalizing forces without being prescriptive of the inner workings of globalization. "For example, individuals as such are increasingly constrained by being members of societies, members of an increasingly thematized and endangered human species and greatly affected by the vicissitudes of international relations."[17]

By mapping the global-human condition in this fashion, Robertson underlines the fact that any analysis of globalization that focuses solely on the nation-state as arbiter of cultural identity and political allegiance is no longer adequate. A case in point is the Ottawa treaty banning anti-personnel landmines. The Ottawa treaty was not originally an agreement proposed by national governments intent on protecting their citizens. To the contrary, pressure was brought to bear on national governments by individuals and groups to adopt the treaty as a result of a massive grassroots global effort largely conducted on the Internet. Individuals in solidarity with this humanitarian cause mobilized support worldwide through local actions that had global effects. In 1997 the Nobel Peace Prize was awarded to Jody Williams and the International Campaign to Ban Landmines, "an umbrella

organization for over one thousand nongovernmental organizations."[18] The contemporary experience of globalization relativizes
and thus transforms the character of the nation-state as unprecedented
pressures from individuals, other nations and concerns for the species as a whole come to bear on the prerogatives of the once sovereign nation-state.

While mapping globalization in this manner attempts to provide a
method towards empirically analyzing and interpreting significant
components of globalization, there are those who reject resoundingly
the very construct of "one world." A global view threatens to impose
an order that barely masks political hegemony and cultural domi-
nance. The rejection of "worldism," one that attempts to explain
human diversity as an epiphenomenon of a foundational world system, is countered by an equally extreme "relativism" that "involves,
for the most part, refusal to make general, 'universalizing' sense of
the problems posed by sharp discontinuities between different forms
of collective and individual life."[19] These contending perspectives bring
into focus the contested relationship between the global and the local
which is critical to Robertson's interpretation of the global field.

The global-local relationship is a contemporary manifestation of
the universal-particular dilemma.[20] The current form, however, of
the universal-particular relationship differs significantly from former
expressions. Where once the universal and the particular were
cognitively and existentially distant and distinct, now they are paired,
"tied together as part of a globewide nexus," such that to speak of
one is to necessarily say something of the other.[21] This is Robertson's
insight: the permeated character of the universal-particular relationship. Contemporary globalization is "a massive, two-fold process
involving *the interpenetration of the universalization of particularism and the particularization of the universal.*"[22] When interpreted in
this fashion, a global focus does not necessarily entail the subordina-
tion of the local, and diversity may not be limited to the particularity
of place.

Robertson notes that Japan represents an interesting example of
the contemporary particular-universal phenomenon. The Japanese
encounter with Chinese cultural repertoires (as expressed in both
Confucianism and Mahayana Buddhism) did not result in the "Chi-
nese-ization" of Japan. Japan enjoys a long history of successfully
selecting and modifying newly introduced cultural elements in such a

way that the resulting cultural products are recognized and promoted as uniquely, genuinely Japanese. Indeed, sociologist Michael Featherstone makes the argument that, from a market perspective, the Japanization of the world (universalism) involves a concerted fidelity to this very particular cultural logic. The Japanese notion of *dochaku* manifests itself in market approaches that seek to tailor the universal to the needs and constraints of the particular. Thus *dochaku* is less about imposing, worldwide, specific Japanese commodities or lifestyles and more about adapting products to meet local market demands. The coinherence of the global and the local in this approach or "glocalism," to use Featherstone's word, concretizes the ever-increasing relational complexity emerging from "processes of relativization." The contemporary "relatively autonomous" existence of nations, individuals, international society and the human species is a thoroughly conditioned existence: each component constrained by the unique and contingent historical fortunes of the other three.[23]

The global-human condition instigates a coming-to-consciousness of how the sundry interactions among diverse forms of life contribute to processes of relativization, construing a picture of global interdependence. Robertson's "attempt to preserve direct attention both to particularity and difference and to universality and homogeneity" flows from his contention that contemporary globalization takes general form: the institutionalization of the universal-particular nexus.[24] This institutionalization is increasingly concretized in the co-inherence of processes shaping individuals, national societies, international society and the idea of humanity. The "global institutionalization of the relationship between universalized particularism and particularized universalism" significantly refigures the global-local relationship.[25] We live in a world where universals make sense only when they are concretized in the particularity of specific human conditions (the particularization of universalism). Simultaneously we live in a world that has come to accept the limitlessness of the particular, that "there is virtually no limit to particularity, to uniqueness, to difference, to otherness" (the universalization of the particular).[26]

Through his cognitive framework of global fields, Robertson argues "for the moral acceptance of [global] complexity" in which contending individuals, nations, international relations and humankind form the primary loci around which globalization is both experienced and thematized.

Arjun Appadurai: Disjunctive Landscapes of Global (Dis)order

Arjun Appadurai, professor of anthropology at the University of Chicago, writes extensively in the area of globalization. His seminal essay, "Disjuncture and Difference in the Global Cultural Economy," appears in several edited volumes and anthologies on the topic of globalization.[27] Fundamental to Appadurai's perspective is the role of imagination in the new global cultural economy. Specifically he investigates how the *social practice of the imagination* functions in the shifting ground of the global present. Like Roland Robertson, Appadurai offers an imaginative construal of globalization; however, where Robertson sees the *conjunction* of juxtaposed social forces, Appadurai sees *disjunctures* and argues for an interpretative framework that attends to "ironies and resistances" that issue from the global juxtaposition of the exotic and the uncanny.[28]

Appadurai notes that prior to the eighteenth century, trade between peoples from different parts of the world occurred only with great effort and expense. The shift in the forces of "cultural gravity" accelerated by European colonialism fashioned both the desire and the means to cross once formidable boundaries.[29] This recent past, however, pales in comparison to the present experience of global flows among peoples, ideas, and commodities. Some have characterized this compression of cultures as an experience of "global village"; but as Appadurai rightly points out, this construal is far too irenic, suggesting a place that is, in fact, no place. "The world we live in now seems rhizomic, even schizophrenic, calling for theories of rootlessness, alienation, and psychological distance between individuals and groups on the one hand, and fantasies (or nightmares) of electronic propinquity on the other."[30]

Appadurai suggests that five broad and significant "landscapes" converge and overlap in a disjunctive global order that resists easy analysis or systemization. These five landscapes are constituted by peoples, technologies, finances, media and ideologies.[31] Appadurai speaks of ethnoscapes (landscapes of peoples, be they tourists or refugees), technoscapes (the proliferation of both low and high technologies), financescapes (the "mysterious, rapid and difficult landscape" of global capital), mediascapes and ideoscapes (which are both "landscapes of images"). Mediascapes refer to ever evolving electronic means of communication and the images, narratives and genres created to carry information. Ideoscapes refer to images of a more political nature and form a patchwork of Enlightenment ideals that have been disembedded from the particular internal logic of the original master narrative.[32] By construing these categories as multidimensional landscapes, Appadurai emphasizes both the fluidity of these relations as well as their perspectival character. These landscapes "are not objectively given relations that look the same from every angle of vision . . . they are deeply perspectival constructs, inflected by the historical, linguistic and political situatedness of different sorts of actors: nation-states, multinationals, diasporic communities, as well as subnational groups and movements."[33]

Appadurai sees the global condition as one of "global cultural flows" where the traffic of persons, ideas, capital and goods follows along "increasingly nonisomorphic paths."[34] This is an unprecedented experience of "deterritorialization" where "the disjunctures have become central to the politics of global culture."[35] The contemporary context of deterritorialization presents ominous challenges. As one of the primary contemporary forces fueling new global fundamentalisms, deterritorialization is also responsible for new markets responding worldwide to the craving of displaced persons for a sense of home. Indeed, the contemporary face of ethnicity has changed profoundly as geographically dispersed peoples make primordial claims of shared identity and construct social-political sentiments and goals (nationhood) that, in some cases, are in direct conflict with the nation-state(s) in which these primordialized persons reside. Thus Serbs and Basques, worldwide, constitute in some sense nations-in-search-of statehood. "Invented homelands" such as the Sikhs' Khalistan, the Palestinians' West Bank, and the Tamils' Sri Lanka express contrasting ways in which deterritorialized persons engage in the ethnic reconstruction of nation-as-state and highlight the beleaguered, even endangered, political notion of the modern nation-state.[36] Geographic separation can intensify cultural-political attachments and feed a variety of primordialisms, including religious fundamentalism.

Diasporas also alter loyalties, re-route the flow of monies and investments, and subject contemporary nation-states to unprecedented social tensions. This remains, however, highly ambiguous territory. Appadurai points out that while some Indians are concerned with how recent Arab investment is changing the service industry in Bombay (hotels and restaurants), other Bombay citizens experience the Arab presence more positively. The corridor of exchange mapped by fellow Indians residing in Egypt and Saudi Arabia provides new conduits for money and luxury items, not only from the Middle East but from throughout the world as well. "The loosening of the holds between peoples, wealth and territories fundamentally alters the basis for cultural reproduction."[37] For Appadurai, this deterritorialized global context is the new and fertile ground for the social practice of imagination.[38]

Beyond contemplation, escapism and fantasy, imagination-as-social-practice plays out new dimensions of not yet realized global interactions of potency and agency. "The imagination is now central to all forms of agency, is itself a social fact, and is the key component of the new global order."[39] Mediascapes offer "image-centered, narrative-based strips of reality" to global audiences whose insatiable appetite for such media exposes the extent to which desires can be manipulated and lives can be re-conceptualized. Whether authored in the form of CNN "news" media, or in the commercial genre of advertisement, or in the entertainment/cultural style of film, images are actively consumed and form a catalogue of potential behavioral repertoires. The dual impact of media and migration is literally reshaping human subjectivities in profound and consequential ways. Appadurai speaks of this as "the mutual contextualizing of motion and mediation."[40] "More people than ever before seem to imagine routinely the possibility that they or their children will live and work in places other than where they were born."[41] Whether these migrations are "diasporas of hope" (the lure of opportunity) or "diasporas of terror" (the agony of oppression), mediascapes narrate an unprecedented range of images and potential life scripts. "For migrants, both the politics of adaptation to new environments and the stimulus to move or return are deeply affected by a mass-mediated imaginary that frequently transcends national space."[42]

One significant arena where the deterritorialized play of imagination can be seen is in the tension between the forces of homogenization and heterogenization. Viewed negatively as cultural hijacking, homogenization is characterized by aggression: the takeover and subsequent displacement of local culture. The flow of products, ideas, and alternative images of the good life threatens shared values and puts cultural distinctiveness at risk. Uncritical assessment of global homogenization processes, sometimes labeled as Americanization or McDonaldization, target the uniforming tendencies associated with the flow of Western cultural commodities into new venues. Appadurai notes, however, "that for the people of Irian Jaya, Indonesianization may be more worrisome than Americanization, as Japanization may be for Koreans, Indianization for Sri Lankans, Vietnamization for Cambodians, and Russianization for the people of Soviet Armenia and the Baltic republics."[43] Moreover, homogenizing forces do not go unresisted; new cultural commodities within a society rarely escape indigenization. Syncretic permutations offer up new expressions that often have their roots in the familiar traditions of a local culture. Democracy, freedom, human rights and sovereignty are Enlightenment ideals that have crossed over into new diasporic public spaces and are being reshaped and indigenized; new meanings emerge from the cultural contexts into which these ideals migrated. The flow of these political ideals into new social contexts triggers values already embedded in the receiving culture and instigates the social practice of augmenting, modifying and transforming the original notion into an indigenized instantiation.[44]

The predicament of the global cultural economy cannot be adequately addressed by models that conceptualize the contemporary world in terms of tensive binaries such as producer/consumer, center/periphery or surplus/deficit.[45] Appadurai's imaginative framework argues for a view of globalization that makes its "complex, overlapping disjunctive order" the starting point for analyzing global cultural complexity, its actuality and its discourses.[46]

Saskia Sassen: Global Cities

Saskia Sassen, professor of sociology at the University of Chicago, looks at the issue of *place* in the new global order and raises questions concerning the sites of globalization.[47] What is the real story about deterritorialization? What are the motives for and the implications of narrating globalization from the optic of hypermobility? Sassen's research, particularly her work at applying a feminist analytic to the question of globalization, searches out the actual sites of economic globalization and uncovers there unseen and devalorized perspectives that nonetheless remain as significant to the success of global cities as the new elites in the growth sectors of specialized services and finance.[48] Global cities are the strategic places where the superabundant flow of capital has transformed national centers into international spaces. However, the transnationalization of capital is only one part of the global equation. The transnationalization of labor, the flow of peoples across national boundaries, be they executives or unskilled laborers, constitutes a worldwide phenomenon that resists antiquated analysis in terms of immigration.[49] In Sassen's words, global cities (New York, Paris, London, Hong Kong, and increasingly Rio de Janeiro and Mexico City) are "denationalized" urban spaces and they constitute the "new geography" of both centrality and marginality.[50]

As denationalized spaces, global cities are embedded in nations, but increasingly have much less in common with cities within their national boundaries. Major cities once considered the apex of particular regions, reflecting the flavor and style of their nation, now appear to be less and less connected to their geographical region. A recent *New York Times* comparison of the 2004 political convention cities of Boston and New York highlighted, among other facts, the number of hotels, transit options, and travelers per day, inadvertently making the case that New York, as a global city, has more in common with London than it has with its colonial sister city.

Global cities have formed "a new geography of centrality" through the global network of concentrated centers of finance and business: "a worldwide grid of strategic places, from export-processing zones to major international business and financial centers."[51] The trading and fiscal activities that drive these cities effectively bind them to each other in ways that transcend physical and political divisions. Mobility, however, has not made location obsolete. The hypermobility of globalization cannot exist without its infrastructures: it is still all about location, location, location. Moreover, "new city users," those highly skilled elites in specialized services (particularly finance and corporate growth sectors), significantly shape the infrastructure of global cities. Elite expectations include not only state-of-the-art (digital, not wired) international business zones but also the compensation of "glamour zones": cities that can sustain five-plus star hotels, high-end restaurants, designer shops and boutiques.[52] This is what is often lost in the rhetoric of globalization: the concrete circumstances that allow global cities to exist at all.

Sassen refocuses attention on the reality that every global city is the result of a wide and disparate range of sub-economies and work cultures. As much as the global economy is dependent on the new elites in finance and special services, it is also dependent on middle- and low-wage workers who provide a vast range of necessary services (delivery, transportation, clerical, janitorial, restaurant and hotel employees, to name only a few). Narrations devoted to the transnationalization of capital often neglect a critical component: the transnationalization of labor and its corresponding cultural and socio-political consequences.[53]

Culturally, economic globalization instigates new processes of identity formation that are refiguring notions of community and membership. The "unmooring" of cultural identities from their originating localities is but one aspect of these global transformations. New alliances and solidarities are transcending national boundaries as deterritorialized peoples engage in processes of reterritorialization. The language of ethnicity, "too often . . . constituted as otherness," cannot adequately describe these processes. The migrations of peoples are better understood as "a set of processes whereby global elements are localized, international labor markets are constituted, and cultures from all over the world are de- and reterritorialized [which] puts them right there at the center along with the internationalization of capital as a fundamental aspect of globalization."[54]

The socio-political consequences of the transnationalization of labor are glimpsed through local practices of valorization and devalorization. Sassen argues that global cities are populated by two types of economic persons: the bearers of corporate capital and the disadvantaged worker. Economic globalization lives only through the local practices that valorize and reward certain roles, positions and life forms, while simultaneously devalorizing others. Focusing on "the material conditions, production sites, and placeboundedness" of globalization, Sassen highlights the "new dynamics of inequality."[55] Traditional economic sectors which remain integral to the success of urban economies are "threatened in a situation where finance and specialized services can earn superprofits."[56] The devalorization of disadvantaged workers is reflected in their absence from most analytics of transnational capital. Sassen notes that "the mainstream account of economic globalization is confined to a very narrow analytic terrain."[57] She maintains that this mainstream version of globalization functions "like a 'narrative of eviction' because it excludes a whole range of workers, firms and sectors that does not fit the prevalent images of globalization."[58] Moreover, even significant "middle-class" professions such as education have felt the refiguring effects of superprofits on global cities. In the early 1990s, the cost of new homes had so outpaced the ability of newly credentialed teachers to buy that some colleges and universities in the San Francisco Bay area began considering housing benefits for teachers who could not qualify for necessary loans in the escalating property market.

Sassen's attention to the concrete instantiation of globalization within world cities allows her to scrutinize the local engines, those overvalued and those devalued, which drive globalizing processes. Her analysis of global cities as strategic sites for the transnationalization of labor as well as capital highlights the conditions and consequences of cultural "unmooring."[59] As Sassen notes, there are as yet no "new forms and regimes to encompass the transnationalization in the formation of identities and loyalties among various population segments which do not regard the nation as the sole or principal source of identification and the associated new solidarities and notions of membership."[60] What the devalued sectors of the global economy lack in power they possess in presence.

As the appearance of "the international human rights regime" demonstrates, there are emerging transnational "sites of normativity."[61] Organizations such as CorpWatch, Public Citizen, Amnesty International, and Global Exchange head a list of hundreds of grassroots organizations linked worldwide and gaining strength through alliances. The World Social Forum, a global gathering of social movement groups, formed as an alternative to the World Economic Forum, meets annually to address the abuses of the current global economic order. The 2004 meeting of WSF in Mumbai, India, hosted close to 75,000 people and included presentations by two Nobel laureates, Shririn Ebadi and Joseph Stiglitz.[62] The solidarities of various human rights alliances transgress national boundaries and expose the inability of state governments to delimit the civic engagement and voice of these residents and citizens. Through careful analysis, Sassen explores the lessons learned "about power through its absence." "Powerlessness is not a silence at the bottom; its absence is present and has consequences."[63]

Strands of Significance

The title of this essay, "Globalization at Large," is a play on Arjun Appadurai's book entitled *Modernity at Large*. In the book, Appadurai contends that "modernity is decisively at large, irregularly conscious and unevenly experienced."[64] I believe this aptly describes contemporary globalization as well. While social theorists vary in their assessment of the origins, the contemporary instigating circumstances, and the degree to which the homogenizing forces associated with globalization are effecting a new world "order," the reality of what Roland Robertson terms "the *comparative interaction* of different forms of life" cannot be denied.[65] Whether globalization is viewed as a new phenomenon or more correctly a new signifier for social and economic processes long shaping our notion of "world," the flow of money, goods, information and peoples has reached a height never before experienced on the planet. Time and space are compressed realities. Simultaneous communication across vast reaches of the globe, coupled with mobile populations of tourists, immigrants, and refugees, permit exotic strangers to live in close proximity in global cities even as they maintain contact with far-off homelands. While the demise of the Soviet Union may have eliminated the bi-polar tension between capitalist and socialist economic systems, the new capitalism dominating global markets may itself prove the most effective in undermining democratic institutions, surpassing any form of Marxism to date. Political economists, like Benjamin Barber, fear for the future of democratic polity in a world where "capitalism run[s] wild because it has been uprooted from the humanizing constraints of the democratic nation-state."[66] Clearly, globalization is at large; it pervades our lives, reshaping our political and economic structures as well as infiltrating our cultural horizons.

Two interwoven strands of significance present themselves: the juxtaposition of cultural worlds, embodied in both mobile individuals and living, authoritative human traditions, and the disembedded character of symbols that have crossed over both geographical and social divides. Once stable and foundational social constructions are thoroughly historicized as multiple worldviews and contending cosmologies collide in the human endeavor of creating and sustaining a life. Cultural worlds are thrown together via digital highways and migratory trajectories. Media and migration contribute in an unprecedented manner to the transgression of cultural boundaries. Contingent circumstances, coercive social forces and cultural repertoires interact, interrogate and work on individuals and communities even as these individuals and communities construe the social worlds that make for a meaningful life. The porous character of cultural boundaries admits difference as readily as it allows for the transfer of once local cultural logics.

This is not to say that homogenization is the order of the day. As this essay has explored, deterritorialization goes hand in hand with some form of reterritorialization; globalizing tendencies produce resistances. The global cultural economy does not undermine distinctive human traditions; on the contrary, it highlights the extent to which peoples may go to distinguish themselves while making sense of their concrete circumstances. Sassen's work, in particular, highlights how powerlessness in economic realms can instigate new politics of presence which draws creatively from multiple cultural repertoires in order to "speak back" to narratives of eviction.

A third strand of significance flows from this: the malleable character of human subjectivities. The porous character of human social life mirrors the interactive character of the human self. The plethora of potential life scripts mediated to individuals through film, entertainment, and advertisement offer a range of life forms to an ever expanding global audience. The superabundance of cultural materials augments and transforms the practices of the imagination and, as Appadurai points out, has profound implications both individually and communally. The ability to consume images and reshape life accordingly (whether by assimilation or resistance) may point to human agency but it does not necessarily point to human freedom.[67] Benjamin Barber notes that mediascapes compose "the actual words and pictures and sounds and tastes that make up the ideational/affective realm by which our physical world of material things is interpreted, controlled and directed."[68] For Barber, the result is the invention of the self as a pseudo-autonomous consumer. By substituting an ideology of choice for freedom, the self is increasingly "defined wholly by want, wish, and the capacity to consume."[69] However understood, the reshaping of human subjectivities by the global context raises profound questions concerning how we are human in a global world.

Theological Implications

If our deepest human questions are intrinsically religious, then the question of our global-human predicament is clearly a new horizon for theological inquiry and critique. Living the Christian mystery in a globalized world presents significant new challenges to our self-understanding as a faith community and our witness to the revelatory gifts entrusted to us. Globalization at large places new demands for faithful, intelligible and transformative theological construals of our "ever ancient, ever new" Christian faith.[70] Given this challenge, what implications and insights might theologians interested in tradition draw from the preceding thinkers? I offer three questions for further study, reflection and *disputatio*.

What Does "Tradition" Mean?

In a globalized world what do we mean when we say "tradition"? The contemporary global context continues to expose how epistemic categories, once thought to be universally understood, need to be reconsidered from within their originating local particularity. For instance, Talal Asad, anthropologist and scholar of Middle Eastern religions, rightly criticizes Western anthropologists who fail to realize that the very idea of "religion" is culturally and historically conditioned; it issues from a particular locale (the West), and its cognitive content as an epistemic category has been shaped by its relationship to other significant categories emerging from early modernity, most significantly the notion of "the secular."[71]

Just as notions of culture, religion and history are receiving new attention, so too, the idea of tradition requires renewed consideration. Anthropologist Corinne Kratz notes that scholars from various disciplines all too often approach the idea of tradition with little reference to how "representations of time, history and identity within particular political contexts" are organized and understood.[72] Recent theological reflection on the notion of tradition in Christianity has paid significant attention to postmodern concerns for the fictive foundational claims of metanarratives as well as the postmodern preference for the particular, the other and the plural. In a recent article, Kathryn Tanner notes that appeals to tradition in Christianity, including more hermeneutically nuanced Gadamerian positions, operate from foundational commitments that postmodern cultural critique calls into question. Seemingly, appeals to tradition are not credible if they fail to address the inescapable fact that all traditions are "invented."

Moreover, Tanner asserts that contemporary appeals to tradition are inadequate if they insist upon any kind of ahistorical continuity effectively guaranteeing the timeless character of these selected truths. For Tanner, the notion of tradition in Christianity has too often eclipsed the serious conflicts that have been part and parcel of the traditioning process. Tanner makes a case for a notion of tradition-as-argument. "Instead of a process of transmission, tradition amounts to a process of argument, among upholders of different Christian viewpoints, whether in the past or the present."[73] Similarly, John Thiel's masterful work, *The Senses of Tradition*, argues for an idea of tradition that differs from "premodern and modern explanations."[74] Through a creative, constructive application of the medieval four senses of scripture, Thiel explicates four senses of tradition and offers a rich, multidimensional, historically responsible interpretative schema that attends to the complex hermeneutical dynamics at work in the Christian tradition's articulation of divine revelation.[75]

As important as these works are, they are also limited by their own perspectival boundaries as academic construals largely informed from within Western theological sources. If we take seriously Kratz's observation that notions of tradition are themselves embedded in particular social, cultural, and political contexts, then we will be curious about the limits of a Western notion of tradition, even one chastened by postmodern cultural critique. What will notions of tradition derived from the cultural sources and experiences of the Latin American, African, and Asian churches look like? How will their particular view of tradition challenge, complement, and correct current reflection towards a theology of tradition? The sheer variety of human traditions demands new assessments of how ideas of tradition function in the localized traditioning processes of diverse communities of Christian disciples.

How Shall We Relate the Past to the Present?

Refiguring the notion of tradition within Christianity is particularly important because of the diachronic relationship of traditions to their pasts. Immanuel Wallerstein notes, "The past can only be told as it truly *is*, not was. For recounting the past is a social act of the present done by men [*sic*] of the present and affecting the social system of the present."[76] Yet, William Faulkner asserts, "The past is not dead. In fact, it is not even past."[77] Embedded in our notions of tradition are our understandings of the past: its influence and authority. Appadurai's disjunctive imaginative view of globalization is tied to his assertion that modernity is much more than a radical transformation of the past. Modernity, according to Appadurai, is a rupture and a break "with all sorts of pasts."[78] Breaks, ruptures, and disjunctions are all significant construals of the global present, particularly in its deterritorialized condition. But, as Saskia Sassen points out, we must also pay close attention to *whom* and *what* the rhetoric of hypermobility serves.[79]

Traditions are also synchronic phenomena; as migrant peoples settle into new spaces the processes of reterritorialization, as uncovered by Sassen's study of global cities, point to strategic sites of cultural and social consequence. Religious traditions play no small role among the sources that guide and sustain people as they construct their corporate and individual lives. How are religious traditions functioning? Clearly, there is ample historical evidence of ambiguity here. Indian theologian Michael Amaladoss notes that although the teachings of the major world religions do not condone violence, in actual practice religious traditions have thwarted human flourishing by failing to reject the abuse of religious sentiments and practices. Repressive cultural-political movements have too readily found religious resources to fund their demonization of those whom they wish to subjugate or annihilate.[80] As Vincent Miller aptly points out, gospel fidelity requires that theologies of tradition attend to the dynamics of both meaning and power in religious traditioning processes.[81]

The global phenomenon of emerging primordialisms, the new and renewed claims for shared identity based in the presumed givenness of ethnic identities, makes the hermeneutical task of traditioning all the more serious. The use of the past to make sense of the present is not a value-free, neutral process. In the words of David Tracy, there are no innocent traditions.[82] Theologically speaking, abstract assertions of grace and the Spirit in some theologies of tradition can mask the contingencies of historical process by which narratives are selected and perspectives authorized/de-authorized. "What is needed is a way of conceiving the dynamics of the Christian tradition that takes into account both the saving meaning it claims to bear and the location of its discourses within the power inequalities that mark human existence."[83]

Can a Truly Catholic Tradition Be Risked?

Globalization at large has altered the landscape of risk and, as Robert Schreiter points out, the accompanying dis-ease has spawned a host of postmodern life forms: ranging from valueless anarchy to insulated enclaves.[84] The shifting ground of the global-human relationship is, indeed, precarious and ambiguous; from the perspective of religious traditions, this global condition raises anew questions about our understanding of revelation, truth, and the mediated transcendence of grace.

For a Roman Catholic theologian, the moral significance of global diversity confirms that the lessons of catholicity have yet to be learned. Diversity within and without requires new discernments from multiple perspectives and mechanisms of critical dialogue to facilitate the necessary theological conversations. For example, attention to diversity within opens the door to subjugated gospel voices that dominate the work of M. Shawn Copeland and Cyprian Davis, and exposes the obviating effect of white privilege on Black Roman Catholic identity.[85] Copeland asserts that the recovered history of African American Catholics testifies: beyond receiving and appropriating the faith, Black Catholics transmitted and mediated the tradition through their faith-filled living amid rejection and open hostility. "There is a Black Catholic subject of Tradition. This subject incarnates protest against the dominant American religious historiography that to be authentically Black and truly Catholic is, at best, impossible, at worst, anomalous."[86]

Beyond the borders of Western cultural formulations of faith, Asian, African, and Latin American Catholics are reconceptualizing the gospel-culture dialog and questioning the foundational presumptions that have controlled the church's approach to inculturation and mission thus far.[87] Michael Amaladoss queries the relationship between revelation and the indispensable (however historically contingent) cultural forms that mediate God's presence to a people. Critical of linear models of tradition as development of a timeless deposit, Amaladoss analyzes the early church's response to the gospel and highlights the internal diversity of the original witnesses to the grace of God revealed in Jesus. "There were four gospels, not to speak of the other pictures that emerge from the letters of Paul, Peter, John and James. There were many apostolic Churches. I think that we should have a new paradigm of history, tradition, and development that integrates this pluralism of experience and expression as internal to it."[88]

Amaladoss's concern for the catholicity of the church expresses itself in a rethinking of the prophetic role of the Christian community in the world. Neither the evangelization of the world, nor the unity of the church, is measured by exterior conformity to creedal formulas and liturgical practices arising out of one particular cultural encounter with the gospel. As important as the originating expressions of Christian faith are, they are not salvific in and of themselves. "In every historical event what is important is the divine-human relationship, not the cultural and temporal circumstances in which that relationship is lived and manifested."[89] Locating the mission of the church within the mission of Christ and the Spirit who are realizing the reign of God at all times and in all places, Amaladoss affirms that, however limited by finitude and sin, all that is human matters to God. "God is present and active in all . . . in ways unknown to us."[90] Herein lies a significant distinction, one that is eclipsed sometimes by too closely associating Jesus with the church. "As risen Christ he is present to all cultures. This is not true of the Church. For the Church this quest to become universal has to be realized through multiple encounters with culture in history. This supposes that it cannot privilege or idolize any one culture."[91]

Theologically speaking, the grace of catholicity is still being realized and this inspires the work of rehabilitating the notion of tradition in a global context. There are dire consequences for a global world that fails at either diversity or unity. When unity is construed as sameness, we risk perpetuating to some degree "narratives of eviction"; when our theories posit incommensurable difference we undermine any claim to shared sources of identity and possibly a shared future. Clifford Geertz has it right, I believe, when he says:

> What we need . . . are not enormous ideas, nor the abandonment of synthesizing notions altogether. What we need are ways of thinking that are responsive to particularities, to individualities, oddities, discontinuities, contrasts and singularities, responsive to what Charles Taylor has called "deep diversity," a plurality of ways of belonging and being, and that yet draw from them—from it—a sense of connectedness, a connectedness that is neither, comprehensive nor uniform, primal nor changeless, but nonetheless real.[92]

The risk of a truly catholic tradition challenges us to discover for our times how the church is universal in and through its diverse, contrastive, yes even, disjunctive particularity.[93] Herein lies, I believe, a new horizon for an ecclesial witness that is both faith-filled and credible.

Notes

[1]Robert Schreiter, C.PP.S., "Major Currents of Our Times: What They Mean for the Church," *Origins* 31, no. 11 (2001): 189-97.

[2]Ibid., 193.

[3]I gratefully acknowledge my indebtedness to scholar and mentor, T. Howland Sanks, S.J. See his "Globalization and the Church's Social Mission," *Theological Studies* 60, no. 4 (1999): 625-52, and his most recent article, "Globalization, Postmodernity and Governance in the Church," *Louvain Studies* 28 (2003): 194-216.

[4]Recent books in the area of theologies of tradition include John Thiel, *The Senses of Tradition: Continuity and Development in Catholic Faith* (New York: Oxford University Press, 2000); Terrence W. Tilley, *Inventing Catholic Tradition* (Maryknoll, N.Y.: Orbis Books, 2000). See also Delwin Brown, *The Boundaries of Our Habitations: Tradition and Theological Construction* (Albany: State University of New York Press, 1994). Orlando Espín's book on tradition (forthcoming 2006) is tentatively titled *An Intercultural Theology of Tradition*. Also forthcoming (tentatively 2005), Gary Macy and Orlando Espín, ed., *Futuring Our Past: Explorations in the Theology of Tradition*.

[5]For a spectrum of views on the topic of globalization see Frank J. Lechner and John Boli, ed., *The Globalization Reader* (Malden, Mass.: Blackwell, 2000) and Patrick O'Meara, Howard D. Mehlinger, and Matthew Krain, eds., *Globalization and the Challenges of a New Century: A Reader* (Bloomington: Indiana University Press, 2000). Other titles include Mike Featherstone, ed., *Undoing Culture: Globalization, Postmodernism and Identity* (London: Sage, 1995); Anthony Giddens, *Runaway World: How Globalization Is Reshaping Our Lives* (New York: Routledge, 2003); Anthony D. King, ed., *Culture, Globalization and the World-System: Contemporary Conditions for the Representation of Identity* (Minneapolis: University of Minnesota Press, 1997); Dani Rodrik, *Has Globalization Gone Too Far?* (Washington, D.C.: Institute for International Economics, 1997); Joseph E. Stiglitz, *Globalization and Its Discontents* (New York: W.W. Norton, 2003); Michael Featherstone, ed., *Global Modernities* (London: Sage, 1995).

[6]Robert Schreiter's working definition of globalization, the simultaneous experience of the compression of space and the extension of modernity, remains a helpful starting point for approaching the question of globalization. See his *The New Catholicity: Theology Between the Global and the Local* (Maryknoll, N.Y.: Orbis Books, 1997), 1-27.

[7]Arjun Appadurai, "Grassroots Globalization and the Research Imagination," *Public Culture* 12, no. 1 (2000): 2.

[8]Schreiter, *The New Catholicity*, 26-27.

[9]Kathryn Tanner, *Theories of Culture: A New Agenda for Theology* (Minneapolis: Fortress Press, 1997).

[10]Ibid., 54.

[11]Roland Robertson's extensive writings in the area of globalization, sociology of religion and culture, and social theory include books, journal articles, edited series and symposium proceedings. Published in multiple

languages, including Japanese, Chinese, and Turkish, he has served on several editorial boards including *The Sociology of Religion* and *Theory, Culture and Society*.

[12]Roland Robertson, *Globalization: Social Theory and Global Culture* (London: Sage, 1992), 8.

[13]"In the broadest sense I am concerned with the way(s) in which the world is ordered. Whereas I am setting out this model of order in what may appear to be formal terms, the intent which actually guides it is to inject *flexibility* into our considerations of 'totality.' In so far as we think about the world as a whole, we are inevitably involved in a certain kind of what is sometimes pejoratively called totalistic analysis. But even though my scheme does involve a 'totalizing' tendency, it does so partly in order to comprehend *different* kinds of orientation to the global circumstances. It will be seen . . . that movements, individuals and other actors perceive and construct the order (or disorder) of the world in a number of different ways. In *that* sense what my model does is to facilitate interpretation and analysis of such variation. So there is a crucial difference between imposing a model of the global field on all the present and potential actors in that field and setting out a model which facilitates comprehension of variation in that field. The latter is an important consideration. My interest is in how order is, so to speak, *done*" (Robertson, *Globalization*, 25-26).

[14]Ibid., 26.

[15]Ibid., 27.

[16]Ibid., 25.

[17]Ibid., 104.

[18]Francis Sejersted, Chairman of the Norwegian Nobel Committee, presentation speech on the occasion of the Nobel Peace Prize, 1997, Oslo, Norway. http://www.nobel.se/cgi-bin/print. Accessed August 10, 2004.

[19]Robertson, *Globalization*, 99.

[20]Ibid., 101.

[21]Ibid., 102.

[22]Ibid., 100.

[23]Ibid., 104. "Specifically, the way in which I tackle the issues of globality and globalization suggests that in order for one to have a 'realistic' view of the world as a whole one must, at least in the contemporary circumstance, accept in principle the relative autonomy of each of the four main components and that, by the same token, one should acknowledge that each of the four is in one way or another constrained by the other three. In one sense, then overemphasis on one to the expense of attention to the other three constitutes a form of 'fundamentalism.' "

[24]Ibid., 100.

[25]Ibid., 103.

[26]Ibid., 102.

[27] Arjun Appadurai, *Modernity at Large: Cultural Dimensions of Global-*

ization (Minneapolis: University of Minnesota Press, 1996), 27-47. This essay was first published in *Public Culture* 2, no. 2 (1990): 1-24. An abridged form of this essay has also been reprinted in *The Globalization Reader*, ed. Frank J. Lechner and John Boli (Malden, Mass.: Blackwell Publishers Inc., 2000), 322-30.

²⁸Appadurai, "Disjuncture and Difference in the Global Cultural Economy," chap. 2 in *Modernity at Large*, 29.

²⁹Ibid., 27-28.

³⁰Ibid., 29.

³¹Ibid., 33-36. "I propose that an elementary framework for exploring such disjunctures is to look at the relationship among five dimensions of global cultural flows that can be termed (a) *ethnoscapes*, (b) *mediascapes*, (c) *technoscapes*, (d) *financescapes*, (e) *ideoscapes*."

³²Appadurai, "Disjuncture and Difference," 33-36.

³³Ibid., 36.

³⁴Ibid., 37.

³⁵Ibid.

³⁶Ibid., 37-38.

³⁷Appadurai, *Modernity at Large*, 49.

³⁸Appadurai, "Disjuncture and Difference," 31.

³⁹Ibid.

⁴⁰Appadurai, *Modernity at Large*, 5.

⁴¹Ibid., 6.

⁴²Ibid.

⁴³Appadurai, "Disjuncture and Difference," 32.

⁴⁴Ibid., 36-37.

⁴⁵Ibid., 32.

⁴⁶Ibid.

⁴⁷Sassen's book titles include *Globalization and Its Discontents: Essays on the New Mobility of People and Money* (New York: The New Press, 1998); *The Global City: New York, London, Tokyo* (Princeton: Princeton University Press, 1991); *Guests and Aliens* (New York: The New Press, 1999). She is currently completing *Denationalization: Economy and Polity in a Global Digital Age* (Princeton University Press, forthcoming).

⁴⁸Saskia Sassen, "Whose City Is It? Globalization and the Formation of New Claims," introduction to *Globalization and Its Discontents: Essays on the New Mobility of People and Money* (New York: The New Press, 1998), xxv-xxvii.

⁴⁹See in particular Sassen's essays "America's Immigration 'Problem' " and "Economic Internationalization: The New Migration in Japan and the United States" which appear as chapters 3 and 4 respectively in *Globalization and Its Discontents*.

⁵⁰Sassen, "Whose City Is It?," xxiv.

⁵¹Ibid., xxv.

[52]Ibid., xxxiii.

[53]"It should be clear by now that powerful international forces are at work behind the outflow of immigrants into the United States. Yet U.S. officials and the public at large persist in viewing immigration as a problem whose roots lie exclusively in the inadequacy of socioeconomic conditions of the Third World, rather than also being a by-product of U.S. involvement in the global economy" (Sassen, "America's Immigration 'Problem,' " chapter 3 in *Globalization and Its Discontents*, 49).

[54]Sassen, "Whose City Is It?," xxxi.

[55]Ibid., xxiii-xxiv.

[56]Ibid., xxiv.

[57]Sassen, "Towards a Feminist Analytics of the Global Economy," chapter 5 in *Globalization and Its Discontents*, 82.

[58]Ibid.

[59]Sassen, "Whose City Is It?," xxx.

[60]Ibid.

[61]"The ascendance of an international human rights regime and of a large variety of nonstate actors in the international arena signals the expansion of an international civil society. This is clearly a contested space, particularly when we consider the logic of the capital market—profitability at all costs—against that of the human rights regime. But it does represent a space where women can gain visibility as individuals and as collective actors, and come out of the invisibility of aggregate membership in a nation-state exclusively represented by the sovereign" (Sassen, "Towards a Feminist Analytics," 99).

[62]CorpWatch, "The Voices of World Social Forum 2004" http://www.corpwatch.org/print_article.php?&id=9588. Accessed August 10, 2004.

[63]Ibid.

[64]Appadurai, *Modernity at Large*, 3.

[65]Robertson, *Globalization*, 26.

[66]Benjamin Barber, *Jihad vs. McWorld*, 2d ed. (New York: Ballantine Books, 2001), xii.

[67]"[W]here there is consumption there is pleasure, and where there is pleasure there is agency. Freedom, on the other hand, is a rather more elusive commodity" (Appadurai, *Modernity at Large*, 7).

[68]Barber, *Jihad vs. McWorld*, 81.

[69]Ibid., 188.

[70]"Three criteriological points drawn from theology in general find an application in christology as well. These are faithfulness to the tradition, intelligibility in today's world, and empowerment of the Christian life" (Roger Haight, *Jesus Symbol of God* [Maryknoll, N.Y.: Orbis Books, 1999], 47).

[71]See in particular Talal Asad, *Genealogies of Religion: Discipline and Reasons of Power in Christianity and Islam* (Baltimore, Md.: Johns Hopkins University Press, 1993) and Talal Asad, *Formations of the Secular: Christian-*

ity, Islam, Modernity (Stanford: Stanford University Press, 2003).

[72]Corinne Kratz, " 'We've Always Done It Like This . . . Except for a Few Details': 'Tradition' and 'Innovation' in Okiek Ceremonies," *Comparative Studies in Society and History* 35, no. 1 (1993): 61.

[73]Kathryn Tanner, "Postmodern Challenges to 'Tradition,' " *Louvain Studies* 28 (2003): 192.

[74]Thiel, *The Senses of Tradition*, vii.

[75]Also see Tilley, *Inventing Catholic Tradition*.

[76]Immanuel Wallerstein, *The Modern World System: Capitalist Agriculture and the Origins of the European World-Economy in the Sixteenth Century* (New York: Academic Press, 1974), 9.

[77]William Faulkner, *Requiem for a Nun* (New York: Random House, 1951), act 1, scene III.

[78]Appadurai, *Modernity at Large*, 3.

[79]Talal Asad notes, "Hannah Arendt had a very different response to mobility in her famous analysis of European totalitarianism. . . . She is . . . aware of a problem that has escaped the serious attention of those who would have us celebrate human agency and the decentered subject: the problem of understanding how dominant power realizes itself through the very discourse of mobility. For Arendt is very clear that mobility is not merely an event in itself, but a moment in the subsumption of one act by another. If people are physically and morally uprooted, they are more easily moved, and when they are easy to move, they are more easily rendered physically *and* morally superfluous" (Asad, *Genealogies of Religion*, 11).

[80]Michael Amaladoss, S.J., "Religions for Peace," *America* 185, no. 19 (2001): 6-8.

[81]Vincent J. Miller, "History or Geography? Gadamer, Foucault, and Theologies of Tradition," in *Theology and the New Histories*, ed. Gary Macy (Maryknoll, N.Y.: Orbis Books, 1999), 56-85.

[82]David Tracy, *On Naming the Present* (Maryknoll, N.Y.: Orbis Books, 1994), 14-15.

[83]Miller, "History or Geography?" 58.

[84]Schreiter, *The New Catholicity*, 13.

[85] See Cyprian Davis, *The History of Black Catholics in the United States* (New York: Crossroads, 1994); Cyprian Davis and Diana Hayes, eds., *Taking Down Our Harps: Black Catholics in the United States* (Maryknoll, N.Y.: Orbis Books, 1998); Cyprian Davis and Jamie Phelps, *Stamped with the Image of God: African Americans, God's Image in Black* (Maryknoll, N.Y.: Orbis Books, 2004); M. Shawn Copeland, "The Cross of Christ and Discipleship," in *Thinking of Christ: Proclamation, Explanation, Meaning*, ed. Tatha Willey, (New York: Continuum, 2003), 177-92.

[86]M. Shawn Copeland, "Tradition and the Traditions of African American Catholicism," *Theological Studies* 61 (2000): 637.

[87]See Michael Amaladoss, S.J., *Beyond Inculturation: Can the Many Be*

One? (Delhi: Vidyajyoti Education and Welfare Society/ISPCK, 1998); Laurenti Magesa, *Anatomy of Inculturation: Transforming the Church in Africa* (Maryknoll, N.Y.: Orbis Books, 2004); Peter Phan, *In Our Own Tongues: Asian Perspectives on Mission and Inculturation* (Maryknoll, N.Y.: Orbis Books, 2003); José Comblin, *People of God* (Maryknoll, N.Y.: Orbis Books, 2003); Jon Sobrino and Ignatio Ellacuría, *Systematic Theology: Perspectives from Liberation Theology* (Maryknoll, N.Y.: Orbis Books, 1997).

[88]Michael Amaladoss, S.J., *Beyond Inculturation*, 29-30.

[89]Ibid., 38.

[90]Ibid., 39.

[91]Ibid., 40.

[92]Clifford Geertz, *Available Light: Anthropological Reflections on Philosophical Topics* (Princeton: Princeton University Press, 2000), 224.

[93]"Through the mission and gift of the Holy Spirit, the Church is born universal by being born manifold and particular" (Yves Congar, *I Believe in the Holy Spirit,* trans. David Smith [New York: Seabury, 1983], 2: 26).

The Global Horizon of Religious Pluralism
and Local Dialogue with the Religious-other

Anne M. Clifford

A revealing encounter prompted this essay on the global horizon of religious pluralism as it actually impacts the lives of many of us. While shopping at a supermarket I simply remarked to a mother dressed in Muslim garb who was transporting a restless three-year-old down an aisle in a grocery cart that her child was beautiful. Her response was softly spoken and heavily accented: "Thank you for not looking away," she said. "So many of you do."

Her words reduced me to silence. Since then I have interpreted this woman-to-woman encounter as an urgent call to me—a Christian, a theologian, and a vowed religious in a congregation that describes its charism in terms of love of neighbor and of reconciliation—to acquire the capacity for a "severer listening"[1] to the religious-other, especially Muslim religious-others in my neighborhood. Such a capacity requires careful consideration of the global religious realities of our time as they are experienced in day-to-day life and of a theology of dialogue with the religious-other that is appropriate for them.

The Global Horizon of Religious Pluralism

In the post 9-11 world, the vocation of the Christian theologian is not the same as it was on September 10, 2001. In the changed global horizon, the Western Christian theologian must take religious pluralism—the persons of other religions in our midst—seriously. The term "globalization," although commonly used with reference to multinational economic realities, is also an appropriate term for the religious pluralities of Earth's people—well over six billion of us.[2] As citizens of the planet, we share a multi-faith world in which 2 billion are at least nominally Christian; 1.3 billion are Muslim; 900 million are Hindu; 360 million are Buddhist; and nearly 14 million are Jewish.[3]

Beyond these statistics is the fact that religion has relevance for the political life of most countries of the globe, providing a source of unity in the midst of the flux of a market economy. Yet in many countries the desire for religious unity (or uniformity) has a powerful shadow-side. Discrimination, violence, and war are being justified on religious grounds. In the wake of both civil and international wars[4] and the threat of religiously motivated violence, a growing number of desperate immigrants are seeking freedom of religious expression and economic survival. For these people "on the move," religion is a source of identity that provides the security of community in enclaves of intimacy. A result of this migration is the impossibility of living in a major city anywhere on Earth (except perhaps in countries that enforce laws forbidding religion, such as North Korea) without coming into contact with some aspect of a religion different from one's own. Religions, once associated almost exclusively with particular regions or nations of the world, now surround us daily.

Robert Schreiter, who has written extensively about theology in a world shaped by globalization, argues that theology today finds itself caught between the global and the local.[5] As a person who does not envision herself engaging in interreligious dialogue on a grand international scale, my primary concern is with dialogue with the religious-other at the local level. Such dialogue presumes mindfulness that the local is linked to complex multi-faith global realities. Those realities prompt feelings of urgency about interreligious dialogue. While religious faith, that extraordinary quality that forms and directs our minds, feelings, and energies, can be a source of "good," providing healing and mutual understanding, it can also unleash division and destructiveness. A growing body of literature written by Christian church leaders and individual theologians gives testimony to the desire to respond to religious pluralism. Most fall into systematic, theoretical categories. Which one, if any, offers help in responding to a felt call to take persons of other religions seriously and to dialogue with them at a local—neighbor to neighbor—level?

In surveying the theological literature on Christianity and the other religions, one notes immediately that some stances rule out dialogue between Christianity and the other religions at the outset. Others are about dialogue, especially articulating *a priori* positions that Christians, especially theologians, should take with them to dialogues with non-Christians. Are the major paradigms and models developed by Christian churches and theologians during the past three decades adequate for meeting the challenge of religious pluralism at the local level?

My thesis is that what is required in this needful time is not theology *about* or even *for* dialogue with people who practice religions other than Christianity, but a theology *of* dialogue that emerges *in* and *from* interfaith neighbor-to-neighbor conversation. My premise is that at the heart of the gospel message is reconciliation, which crosses social barriers in its offer of peace. Integral to a theology of religious dialogue seeking reconciliation is careful attention to the self-other relationship, including the risk of extending one's self to the other, with all the vulnerability that such an extension requires.

Christian Responses to Religious Pluralism: Theologies *about* Dialogue

A logical starting point is a survey of major existing positions on interreligious dialogue with an accompanying discernment of their pros and cons. The Christian response to the plurality of religions is usually analyzed in terms of three paradigms: exclusivism, inclusivism, and religious pluralism.[6] Paul Knitter provides a more nuanced analysis in terms of four models: "replacement," "fulfillment," "mutuality," and "acceptance."[7] Privileging their own tradition over all others, Christians who hold an exclusivist/replacement position reserve saving truth to Christianity. For them, salvation lies in following one path, the path of Jesus Christ, the Savior.[8] Although not all exclusivist/replacement defenders find no value in non-Christian religions,[9] this paradigm/model offers nothing of value for dialogue beyond toleration of the religious-other.

Inclusivism

Inclusivism, Knitter's "fulfillment model," is more complex and multi-faceted than the first paradigm/model. Knitter captures the "heart" of this model in what it confirms: "God's love is universal, extending to all peoples, but also . . . God's love is particular, made real in Jesus the Christ."[10] These Christian theologians recognize not only that non-Christians may be saved, but also in some cases that their religions may be ways to salvation, even though they are deficient.[11]

Inclusivists do not see the religious-other as a threat, but do envision religious diversity as included in a single religious worldview—their own. What is valued in the other religions is what counts most in one's own. Inclusivism is not foreign to non-Christian religions. Muslims have long held the belief that Islam is spacious enough to encompass all other religions, especially Judaism and Christianity, because it supersedes them as the definitive culmination of all monotheistic traditions.

Since the Second Vatican Council the official Roman Catholic position has been a form of inclusivism/fulfillment.[12] Interreligious dialogue has been most recently addressed in the Declaration *Dominus Iesus*,[13] which supports "the unicity and salvific universality of the mystery of Jesus Christ and the Church" (§3). At the outset *Dominus Iesus* stresses that the Roman Catholic Church rejects nothing of what is true and holy in non-Christian religions and in fact has a high regard for the manner of life and conduct, the precepts and teachings, which, although differing in many ways from its own teaching, nonetheless reflect the truth that enlightens all people (§2). Praise for truth found in the other religions, however, must not be confused with acceptance of relativism, which the authors of *Dominus Iesus* associate with pluralist theologies of religion (§5). Dialogue has limits made evident by distinguishing between theological faith and belief. *Dominus Iesus* states:

> If faith is the acceptance in grace of revealed truth, which "makes it possible to penetrate the mystery in a way that allows us to understand it coherently" then belief, in the other religions, is that sum of experience and thought that constitutes the human treasury of wisdom and religious aspiration, which man in his search for truth has conceived and acted upon in his relationship to God and the Absolute (§7).

This distinction, *Dominus Iesus* bemoans, is often ignored in current theology.

Thus, theological faith (the acceptance of the truth revealed by the One and Triune God) is often identified with belief in other religions, which is religious experience still in search of the absolute truth and still lacking assent to God who reveals himself. This is one of the reasons why the differences between Christianity and the other religions tend to be reduced at times to the point of disappearance (§7).

Such reduction compromises the truth claims upon which Roman Catholicism is founded and results in relativism.

Among the truth claims that *Dominus Iesus* emphasizes is the statement: "it must be firmly believed that 'the [Roman Catholic] Church . . . is necessary for salvation,' because Christ the one mediator of salvation is present in his body which is the Church" (§20). This emphasis on the necessity of the intermediary role of the Catholic Church in salvation has proved to be problematic for Protestants and for representatives of other religions because, although *Dominus Iesus* expresses openness to the religious-other (§2), it sets up walls of demarcation that devalue non-Catholic churches and support Roman Catholic supremacy over other religious traditions. Put simply, the inclusivism that *Dominus Iesus* affirms is in tension with an ecclesiastical exclusivism.

Dominus Iesus lends itself to the conclusion that exclusivist/replacement and inclusivist/fulfillment paradigms are more alike than different. They honor the uniqueness of Christianity and the significance of Christ as truths to live by. They lend themselves to thick religiosity, because the truth to which they are committed finds expression not only in doctrines, but also in worship, ethics, and communal-relational practice. Both envision Jesus Christ as normative for salvation in either an exclusive or absolute sense.[14]

Pluralism

We turn now to the paradigm of pluralist theologies of religion. Both the exclusivism/replacement and inclusivism/fulfillment models negatively assess the pluralist theologies of religion paradigm. Pluralist theologies of religion are judged to assume that it really does not matter what religion one is committed to. According to some of their many critics, religious pluralists are motivated by "political correctness," with a resulting relativism that lends itself to religious indifference. Religious indifference is but a step away from a sweeping contempt of religion: Why should one believe in any religion at all?

Knitter, himself a theological pluralist, provides a helpful response to critiques of relativism directed to the pluralist paradigm by effectively analyzing the many positions associated with religious pluralism in terms of "mutuality" and "acceptance" models. Superficial critiques of religious pluralists fail to take into consideration the considerable differences in the positions of theologians whose theologies might fit under the broad category of religious pluralism. Although those who take a mutuality position are committed to honoring a "level playing field" of dialogue among equals, there are significant differences where Jesus Christ is concerned.

John Hick's position, for example, rejects Christian absolutism on the grounds that it has provided validation for political and economic evil.[15] Integral to his rejection of Christian absolutism and triumphalism is his treatment of Jesus Christ as a symbol, a metaphor among many, not to be taken literally. He holds that "the great world [religious] traditions constitute different conceptions and perceptions of and responses to the Real from within the different cultural ways of being human."[16] Pluralist theologies of religion in company with Hick share a fundamental theocentric approach, which holds that the great world religions constitute varying, yet partial conceptions of one ultimate, mysterious divine or transcendent Reality. It logically follows that religious terms for an impersonal ultimate Reality, like Brahman, as well as personal names such as Yahweh, Christ, Allah, and Shiva are merely different culturally influenced ways of naming and connecting with the Real.

A shortcoming of Hick's position for a person who seeks a theology *of* dialogue with the religious-other is that his theism is religiously thin—a philosophical hypothesis put forward to support a common grounding for all religions. An "object" of speculation, the "Real" is removed from all the thick elements that give religions and the people who practice them daily their own religious identities. Religions can be said to be true (or salvific), in so far as they contribute to the transformation of human existence from self-centeredness to Reality-centeredness. Hick's rejection of Christian triumphalism where salvation is concerned has merit, but his conviction that all ways to salvation are variations of a common theism and are, therefore, equally valid is a generalization of questionable merit. Such a position honors the principle of "dialogue among equals" but at the expense of the central convictions of the Christian tradition about Jesus Christ.

Knitter provides an understanding of Jesus in the "mutuality model." He conceives of the significance of Jesus Christ in terms of a sacramental-Spirit Christology in which Jesus is normative for Christians, while at the same time recognizing that other representations of God can also be universally normative.[17] What this implies is that Christians truly encounter the fullness of God's saving love in Jesus the Christ, but they cannot maintain that this fullness is limited only to Jesus.

The "acceptance model" in the religious pluralism paradigm includes several positions. One is postliberal and argues that religions are so different as to have nothing in common. The culture-bound linguistic concepts of one religion cannot be translated into the conceptual language of the other. There is no possible bridge to span the gap between religions. Also, there is no common core, including an underlying theism or ethics to unite them. Therefore, they are incommensurable. With the possibility of translation ruled out *a priori*, it would seem that there is no hope for a dialogical middle, no potential for deep conversation between persons practicing different religions.[18]

The postliberal form of the "acceptance model" stands in contrast to the position of comparative theologians, such as Francis X. Clooney, who seek a foundation for a pluralist theology of religion in dialogue with the religious-other rather than in *a priori* theological convictions, whether Christian or theistic.[19] The invitation of the comparative theologians' approach is to move from globalizing theologies about dialogue and for dialogue to a theology of dialogue. Clooney's focus on theology of dialogue is primarily textual, requiring a sophisticated grasp of the original languages in which classical Hindu texts were written.[20] He envisions theology rising from the dialogue itself.

For the non-specialist in a religion other than Christianity, is a theology *of* dialogue possible? In particular, without the benefit of in-depth study of a non-Christian religion and its primary sources, is a theology of dialogue possible without slipping into a facile homogeneity or into a surrender to incommensurability?

Toward a Local Theology *of* Dialogue

The treatment of the major models of the theology of religions serves as an argument for a different approach. If we presume that a theology *of* dialogue is not only possible but also desirable for persons of good will and that it will take us beyond approaching the dialogue table with preconceived globalizing theologies about the other religions and that it will not require sophisticated expertise in the religious texts and practices of the religious-other, then what is required?

A tenable response to these questions is offered by Michael Barnes, S.J., lecturer on Christianity and interreligious dialogue and the director of the Centre for Christianity in Dialogue at Heythrop College, University of London, and director of the Jesuit-sponsored De Nobili Dialogue Centre.[21] For Barnes, the preliminary answer to the question is that Christians must not only move beyond an inclusivism that seeks to demonstrate how other religions may be included within the Christian dispensation,[22] but also beyond pluralist theologies of religion that provide visions of family resemblance "above the action."[23] Hypotheses that gloss over the historical and cultural complexities of the different religious traditions that we encounter in our neighborhoods do not serve us well. What we must do is develop a theology of dialogue in which the primary focus is on "the other" and not on "religion." Such a theology of dialogue will be an ethical theology that respects the other without slipping into the relativism of incommensurability.[24]

Barnes's ethical theology of dialogue is informed by philosophical and social theory that is concerned with human subjectivity and the question of the self in relationship to "the other." As his argument for an ethical theology of dialogue with the religious-other unfolds, several points of emphasis emerge:

1. Interfaith dialogue is a practice of faith that listens for possible "seeds of the Word" in the self's relationship to the religious-other.[25] Listening for "seeds of the Word" requires openness to what God may be revealing in the context of the encounter with the religious-other as other.

2. Dialogue with the religious-other is concerned less with achieving consensus, of articulating a common point of view, than with creating a space for the possibility for deep conversation between persons. This requires resistance to *a priori* positions and to premature closure dictated by extraneous forces.

3. Interfaith dialogue presumes that the Christian theologian will work toward establishing a relationship with the other, without eradicating the otherness of the other. This type of relationship challenges and reshapes one's own identity. The medium for establishing relationship is narrative.

4. Interfaith dialogue calls for on-going negotiation of the "middle

ground" of human interaction, which, due to a long history of conflict and violence between and among religious groups at various junctures of history, may be experienced as a "broken middle," as a present haunted by the "uncanny ghost" of the past.

Each of these four major positions is informed by elements of the philosophers Emmanuel Levinas and Paul Ricoeur, and the social scientist Michel de Certeau.

"Seeds of the Word"

The first point of emphasis calls for discerning "seeds of the Word" in interfaith dialogue. Other Christian theologians have also given attention to "seeds of the Word." Jacques Dupuis, for example, devotes chapter 6 of *Christianity and the Religions* to *logos spermatikos* ("seed-bearing Word").[26] Dupuis unpacks this symbol, as it was understood by the early Fathers, in support of the "universality of the Word." Although Barnes and Dupuis both give attention to "seeds of the Word," each conceives of his project differently. Dupuis develops a theology for "a pluralistic inclusivism." Barnes's project, although it shares with Dupuis "openness to the faith of the other in its difference,"[27] seeks to provide a thick phenomenological description of what such openness entails when the self is actually engaged in dialogue. Also and very importantly, Barnes does not speak of his project in inclusivist/fulfillment terms.

While not apologizing for his Christian identity, Barnes is judicious about honoring the religious-other without imposing or extrapolating from the other elements most prized by Christianity. In this regard Levinas, in particular, provides Barnes with a basic direction for his ethical theology of dialogue with the religious-other. It is not possible here to provide a full exposition of Barnes's treatment and appropriation of Levinas's ideas. What requires attention is Levinas's position on ethics and his use of the terms "Same" and "Other."

Dialogue with the Other

Disenchanted by the trajectory of Western philosophy, especially its totalizing ontology, Levinas envisioned philosophy as properly in the service of ethics. In his conception of ethics as first philosophy, Levinas rejects Western philosophy's preoccupation with Being—"the Same"—at the expense of what lies outside the totality of Being as transcendent, exterior, infinite, alterior—"the Other." Levinas stresses that ethics must be distinguished from ontology, for ontology as totality admits of no exteriority, of no other. He stresses: "the Other is in no way another myself, participating with me in a common existence."[28] Levinas's conception of the other is radical. Exteriority is required: the self and the other must be external to one another in a strong sense. If this is not the case, then there is only all-encompassing totality at the expense of alterity. The other cannot be integrated into the consciousness of the self. The exteriority of the other cannot be represented, because for Levinas representation is assimilation and assimilation taints the absolute exteriority of otherness. The other cannot become an object of knowledge or experience. If it does, "egology" results and the "I" becomes a "living from" that uses up the other in order to fulfill its own needs and desires. For Levinas ethics is situated in an "encounter" with the other that cannot be reduced to a symmetrical "relationship."

Obviously, "ethics" in Levinas's sense does not mean what is typically referred to as "morality," particularly, a religious code of conduct prescribing how one should act. For Levinas "ethics" is a calling into question of the "Same." This calling cannot occur within the egoistic spontaneity of the "Same"; it is brought about only by the other.[29] Barnes's application of Levinasian ethics to dialogue with the religious-other means that the boundaries of the religious-other are not drawn by the Christian on Christian terms. The religious-other cannot be placed somewhere else for the sake of the comfort of the Christian self. An ethically demarcated sense of the other must be maintained.

The chapter in *Theology and the Dialogue of Religions*, in which Barnes treats Levinas's thought most extensively, is suitably entitled "Facing the Other."[30] This title resonates with Levinas's insistence that "ethics is the spiritual optics"[31] and his resistance to the imperialism of Western philosophy that results in the reduction of "the Other" to "the Same" "by interposition of a middle and neutral term that ensures the comprehension of being."[32] For Barnes, resistance to the reduction of the religious-other to "the Same" of Christianity, is a form of *kenosis*, which implies passivity, especially the passivity of listening for the injunction coming from the other, of waiting within the space shared by the other for the utterance of the Word. The self embraces the passive experience of relationship to the Other. Barnes speaks of a passivity as attestation of otherness in which self-identity is forged.[33] This forging resists totalizing tendencies inherent in *a priori* systematic theological positions. This requirement presumes that God's word continues to be spoken in the dialogue with the religious-other and not in ways that the Christian churches can assume already to know.

The second position is concerned with dialogue with the religious-other. Dialogue calls for relinquishment of a demand for arrival at consensus (cf. Levinas's totalizing Same). For Barnes the specific results of dialogue with the religious-other are less significant than the continuing, fundamental, and potentially life-changing encounter that is promoted by the practice of entering again and again into conversation.[34] Dialogue over time may take many forms and implies an on-going process of return and departure.

Relationships in Dialogue

This brings us to the third and closely related position concerned with relationships made possible in and through dialogue. In the first two positions Barnes draws from the thought of Levinas, however, where relationship is concerned, he finds shortcomings in Levinas's thought. Barnes notes the problem of the radical separation between the self and the other in Levinas's ethics. Barnes writes: "Through language, produced in the face-to-face encounter, the 'abyss of separation' is not filled—indeed, says Levinas, it is confirmed."[35] Is the separation of the self and the other an abyss that cannot be bridged? Is mutual relationship not possible? Ricoeur offers a helpful response. Ricoeur argues that when the face of the other raises itself before me, "it is not an appearance that I can include within the sphere of my own representations . . . the face is not a spectacle. Rather it is a voice."[36] For Ricoeur, Levinas unnecessarily leaves no room for dialectical movement between the great meta-categories of "Same" and "Other." This strikes Ricoeur as inappropriate because the self is left with solitude without solicitude. Therefore, the exteriority of the other cannot be expressed in the language of relationship.[37] Ricoeur, according to Barnes, expands the ethical philosophy of Levinas by moving away from the co-existence of separate egos to the hermeneutical language of testimony in which the self is continually summoned to respond to the voice of the other. Ricoeur writes: "It is in me that the movement coming from the other completes its trajectory: the other constitutes me as responsible, that is as capable of responding. In this way, the word of the other comes to be placed at the origin of my acts."[38] In the place of the ego, concerned for maintaining its own continuity in time, arises the self formed in dialogue, in intersubjectivity not possible without alterity.[39]

Barnes finds Ricoeur's nuanced explanation of relational identity useful for his ethical theology of dialogue. The self for Ricoeur is constituted by an inextricable tie between a selfsameness (*idem*-identity) and a selfhood or ipseity (*ipse*-identity). The self's *idem*-identity is that which gives the self, among other things, its spatio-temporal sameness. Its *ipse*-identity gives it its unique ability to initiate something new and imputable to himself or herself.[40] About the significance of Ricoeur's distinction for dialogue with the religious-other, Barnes writes: " '*Idem*-identity,' in its concern to maintain the continuity and coherence of the individual, sets itself over against the other, whereas '*Ipse*-identity' gives us the subject in dialogue with the other, where it is challenged and shaped anew by a complex and pluriform otherness in which it is always imbedded."[41] By this Barnes means that in and through the relationship made possible by dialogue with the religious-other, one's own religious identity (as a Christian) is confirmed and, as we shall see in his fourth position, is also purified of gratuitous assumptions and narrow and prejudicial notions.

Important to Barnes's understanding of dialogue is the role of narrative in the relationship of self to others. The Christian and the religious-other speak from their own identity-forming narratives. According to Ricoeur, other persons and their narratives are always constituents in an individual's personal identity and narrative. Furthermore, narratives show that from the standpoint of ethics there is a primacy of the other-than-self over the self. The responsive self does not aim primarily at autonomy, nor does the self shrink from every sort of heteronomy. Rather, the responsive self lives in anticipation that responsiveness to others can and will bring about something more for all engaged in the dialogue.[42] This position, although not addressed by Barnes, fits Ricoeur's notion of dialogue as mediation. In a debate with Hans-Georg Gadamer, Ricoeur addresses dialogue and states: "In dialogue I have to encounter the other as he is, I have to presume that he *means* something, that he *intends* something and I have to bring myself into that which is meant and intended."[43] Ricoeur further points out that the philosopher proceeds by progressive mediation. Surely this is also the case for the theologian engaged in dialogue with the religious-other. Religious narrative in the form of texts and practices is the medium of the mediation.

The Negotiated Middle

This brings us to the fourth position upon which Barnes founds his ethical theology of dialogue: his attention to the realities of the "negotiated middle," which, due to a long history of conflict and violence, may be experienced as a "broken middle." De Certeau speaks of the "broken middle" in dialogue as the present haunted by the "uncanny ghost" of other persons, other stories, other experiences, which, once marginalized to the borders of the known and familiar, manage to insinuate themselves into the center of dialogue. For de Certeau, this leads to "heterology": a phenomenology of the other, what Barnes calls "the returning other."[44] The "returning other" continues to affect the present, often in ways that block dialogue or, at the very least, slow its processes.[45]

In this regard, Barnes notes the importance of Ricoeur's critique of historians who, on the one hand, see history as a re-enactment of the past in the present, and those who, on the other hand, see in history an affirmation of temporal distance. As a corrective to the extremes of both positions, Ricoeur brings into play not only "the Same and the Other," but also the "Analogous," which for Ricoeur is the resemblance between relations rather than between terms. On this basis, Barnes proposes that theology that rises from the experience of interfaith dialogue—"being set in the 'middle,' between the same and the other—will utilize a dialectical process to re-imagine a history of interfaith relations." This re-imaging does not gloss over the history of conflict (in fact it requires a hermeneutics of suspicion to attend to it), but it also does not let such history be a barrier to discerning openness to possible "seeds of the Word" in the present.[46]

Christianity as a School of Faith

The theoretical framework developed by Barnes, with its attention to the self-other dynamics of dialogue, is but a prelude to the ethical theology of dialogue, which emerges when one risks viewing Christianity as a "school of faith," a community called not just to teach others but to learn from them as well. This learning does not require abandoning or even bracketing one's faith. Barnes stresses: "I make no apologies for writing as a convinced believer in the God of Jesus Christ."[47] But it does presume that one is willing to have his/her Christian faith shaped in the context of interfaith and expressed in mutual self-other relationship.

In a multifaith world, entrance into the "school of faith" with the religious-other springs from belief in the incarnation—God's love embodied and poured out into a world shaped by history and culture. Barnes's "school of faith" experiences include dialogues with Hindus and Sikhs in Southall (west London).[48] These experiences heighten his awareness of the highly complex role that religion and faith play in the formation of human identity.

In Barnes's conception of the "school of faith," dialogue springs from the same roots as the church's liturgy, the formative experiences of Christian community in which Christians tell and celebrate the story that unites them. Barnes, therefore, connects his notion of "a school of faith" to the Eucharist as the place in which the church learns how to be itself. Barnes likens this learning to Levinas's notion of the "liturgy of study."[49]

For Levinas, the liturgy is the work of the people. The liturgy of study is concerned with faithful obedience. The obedience of liturgy is not merely ritual enacted in accord with the prescriptions of tradition. For liturgy not to be reduced to "mere ritual" it must become ethical with an orientation "for-the-Other."[50] In liturgy the church opens the horizons of contemplation while narrating what the church knows in faith—the narrative of how this people, gathered in space and time, has been reconciled to God. Eucharist brings worship and ethics together in mutual indispensability.

Barnes stresses that liturgy is also the work of God. The content of what is learned at Eucharist rises from giving thanks for God's act of welcome and hospitality. From God's act through Jesus Christ, the Christian community learns generous hospitality toward the other, learns how to act as host and respond as guest.[51] Barnes writes: "[At Eucharist] the church learns how to be itself: through the practice of return and repetition which, in giving thanks for God's act of welcome and hospitality, links the faithful liturgical practice of *this* [emphasis his] community here and now with the story of its origins and the promise of its fulfillment."[52]

The Eucharist also anchors the community in its own history, a history re-membering the broken body of Christ. This is also part of the dynamic of return and repetition. The church is formed after the manner of Jesus facing the otherness of his own death, while considering the violent death of many in our own time, especially killings motivated by religious prejudice or rationalized on religious grounds. In dialogue with the religious-other, the movement toward reconciliation is sometimes slow and painful. This underscores the Christian's need for willingness to be led to the truth by the Spirit, willingness to listen, to learn, and to participate in God's own mission.[53]

In a sense, for Barnes dialogue with the religious-other *is* mission. It is being sent by the trinitarian God revealed in Jesus Christ to engage in the trinity of listening-learning-participating in dialogue with the religious-other. Often this mission requires patient "dark night" waiting for "seeds of the Word" to be revealed.[54] In the "negotiation of the broken middle" no neat pattern of progress is likely. In summing up the dynamic of the process of dialogue with the religious-other, Barnes writes:

> [A] Christian theology which would seek to grapple with the "context of otherness" will be contemplative in discerning possible "seeds of the Word"; it will be ethical in its responsibility before the face of the other; it will be liturgical in constantly returning to the "broken middle" to the formative experience of community; and if it is to be properly Christian, then it will be Trinitarian in the way it discerns in that dialogue between Father and Son, which is eternally generated in the love of the Spirit, the prime analogue of all human encounter and relationship.[55]

Conclusion

Conflict and violence between and among peoples who practice Abrahamic religions around the globe challenged me to delve into the area of interreligious dialogue. However, a simple encounter with a Muslim mother and child in a local supermarket, of Christian self and Muslim other in the midst of the daily, called me to reflect deeply on dialogue with the religious-other on a local neighbor-to-neighbor level. The call to reflect deeply about what is entailed in a theology *of* dialogue with the religious-other drew my attention to the need for a "severer listening" that resists confusing the common context of conversation with a "common core" that reduces the religious-other to the "Same" of my religion. "Severer listening," however, is but a step toward reconciliation—here envisioned as bridging the broken middle—with the religious-other who is also my neighbor. Reconciliation, of course, is primarily God's work. It is something we discover as gift and grace, rather than achieve by our own efforts.

Reconciliation, however, is not only God's activity, it is a multidimensional human reality that involves people coming to terms with who they are in relationship to otherness. This is basic to a theology of interfaith dialogue. Interfaith dialogue that respects the otherness of the religious-other can take many forms at the local level, including:

1. *Dialogues of life* with the religious-other seen face to face as both other and as neighbor, with space made for solicitude, for empathetic listening to the sorrows and joys of daily living;

2. *Dialogues of action* with collaboration with the religious-other in the promotion of justice to counter religiously motivated prejudice, and in agency, especially on behalf of children and infirm elderly;

3. *Dialogues of religious experience* where spiritual riches, such as beloved narratives and ways of praying and searching for God, can be shared and learned from.[56]

These forms of dialogue are not listed in chronological progression, but in a progression of hope for unfolding relationship.

In each type of dialogue with the religious-other, the "isms" of exclusivism, inclusivism, and religious pluralism must yield to the desire of crossing the threshold of reconciliation and new possibility. If any *a priori* stance is to be brought to the dialogical middle, it is the recognition that claims to religious truth are not only provisional, but also are eschatological. Persons who identify with one or another of the three "isms" speak what they believe is truth. Yet none of us, including the church, can know with certainty the total reality of what remains other and utterly mysterious. No one can know the extent of God's salvific action at work in people of good will. The extent to which the global horizon of religious misunderstanding and conflict might be healed and transformed by local efforts of tending the "seeds of God's Word" in dialogue with the religious-other, neighbor to neighbor, will be revealed only at the end.

Notes

¹This term is found in Adrienne Rich's poem, "Transcendental Etude," in which she urges a "severer listening, cleansed of oratory, formulas, choruses, laments" to make room for "a new language," originally published in *The Dream of a Common Language* (1978) and republished in *The Fact of a Doorframe: Poems Selected and New 1950-1984* (New York: W. W. Norton, 1984), 266-67.

²This data gathered in 2001 can be found at http://www.adherents.com; accessed 5/15/04. To round out the statistical picture, there are perhaps at least 850 million secularists, agnostics, and atheists with no religious affiliation.

³This figure includes a large number of non-practicing ethnic Jews.

⁴Deadly conflicts with links to religion continue in Israel/Palestine and other parts of the Middle East, Armenia/Azerbaijan, India/Pakistan, Russia/Chechnya, the Philippines, and in many countries and regions of sub-Saharan Africa.

⁵See especially Robert J. Schreiter, *The New Catholicity: Theology between the Global and the Local* (Maryknoll, N.Y.: Orbis Books, 1997).

⁶These paradigms were first presented by Alan Race, *Christians and Religious Pluralism* (Maryknoll, N.Y. Orbis Books, 1983).

⁷Paul F. Knitter, *Introducing Theologies of Religions* (Maryknoll, N.Y.: Orbis Books, 2002).

⁸Christian exclusivists tend to look to biblical warrants for their positions such as the words attributed to the apostle Peter about Christ, "There is salvation in no one else, for there is no other name under heaven given among mortals by which we must be saved" (NSRV, Acts 4:12).

⁹Knitter's analysis divides those who subscribe to the "replacement model" into total replacement and partial replacement. The former holds that there is only "one true religion"—Christianity; the latter allows that non-Christian religions have some value because to varying degrees they at least have some general or natural revelation. Yet all non-Christian religions are seriously deficient because they do not accept the biblical witness of Jesus Christ as Savior and do not offer salvation; see *Introducing Theologies of Religion*, 26-36.

¹⁰Ibid., 63.

¹¹Among the key proponents are Roman Catholic theologian Karl Rahner, advocate for "anonymous Christianity" (Karl Rahner, "Anonymous Christians," in *Theological Investigations*, vol. VI [New York: Crossroad, 1982], 390-98, and additional articles in *Theological Investigations*, vols. V and XIV]), and evangelical Protestant Clark H. Pinnock, advocate of the "universality axiom," which posits that God's saving grace is for the entire race because God desires the salvation of all persons (Clark H. Pinnock, "An

Inclusivist View," in *Four Views on Salvation in a Pluralistic World*, ed. Dennis L. Okholm and Timothy R. Phillips [Grand Rapids: Zondervan, 1996], 93-122). I offer these two examples to illustrate the wide spectrum of theological commitments included in this paradigm/model.

[12]Recommended are *Nostra Aetate* ("Declaration on the Relationship of the Church to Non-Christian Religions"); *Ad Gentes* (Decree on the Church's Missionary Activity), nos. 3, 9, 11, 18-21; *Gaudium et Spes* (Pastoral Constitution, The Church in the Modern World), nos. 22, 28, 29, 38, 92, 93; *Lumen Gentium* (Dogmatic Constitution on the Church), no. 16.

[13]Congregation for the Doctrine of the Faith, "Declaration Dominus Iesus: On the Unicity and Salvific Universality of Jesus Christ and the Church," *Origins* 30 (Sept. 14, 2000): 209-19. (Of related interest, see International Theological Commission, "Christianity and the World Religions," *Origins* 27 (Aug. 14, 1997): 149-66.

[14]A curious element in the positions of both groups is their neglect to give specific and in-depth attention to their preferred interpretations of salvation. Is the understanding of salvation in Christ informed by 1) a *Christus Victor* interpretation—a) ransom of the devil, or b) a cosmic battle in which Christ is the victor over sin and death; 2) a satisfaction atonement interpretation— a) Anselm's position that Christ's death restores God the Father's offended honor, or b) Luther's substitutionary penal suffering of Christ with Jesus punished in our place; 3) an exemplar of love interpretation (Abelard's depiction of Jesus' death as the act of a loving God); or something else? In the claim that Jesus Christ is the true and normative source of salvation, where do Jesus' life and teachings come into play?

[15]John Hick, "The Non-Absoluteness of Christianity," in *The Myth of Christian Uniqueness: Toward a Pluralistic Theology of Religions*, ed. John Hick and Paul F. Knitter (Maryknoll, N.Y.: Orbis Books, 1989), 17.

[16]John Hick, *An Interpretation of Religion: The Challenge of Other Religions* (Oxford: Basil Blackwell, 1989), 376.

[17]Knitter, *Introducing Theologies of Religions*, 156. Knitter sees Roger Haight's spirit christology as contributing to the mutuality model. See Roger Haight, *Jesus Symbol of God* (Maryknoll, N.Y.: Orbis Books, 1999), 156.

[18]Among the major representatives of this model are George Lindbeck, Paul Griffiths and Joseph Augustine DiNoia, each of whom affirms that only in Christ is salvation offered, while accepting that other religions may also be God-willed with their own particular contributions for the persons who practice them (Knitter, *Introducing Theologies of Religions*, 173-91).

[19]Ibid., 203.

[20]Francis X. Clooney, "Theology and Sacred Scripture Reconsidered in the Light of a Hindu Text," in *Theology and Sacred Scripture, College Theology Society Annual Volume 47 (2001)*, ed. Carol J. Dempsey and William P. Loewe (Maryknoll, N.Y.; Orbis Books, 2002), 211-36.

[21]The center is named after a seventeenth-century Italian Jesuit missionary

who spent nearly fifty years of his life in South India. The aim of the center is to provide a hospitable space where people of different faiths can meet in an atmosphere of prayerful peace and mutual respect. There is a regular event at De Nobili on the first Sunday of every month from October to July. For more information, see http://www.jesuit.org.uk/ interfaith/denobilihouse.htm; accessed on 9/15/04.

[22]In 1989 Barnes expressed his conviction in this way: "A religious tradition can no more see the other as a cut-down or amended version of itself than a man can afford to regard a woman as a sort of secondary image of his own superior maleness" (*Christian Identity and Religious Pluralism, Religions in Conversation* [Nashville: Abingdon Press, 1989], 131).

[23]John Hick's form of religious pluralism fits this description. Barnes is critical of religious pluralism because it is proposed as the only reasonable alternative to exclusivism and inclusivism. See *Theology and the Dialogue of Religions* (Cambridge: Cambridge University Press, 2002), 14 and *passim*.

[24]Ibid., 13-15.

[25]"Seeds of the Word" is a patristic concept that Barnes traces to Justin Martyr and Irenaeus (Barnes, *Theology and the Dialogue of Religions*, 5). It is also found in *Nostra Aetate* ("The Declaration on the Relation of the Church to Non-Christian Religions"), #11.

[26]Jacques Dupuis, S.J., *Christianity and the Religions: From Confrontation to Dialogue* (Maryknoll, N.Y.: Orbis Books, 2001), 147-56.

[27]Ibid., 230.

[28]Emmanuel Levinas, *Time and the Other*, trans. Richard A. Cohen (Pittsburgh: Duquesne University Press, 1987), 75.

[29]Levinas employs a style of writing that endeavors to resist ontology's totalizing grasp. In an often quoted and key passage on ethics, the other, and the same, Levinas writes: "We name this calling into question of my spontaneity by the presence of the Other ethics. The strangeness of the Other, his irreducibility to the I, to my thoughts and my possessions, is precisely accomplished as a calling into question of my spontaneity as ethics. Metaphysics, transcendence, the welcoming of the Other by the Same, of the Other by Me, is concretely produced as the calling into question of the Same by the Other, that is, as the ethics that accomplishes the critical essence of knowledge" (*Totality and Infinity*, trans. Alphonso Lingis [Pittsburgh: Duquesne University Press, 1969], 29).

[30]Michael Barnes, "Facing the Other" (chap. 3), in *Theology and the Dialogue of Religions*, 65-96.

[31]Levinas, *Totality and Infinity*, 78.

[32]Ibid., 43.

[33]Barnes, *Theology and the Dialogue of Religions*, 68. (In this regard, the influence of Ricoeur and *Oneself as Another* can be detected, see especially p. 189).

[34]Ibid., 71.

[35]Ibid., 113.

[36]Paul Ricoeur, *Oneself as Another*, trans. Kathleen Blamey (Chicago: University of Chicago Press, 1992), 336. Ricoeur, although accepting of some of Levinas's insights, is critical of others. Central to Ricoeur's philosophy of selfhood are multiple nuanced descriptions of the correlation between the self and the other. The self is not grounded within itself, but linked to otherness, others, and the unnamed Other.

[37]Ibid.

[38]Ricoeur, *Oneself as Another*, 336.

[39]Barnes, *Theology and the Dialogue of Religions*, 119.

[40]Ricoeur, *Oneself as Another*, 35.

[41]Barnes, *Theology and the Dialogue of Religions*, 105.

[42]Ricour, *Oneself as Another*, 165-68.

[43]"The Conflict of Interpretations: Debate with Hans-Georg Gadamer (1982)," in *A Ricoeur Reader: Reflections and Imagination*, ed. Mario J. Valdés (Toronto: University of Toronto Press, 1991), 234-35.

[44]Barnes, *Theology and the Dialogue of Religions*, 62; see also 26, 98.

[45]This, according to Barnes, is what de Certeau means by "heterology," ibid., 26 and *passim*.

[46]Ibid., 125.

[47]Ibid., xi.

[48]I have not provided any specifics from Barnes's treatment of the religions of India because concern about Muslim-Christian relations is what prompted this paper. Religious preference surveys indicate that around seven million people in the United States practice Islam; see http://www.allied-media.com; accessed 5/18/04.

[49]Barnes first introduces this theme in *Theology and the Dialogue of Religions*, 109, citing Levinas's *Nine Talmudic Readings* (1990) and *In the Time of Nations* (1994).

[50]Barnes, *Theology and the Dialogue of Religions*, 190.

[51]Ibid., 193. The root word for hospitality in Latin, *hospes*, can be translated as "host" and as "guest."

[52]Ibid., 201.

[53]Ibid., 227.

[54]Ibid., 211, 245.

[55]Ibid., 245.

[56]The terms in italics are borrowed from Pontifical Council for Interreligious Dialogue and Congregation for the Peoples, *Dialogue and Proclamation: Reflections and Orientations on Dialogue and the Proclamation of the Gospel of Jesus Christ* (1991), accessed on 5/20/04, http://www.vatican.va/roman_curia/pontifical_councils/interelg/documents/rc_pc_interelg_doc_19051991_dialogue-and-proclamatio_en.html but developed differently here.

Toward an Ecology of Salvation

Sally Kenel

Many contemporary theologians acknowledge the potential fruit-fulness, and even the necessity, of examining Christian doctrine through an ecological lens. Indeed, in her keynote address at the 2004 Annual Convention of the College Theology Society, Elizabeth Johnson identified concern for the earth/cosmos as part of theology's "new horizon."[1] Yet, in a certain sense, the turn to ecology is hardly new: the College Theology Society itself has already devoted two conventions to the topic, one in 1990 and one twenty years earlier, in 1971.[2] Although reflections at these meetings could not help but be influenced by Lynn White's 1967 indictment of Christianity as playing an integral role in promoting disregard for the earth,[3] there were constructive efforts as well.[4] Since 1990, moreover, reflection on the relation of ecology and theology at annual conventions has continued in a section devoted to the topic. And there is much more.[5]

Despite this attention, ecology remains part of theology's new horizon, at least in part because adopting an ecological worldview calls for a re-centering of theological thought.[6] This paper considers the implications of ecology for one area of systematic theology, soteriology. After reviewing the traditional concept of "the economy of salvation" and its inadequacy in describing salvation's scope, the paper will examine the potential of wisdom christology and the theme of reconciliation as possible carriers for a contemporary ecological salvation story.

The Economy of Salvation

The phrase "the economy of salvation" was coined in early Christianity and is used eighteen times in the *Catechism of the Catholic*

Church. The phrase has, if nothing else, staying power. Although the *Catechism* proffers no definition, it makes its origin in Trinitarian theology clear:

> The Fathers of the Church distinguish between theology (*theologia*) and economy (*oikonomia*). "Theology" refers to the mystery of God's inmost life within the Blessed Trinity and "economy" to all the works by which God reveals himself and communicates his life. Through the *oikonomia* the *theologia* is revealed to us; but conversely, the *theologia* illumines the whole *oikonomia*. God's works reveal who he is in himself; the mystery of his inmost being enlightens our understanding of all his works. So it is, analogously, among human persons. A person discloses himself in his actions, and the better we know a person the better we understand his actions.[7]

The economy of creation and the economy of salvation, then, described the "external" activity of the Trinity and constitute parts of "the whole divine economy." The "economy of salvation" effectively emphasized the divine role, the "household management," of salvation. What is not as clear, however, is the nature and extent of the household being managed. "Economy," then, is a term that refers to the way God does salvific work, but does not clearly elucidate what or whom this divine work benefits.[8]

While affirming the value of the term "economy" in providing access to an important dimension of the mystery of the Trinity, it keeps the focus on the managerial side of salvation. The corresponding lack of consideration of the scope of salvation has permitted, if not encouraged, an anthropocentric bias. This bias is increasingly difficult to support in light of the general ecological principle of the interrelatedness of all things. The *scope* of salvation merits theological reflection. I propose here to consider an "ecology of salvation." Derived from the same Greek root (*oikos*) as economy, ecology (literally, the study of the household) calls attention to what or who is being managed, in this case, being saved. Is the object of God's saving work individuals, society, the world?

Contemporary Salvation Stories

Salvation stories begin with the premise that things are not as they should be. That this is the case cannot be debated. The complexity and ambiguity of the universe imply that a simple story of salvation where a mythic hero comes down from above to solve all problems no longer works. Although many refuse to admit it, neither do typical Enlightenment stories where reason triumphs and human progress continues unabated. The situation of the world today is one in which humans cannot be viewed in isolation; all parts of the household, the cosmos, interrelate. Even the best efforts of humans, moreover, may contribute to increasing degeneration and destruction. "The chaotic, contingent, threatened character of existence and the fragility of the human project" call for a type of salvation narrative that Elizabeth Johnson has called "historical contingent." Such a narrative, she says, "tells the story of the joyous, Spirit-filled ministry of Jesus, his unjust suffering and death, and his rising to new life in such a way that God can be seen to draw near in the midst of historical discontinuities rather than in bypassing them."[9] This is most centrally a wisdom story.

Although there was a time when the wisdom tradition was considered theologically inferior, twentieth-century Christian feminists in particular were active in reappraising and subsequently retrieving this strand of biblical thought. In what many consider the best exposition of the wisdom tradition to date, Elizabeth Johnson thoroughly probes its place in the Jewish tradition as well as its use among early Christians to understand Jesus. Johnson's goal, establishing "A Biblical Basis for Non-Androcentric Christology," circumscribes its value.[10] Australian theologian Denis Edwards has explored the ecological potential of the wisdom tradition, examining its value as the basis of a non-anthropocentric christology. Arguing that "Wisdom categories can provide the basis for an authentic interpretation of the life and ministry of Jesus,"[11] Edwards, like Johnson, identifies Jesus as Wisdom's teacher and prophet and as a practitioner of inclusive table companionship whose healing ministry anticipates the fullness of the reign of God. With Jesus' persecution, death, and resurrection, moreover, the association with wisdom is so enriched that "Jesus, the great teacher of wisdom—one so closely associated with wisdom in his lifetime—is, after his death and resurrection, understood to be divine Wisdom."[12]

Understanding Jesus as Wisdom incarnate provides a link between creation and salvation. Present with God at creation as "a skilled co-worker" (Prv 8:30; Wis 7:22; 8:6), "Wisdom takes delight in the company of human beings" (Prv 8:31), builds her house among them, and "invites all to her feast" (Prv 9:3-5).[13] As Edwards reprises it, "Wisdom revealed in the marvels of creation now makes her home among human beings." In incarnational terms, Wisdom does not merely become human, but enters into the created order in a new and particularized way in Jesus of Nazareth. The words of Jesus are words of Wisdom; the ministry of Jesus reveals the way of Wisdom; the foolishness of the cross is the Wisdom of God; the scope of Wisdom's salvation is all creation.[14]

Not all agree with Edwards's assessment that wisdom christology offers the best version of a contemporary salvation story. After examining the ecological potential of six contemporary christological motifs (prophetic, wisdom, sacramental, eschatological, process, and liberation christologies), Sallie McFague, for example, makes a case for two: prophetic and sacramental. Claiming that her ecological christology can be encapsulated by the phrase, "God with us," McFague argues "this Christology would be very 'high' and very 'low' " in that it "focuses on the ministry of Jesus of Nazareth for the content of our praxis towards oppressed people and deteriorating nature and on the incarnation and resurrection for its range and promise."[15] As always, McFague acknowledges that her own social location (white, North American, middle-class feminist) may bias her work, and is open to the idea that there are other ways to develop an ecological christology.

I also am a white, North American, middle-class feminist, and I endorse McFague's claim that "God with us" is the basic christological insight. I agree, too, that from an ecological perspective, both high and low christologies have value. However, I find that wisdom christology has more to offer than McFague recognizes. Wisdom christology encompasses both the prophetic and sacramental dimensions that she judges crucial and expands them. McFague is not untouched by the ecological potential of wisdom christologies, but ultimately she chooses not to formally adopt this motif as her christology because she finds that it says too little about the cross.[16] Not only is her reason for rejecting wisdom christologies unsubstantiated, her adherence to the prophetic motif limits the ecological character of her christology, and her sacramental christology employs the concept of Wisdom incarnate to broaden its scope.[17]

The wisdom motif as developed by Edwards encompasses both McFague's low and high christologies. As Wisdom's prophet, Jesus lives according to the way of Wisdom and proclaims this way as the path of discipleship. Thus, as Edwards contends, "a Wisdom Christology which is faithful to the gospel will be a theology of liberating practice,"[18] that is, a prophetic one. At the same time, viewing the incarnation in wisdom categories leads to an inclusive, cosmic view of salvation. As the early church testified, Jesus in his life, death, and resurrection evokes recognition as the Wisdom of God, and this insight underpins the move to understand him within the already existing cosmic wisdom categories. Using the one motif, wisdom, to express both low and high christologies has an added advantage. Much like the interrelationship of *theologia* and *oikonomia*, in wisdom christology the functional is the basis for the ontological, and the ontological in turns gives meaning to the functional. In Jesus we have a particularized form of God's Wisdom, a saving Wisdom that encompasses all creation.

Saving Wisdom

Using wisdom categories to expand the scope of salvation stories to all creation raises the question of the theme of these stories. Inasmuch as Edwards sees salvation as coextensive with creation, his view of salvation in wisdom categories does not feature sin. Rather, he argues:

> [S]alvation is a bigger concept than simply the forgiveness of sin. Nonhuman creatures, and the universe itself, do not sin. Yet they will be transfigured by the saving love of God revealed in Jesus in what the scriptures call the New Creation. Salvation, redemption and reconciliation include the forgiveness of sins, but they are larger concepts embracing the transformation of the universe.[19]

Thus, the concept of transformation becomes the theme of his version of the salvation story, which he condenses into a two-step schema: "1. *God's transformation of the whole universe. . . . 2. God's self-offering in saving grace to human beings and the invitation to them to participate in a human way in the divine work of on-going creation and redemption.*"[20] The expansion of the scope of salvation to the cosmic frees Edwards's soteriology from an anthropocentric bias.

In addition to particular problems with Edwards's work,[21] one might follow Roger Haight in claiming wisdom christologies carry an anthropological bias. Haight claims that "there is a high correlation between these wisdom christologies and the theme of revelation."[22] Haight bases his argument largely on his interpretation of the hymn found in Philippians 2. Noting that its context, "Have among yourselves the same attitude that is also yours in Christ Jesus" (2:5), makes the hymn a plan for Christian living, Haight concludes that "as the wisdom of God, Jesus reveals both the true nature of human existence and also the nature of God."[23] The anthropological focus of this wisdom christology is undeniable. How does salvation understood as revelation work on a more comprehensive level, at the level of the cosmos? While nature has a long history of being considered a means of God's revelation, how does it receive revelation? Are we to affirm such romantic insights as Richard Crashaw's epigram on the marriage feast of Cana, "The conscious water saw its God and blushed"?[24]

However, wisdom christologies are also connected with reconciliation. The basis for Haight's adopting revelation as the salvation theme associated with wisdom christologies is but one of the three New Testament texts he uses to show the development of wisdom christologies. One of the others, also a hymn, Colossians 1:15-20, presents a different understanding of salvation, but Haight comments on only part of this text. He is content to show that the first three verses reflect an understanding of Jesus the Wisdom of God within the context of the larger wisdom tradition.[25] Omitted from Haight's analysis, the last two verses have direct bearing on salvation: "For in him all the fullness was pleased to dwell, and through him to reconcile all things for him, making peace by the blood of his cross [through him], whether those on earth or those in heaven" (Col 1:19-20). Here reconciliation, not revelation, is offered as an image of salvation. Inasmuch as this passage is derived from a hymn based on the figure of Wisdom, it would seem that the theme of reconciliation merits consideration as the theme of wisdom stories of creation.

While the anthropocentric focus of Haight's revelation theme makes its relevance to an ecology of salvation suspect, Edwards's proposition that "the world is in need of transformation," although suffering from generality, is incontestable. As we have seen above, to be meaningful a contemporary salvation narrative must address serious, multifaceted issues. It must offer hope to every other part of the universe as well as to the cosmos as a whole. It must address the human situation as part of the cosmos in such a way that individual psychological health and social-political well-being, while not the only considerations, are still cherished. The hymn in Colossians 1:15-20 recommends reconciliation as the theme of a soteriology rooted in wisdom christology. Certainly reconciliation is more specific than transformation. Is reconciliation a sufficiently robust theme for a salvation story of the historical-contingent character described by Johnson? What do particular situations in our world today bring to our understanding of reconciliation? Such questions cannot be answered without at least some consideration given to the ills that call for salvation today.

An Ecological Window

Although there are any number of aspects of the world that one might choose to demonstrate that the cosmos is in need of salvation, I will focus on but one, global warming, a story of the interplay of air, ocean, and land. At a given time, when observed from a distance, the ocean appears to be constant, showing nothing of its dynamic, complex nature. It is impossible to see, for example, that the sea itself is home to myriads of creatures that in turn support life. Neither are the various ocean currents visible: there is no sign of the circulation of colder water to the sea bottom nor of the major currents that play an important role in regulating the temperature of the adjoining land. Changes, however are taking place. Studies show that melting glaciers and increased snowfall, for example, are affecting the ocean's salinity. Using the period of 1950-1959 as a baseline, scientists have determined that the water in the North Atlantic is colder and fresher than it used to be, while that of the tropical Atlantic is saltier. These changes in water density in turn influence ocean currents—in particular those that moderate the weather of the northern hemisphere.[26] Today, much of the fresh water entering the North Atlantic comes from the melting of Greenland's ice cap, a phenomenon many scientists consider a by-product of global warming. However, it must be remembered that in addition to temperature, ocean currents are determined by a variety of factors including winds, tides, the shape of the ocean floor, and so on.

With air quality a regular feature of weather reports, awareness of fluctuations in the earth's atmosphere, at least on a daily basis, is common. Long-term effects of air quality are also receiving more attention, with knowledge of the gradual warming of the earth since the late nineteenth century becoming widespread. In general, this rise in temperature is attributed to the fact that industrialization with its increased combustion of fossil fuels has led to an increased release of carbon dioxide and water vapor, and these and other gases keep more of the earth's radiant energy in the atmosphere, warming both land and sea—in short, the greenhouse effect. However, while the relationship of the combustion of fuels to global warming appears simple, it cannot be applied directly to every place on earth. Ironically, as the melting of the Greenland ice cap, itself a product of global warming, adds cold, fresh water to the Atlantic it disrupts ocean currents in such a way that the predicted result is a colder northern hemisphere. In fact, scientists claim that long before humans were burning fossil fuels, ocean currents kept the northern hemisphere so cold that what is now part of New York City was the terminal moraine of the Wisconsin ice sheet.[27] While there is no doubt, especially in recent years, that human activity has exacerbated the factors that work toward major planetary changes, it would be the height of hubris to imagine that humans control the entire universe. On the other hand, denial reaches its depths when humans refuse to take responsibility for the escalation of what are at times catastrophic changes in the contemporary world.

Even in such an abbreviated form, this particular earth story suggests several elements that have bearing on the earth's need for salvation. First, it confirms the general principle of the interrelatedness of all things and demonstrates the complexity of these relationships. Second, while limiting human responsibility for planetary and usually destructive changes, it also limits the effectiveness of the human role in the salvation of the universe. Finally, the outcome, or what salvation means for the cosmos in the face of augmented global warming, is ambiguous. If reconciliation can serve as the theme of a salvation story of the earth, then, at the very least, it must have some bearing on these elements. Or, to put it another way, we need to use the story of the earth's need for salvation to refine our understanding of reconciliation.

Reconciliation in the Ecology of Salvation

At first glance, the definition of reconciliation as bringing harmony, peace, or concord and an end to discord, disruption, and conflict seems promising as a theme for an ecological story of salvation. Harmony, in particular, with its denotation of unity and order produced by the interrelating of various parts readily embraces what many understand as the ecological ideal of balanced equilibrium. Also the notion of reconciliation as *bringing back* harmony indicates that it is a process of reaching unity and order by restoring relationships that pre-date a current chaotic state. Our reflections on global warming indicate, however, that determining the nature of that earlier ideal state is not as simple as one might think. Would it be a return to the pre-industrial clean air of the seventeenth century or the ice age that pre-dates human existence? Thus, as an ecological salvation theme, reconciliation as the restoration of harmony or order is in need of modification.

Most scientists no longer endorse the notion that the earth can be broken down into a series of discrete ecosystems, each with its own ideal state of dynamic equilibrium or homeostasis. Rather, as Daniel Botkin claims, the new ecology is one of *Discordant Harmonies*:

> Until the past few years, the predominant theories in ecology presumed ... a very strict concept of highly structured, ordered, and regulated, steady-state ecological systems. Scientists know now that this view is wrong at local and regional levels ... that is, at the levels of populations and ecosystems. Change now appears to be intrinsic and natural at many scales of time and space in the biosphere.[28]

This new ecology suggests that reconciliation should not be viewed as the achievement of some overall permanent state where change exists only on the microscopic level while the larger picture is one of unchanging serenity. Rather, from an ecological perspective, reconciliation is of the moment—harmony exists for now, but if one element holds the note too long there is discord. Reconciliation in this sense is better understood as a process that makes harmony possible, but, because of the variable nature of the universe and human freedom, cannot guarantee it.

Such a complex understanding of reconciliation is not foreign to the gospels, where some of Jesus' sayings present him as a cause of division not the Prince of Peace. "Do not think that I have come to bring peace upon the earth. I have come to bring not peace but the sword" (Mt 10:34). This discord reaches right into the family, so that "one's enemies will be those of his own household" (Mt 10:36). In first-century Jewish Palestine, Jesus' teachings did indeed bring the sword, in the form of the cross. While pointing to the fact that things were not as they should be, however, the crucifixion of Jesus is not the last word. Rather, in the post-resurrection appearances the message of Jesus becomes, "Peace be with you" (Lk 24:36). Flowing from his life, persecution, and death, the peace of Jesus is a far cry from what Robert Schreiter calls a "false reconciliation" or a "hasty peace," the sort of peace that "covers up the enormity of what has been done and tries to foreshorten the process."[29] The peace that Jesus brings is the peace described in the hymn in Colossians 1—a peace initiated by God, revealed in the cross, and part of an ongoing process, the "ministry of reconciliation" (2 Cor 5:18) in which the whole cosmos participates.

Here, as the situation of the earth demands, reconciliation is understood as process, and, as ministry suggests, a participative process cosmic in scope. Of course, not all participation is equal. I am not suggesting that the ocean can consciously regulate its temperature. Nor do I wish to say that humans should or even can fix everything, or that reconciliation means restoring the original, unspoiled world. Rather, reconciliation is an ongoing restructuring and renewing of the cosmos in the face of ever-changing forces. It is a continual reestablishing of relationships as the universe expands, the sun slowly ages, evolution continues, the Greenland ice cap melts, nations wage war, and humans murder, rape, and consume an unseemly portion of the earth's goods. It is within such pandemonium that reconciliation conveys its true meaning and hope for the future lives on. It is in reconciling this chaos that the creative and salvific love of God can be seen as one force—as Wisdom, ever present in the cosmos, valuing what is and at the same time promising more.

Conclusion

Part of theology's new horizon comes from shifting the context of reflections from the anthropological to the cosmic. Rather than starting with individual humans and working outward to society and then to the world, theologians are encouraged to look at the universe and only then at the various species, including humans, who call it home. In this view, the earth is not a closed system where physical and chemical equilibrium can be established, nor are humans isolated, superior beings. All the earth and its inhabitants are part of a very complex cosmos. Such a perspective is in keeping with the first creation story in Genesis where even prior to the creation of humans, God finds the products of divine work good. While humans, moreover, are responsible for at least exacerbating a good number of the earth's current problems, no amount of conservation or recycling or simple living can lead to a totally sustainable world.

Soteriology is necessarily influenced by such a worldview, and for salvation stories to be correspondingly meaningful their scope must move yet beyond the human. Interpreting Jesus as the Wisdom of God provides a way of understanding salvation that appreciates its cosmic scope. God, who through divine wisdom created the world, has, in Jesus of Nazareth made the world home. As the way of wisdom, the saving work of Jesus, while coextensive with creation, is not complete: hence the call for an ongoing "ministry of reconciliation" that includes our participation in the ecology of salvation. But beyond creation's participation, God who has given us "the ministry of reconciliation" is even now "reconciling the world to himself in Christ" so that "whoever is in Christ is a new creation." (2 Cor 5:17-19). United in the process of reconciliation, the entire household, all creation, groans, hoping for its "share in the glorious freedom of the children of God" (Rom 8:19-22).

Notes

[1]Elizabeth A. Johnson, "Horizons of Theology: New Voices in a Living Tradition," 10-13 above.

[2]The convention theme in 1990 was "An Ecology of the Spirit: Religious Reflection and Environmental Consciousness"; and in 1971, "That They May Live: Ecological Reflections on the Quality of Life."

[3]Lynn White, Jr., "The Historical Roots of Our Ecological Crisis," *Science* 155, no. 3767 (March 10, 1967): 1203-07.

[4]See, for example, Michael Barnes, ed., *An Ecology of the Spirit: Religious Reflection and Environmental Consciousness.* The Annual Publication of the College Theology Society 36 (Lanham, Md.: University Press of America, 1994).

[5]From 1996 to 1998, for example, a series of conferences on world religions and ecology took place under the leadership of the Harvard University Center for the Study of World Religions. Of particular interest here is the volume *Christianity and Ecology: Seeking the Well-Being of Earth and*

Humans, ed. Dieter Hessel and Rosemary Radford Ruether (Cambridge: Harvard University Press, 2000.)

[6]For an assessment of the difficulties ecology poses for traditionally trained theologians as well as strategies for overcoming them, see John B. Cobb, Jr., "Theology and Ecology," <http//www.religion-online.org/cgi-bin/relsearched.ddl/showarticle?item_ed=1492 (1990).

[7]*Catechism of the Catholic Church* (New York: Doubleday, Image, 1995), #236, 70.

[8]Irenaeus of Lyons offers a clue to the early understanding of the scope of salvation. He argued that salvation is extended to Adam as part of God's handiwork and in doing so made reference to "the whole economy of salvation regarding man" (*Adversus Haereses,* <http//www.newadvent.org/fathers0103323.htm (inter 180/199 C.E.): Book III, Chap. 23, #1). Irenaeus summed up the encompassing economy of salvation in his theme of the recapitulation of all things. The soteriological concerns in the second century C.E., however, centered more on human salvation, in particular what happened to those who had lived before Christ. Could they be saved? Iranaeus' response is a firm yes:

> For it was not merely for those who believed in Him in the time of Tiberius Caesar that Christ came, nor did the Father exercise His providence for the men only who are now alive, but for all men together, who from the beginning, according to their capacity in their generation have both feared and loved God, and practiced justice and piety towards their neighbours, and have earnestly desired to see Christ and to hear his voice. Wherefore He shall, at His second coming, first rouse from their sleep all persons of this description, and shall raise them up, as well as the rest who shall be judged, and give them a place in His kingdom (*Adversus Haereses*, Book IV, Chap 22, #2).

Irenaeus, at the very least, extrapolates salvation as a manifestation of God's loving care backward in history to Adam and through him to all creation.

With the Council of Nicea and its creedal formula, "for us men and for our salvation," however, an anthropocentric concept of the salvation soon became the norm. Dropping the English "men" does bring the translation closer to the gender-inclusive Greek and Latin, but the remaining "us" clearly refers to human salvation. Certainly, the Fathers of the council were more interested in understanding Jesus as God than in clarifying God's role in saving the world. Nonetheless, the fact is that we are left with an anthropocentric view of salvation that is regularly professed liturgically.

Given the Nicene context, it is not surprising that, for the most part, mainstream discussions of salvation focus on the human. Yet, although Anselm's question, *Cur Deus Homo?*, and the satisfaction theory that he offers as answer clearly refer to human salvation, it must be admitted that payment of the debt does have a corollary for the world in that the restoration of God's honor is related to the restoration of the proper order of creation (see Anselm of Canterbury, *Cur Deus Homo?*, <http://www.ewtn.com/library/ CHRIST/CURDEUS.HMT, [1098]: Book I chap 13: "Nothing less was to be endured, in the order of things, than that the creature should take away the honor due the Creator and not restore what he takes away."). Yet the economy of salvation remains anthropocentric. Was the incarnation necessary or merely fitting? Is justification a matter of faith or works? Is salvation individual or social? All these questions pertain to humans. Thus, although the term "economy" refers to God's external work in and for the world, the scope of salvation, unlike creation, has been limited to humanity.

[9]Elizabeth A. Johnson, "Jesus and Salvation," *Proceedings of the Catholic Theological Society of America* 49 (1994): 7-10.

[10]Elizabeth A. Johnson, "Jesus the Wisdom of God: A Biblical Basis for Non-Androcentric Christology," *Ephemerides Theologicae Lovanienses* 61 (1985): 261-94.

[11]Denis Edwards, *Jesus the Wisdom of God: An Ecological Theology* (Maryknoll, N.Y.: Orbis Books, 1995), 50.

[12]Ibid.

[13]Ibid., 70.

[14]Ibid.

[15]Sallie McFague, *Life Abundant: Rethinking Theology and Economy for a Planet in Peril* (Minneapolis: Fortress Press, 2001), 167.

[16]Ibid., 163.

[17]The cross is an essential christological theme for McFague because it is the basis for the "cruciform lifestyle" she advocates as the ground of ecological praxis. "For us privileged Christians a 'cross-shaped' life will not be primarily what Christ does for us, but what we can do for others. We do not need so much to accept Christ's sacrifice for our sins as we need to repent of a major sin—our silent complicity in the impoverishment of others and the degradation of the planet" (McFague, *Life Abundant*, 14). McFague seems to have missed the point that, as the first four chapters of 1 Corinthians indicate, wisdom christology from its inception has been cruciform. The heart of the New Testament contrast between human wisdom and divine wisdom is that the latter is revealed in the cross. "For Jews demand signs and Greeks look for wisdom, but we proclaim Christ crucified, a stumbling block to Jews and foolishness to Gentiles, but to those who are called, Jews and Greeks alike, Christ the power of God and the wisdom of God. For the foolishness of God is wiser than human wisdom, and the weakness of God is stronger than human strength" (1 Cor 1:22-25).

In McFague's view, prophetic christologies offer an answer to the question of what constitutes a Christian ecological, economic praxis, and suggest "that all the language about justice, rights, care and concern that Christians believe the human neighbor, especially the oppressed neighbor, deserves should be extended to the natural world" (McFague, *Life Abundant*, 167). In other words, it is praxis dependent upon extrapolating social responsibility to the ecological level. Or, to put it in biblical terms, it is praxis based on covenant rather than creation. While one can argue that a covenantal soteriology includes the Noahic covenant made with all creatures, a more restricted view is commonly held. Indeed, the *Catechism* (§705, 204) states unequivocally that "the promise made to Abraham inaugurates the economy of salvation. . . ." Irenaeus, as we have seen, disagrees. For him, salvation is extended back beyond Abraham to Adam, so that, as the book of Genesis indicates, covenant is situated within creation. Positioning humanity within creation is one of the hallmarks of the wisdom tradition in general and it offers a correspondingly broader context for christology.

To comply with her contention that ecological christologies must also be "high," McFague balances the prophetic dimension with a sacramental one. Jesus is more than a prophet; he is "God with us." Emphasizing that sacramental christology is incarnational, McFague argues that the Word is made flesh uniquely but not exclusively in Jesus. God is incarnate in all creation, and this God-filled creation, in turn, testifies to the value of the physical. Thus, in its sacramental form, McFague's christology reflects the values of inclusion and embodiment:

> Incarnational Christology valorizes matter; moreover it focuses the justice and care of the prophetic dimension of Christology on physical needs and well-being. Incarnational Christology means that salvation is neither solely human nor spiritual; it must be for the entire creation and it must address what makes different creatures and ecosystems flourish. Incarnational Christology says that God wants all of nature, human beings and all other entities, to enjoy well-being in body and spirit. Incarnational Christology, then, expands the ministry and death of Jesus, the model for Christians of "God with us," to envelop the entire universe (McFague, *Life Abundant*, 169-70).

However, McFague herself acknowledges that her incarnational christology cannot be based on a strict Logos and, hence exclusive, christology in which God is embodied solely in Jesus. Rather, she admits that along with spirit christologies, wisdom christologies broaden the scope of embodiment in that "both include other life-forms." Specifically, "Wisdom makes her home in all creation" (McFague, *Life Abundant*, 169). Thus, the use of previously rejected wisdom categories enables McFague to develop her high, incarnational christology. The qualities of embodiment and inclusion that characterize her sacramental theology serve, in turn, to focus her prophetic christology on specific needs and, at the same time, to extend her christology far beyond the "for us men and for our salvation" formula.

[18]Edwards, *Jesus the Wisdom of* God, 63.

[19]Ibid., 145.

[20]Ibid., 150.

[21]Two other concerns can be seen in Edwards's work. First, the participative role of humans in the divine work of salvation that Edwards describes emphasizes the discontinuity of humans with the rest of creation. By not dealing with sin and the human need for salvation, Edwards runs the risk of undervaluing the continuity of humanity with all creation. By simply referring readers to his previous treatments of Christian anthropology, Edwards misses an opportunity to highlight Jesus' activity as a catalyst for human transformation in first-century Palestine, a dimension that confirmed the early Christian identification of him with the figure of Wisdom. Some comments on the gospel presentations of Jesus' calls to conversion, however brief, would have been helpful in establishing the concrete particulars of transformation. Without such grounding, one may devalue the earthly life of Jesus and, by implication, the earth and its inhabitants as well.

Second, Edwards contends "in a wisdom Christology it becomes clear that the Wisdom revealed in a rainforest is revealed in a new and staggering way in the crucified One. The resurrection of Jesus crucified can be grasped as the beginning of the transformation of the whole universe" (Edwards, *Jesus the Wisdom of God*, 153). Although he broadens the scope of incarnation to include the cosmos (rainforest) as well as Jesus, the nature of the transformation Edwards anticipates remains vague. If humans are to get beyond the anthropocentric and purely eschatological hope that the resurrection means that what happened to Jesus will happen to us, we need to sharpen our understanding of the cosmic need for transformation. The best way to do this, it seems, would be to study particular aspects of the world that demonstrate its need of salvation. In this way, not only will the resurrection hold out hope for transformation, but the concrete situation of the world will tell us something of what this transformation will be like.

[22]Roger Haight, *Jesus Symbol of God* (Maryknoll, N.Y.: Orbis Books: 1999), 171.

[23]Ibid., 172.

[24]Richard Crashaw, "Translation of His Own Epigram on the Miracle of Cana—St. John's Gospel (ch. II)," <http://www.worldof quotes.com?topic/Wine-and Spirits/1/.

[25]Haight, *Jesus Symbol of God*, 169.

[26]Andrew C. Revkin, "An Icy Riddle as Big as Greenland," *New York Times,* 8 June 2004, F4.

[27]Margaret Mittelbach and Michael Crewdson, *Wild New York: A Guide to the Wildlife, Wild Places and Natural Phenomena of New York City* (New York: Random House, 1997), 35.

[28]Daniel B. Botkin, *Discordant Harmonies: A New Ecology for the Twenty-First Century* (New York: Oxford University Press, 1990), 10;

quoted in David Toolan, *At Home in the Cosmos* (Maryknoll, N.Y.: Orbis Books, 2001), 106.

²⁹Robert J. Schreiter, *Reconciliation: Mission and Ministry in a Changing Social Order* (Marynoll, N.Y.: Orbis Books, 1992), 21.

Cohabitation and Entry into Marriage

Two Diverse Trajectories and the Future of Catholic Theology

Randall Jay Woodard

In a particularly strong statement, John Paul II once claimed, "The future of the world and of the Church passes through the family."[1] This may be a worrisome claim because, as Michael Lawler put it, "In the western world, marriage is in a crisis."[2] For some, this crisis consists of a lack of conformity to "traditional" norms concerning marriage and the family.[3] Yet others see this "crisis" as a positive movement away from patriarchal family systems that have historically subjugated women and children.[4] Moreover, "family" itself is no longer a univocal term, if it ever was one.[5] Regardless of one's evaluation of the "crisis," the way many in the Western world experience marriage and family life has been radically transformed.

Several new trends currently affect marriage and the family in the United States. One is the frequency of couples living together as husband and wife before marriage. Forty to sixty percent of Americans cohabit before marriage.[6] This statistic is as true of Catholics as other Americans, even though the official teaching of the Catholic Church is opposed to premarital cohabitation.[7] That a significant number of Catholics cohabit while the church opposes any sort of cohabitation or "trial marriage" is a significant component in this "crisis."

Anglican layperson Adrian Thatcher asks the critical and pressing question: "What are the churches to say and do about the widespread practice of cohabitation prior to marriage, inside and outside of the churches?"[8] Does the Catholic Church have anything to say about this practice? Are approximately half of those entering into marriage quite simply "living in sin"?

Two patterns of response to this question can be discerned, a "traditional" response and a more "innovative" theological reevaluation of cohabitation that proposes certain circumstances in which it might understandably take place. This paper shows how consent plays an important role in contemporary canonical and theological understandings and evaluations of cohabitation. It then assesses the positive aspects and limitations of each response in order to offer insight into the contemporary situation and the future of Catholic family life.

Broadly speaking, cohabitation refers to non-married persons living together in an intimate relationship. Thatcher classifies cohabiters into three different categories based on their intentions for living together:

> The first type is "temporary or *casual* cohabitation," entered into with little thought or commitment; the second type is conscious *preparation for marriage* or "trial marriage"; the third type functions as a *substitute for marriage* either because the couple is opposed to marriage as an institution, or because they live in a society where cohabitation is an institution already.[9]

This paper uses the term "cohabitation" only to signify a relationship between a man and a woman who are not married, are committed to one another, intend marriage, and are living together as husband and wife on a transitional basis. The lack of commitment in "casual cohabitation" and the disregard for marriage in the third type are not relevant to a study of entry into marriage.[10] The second type is similar to Michael Lawler's "pre-nuptial" cohabitation which indicates the couple's intention to marry: "marriage is consciously intended to follow" the time of cohabitation.[11]

A Traditional Approach to Cohabitation

Although a variety of circumstances motivate couples to cohabit before marriage (such as getting to understand the person's lifestyle, testing compatibility, and financial benefits), many approaching cohabitation "traditionally" focus on the issue of fornication.[12] This

approach finds intimate sexual expression fitting only when commitment has been formally and liturgically expressed. It claims that most,
if not all, motivation to cohabit could be satisfied without intimate
cohabitation. A couple does not need to be in a sexually active cohabiting relationship to save money or discover if they are compat-
ible.

The Catechism of the Catholic Church clearly defines this approach:

> Some today claim a *"right to a trial marriage"* where there is
> an intention of getting married later. However firm the
> purpose of those who engage in premature sexual relations
> may be, "the fact is that such liaisons can scarcely ensure
> mutual sincerity and fidelity in a relationship between a man
> and a woman, nor, especially, can they protect it from
> inconstancy of desires or whim." Carnal union is morally
> legitimate only when a definitive community of life between a
> man and a woman has been established. Human love does not
> tolerate "trial marriages." It demands a total and definitive
> gift of persons to one another.[13]

John Paul II expands on the position held by the catechism in
several of his works. He emphasizes human dignity as the foundation for his theology of marriage.[14] In particular, there is an underlying concern that individuals not become a means for manipulation
that underlies his effort on behalf of those entering into marriage. In
Familiaris Consortio, John Paul II addressed two "irregular situations": "trial marriages" and "de facto free unions." He asserted
that sexuality must be an act of total self-giving; it must reflect and
promote the true dignity of the human person and mirror the covenant love between Christ and the church. For John Paul II, marriage
is "the covenant of conjugal love freely and consciously chosen,
whereby man and woman accept the intimate community of life and
love willed by God himself. . . ."[15] Sexuality, he writes:

> concerns the innermost being of the human person as such. It
> is realized in a truly human way only if it is an integral part of
> the love by which a man and a woman commit themselves
> totally to one another until death. The total physical self-
> giving would be a lie if it were not the sign of a personal self-

giving, in which the whole person, including the temporal dimension is present: If the person were to withhold something or reserve the possibility of deciding otherwise in the future, by this very act he or she would not be giving totally.[16]

When addressing irregular situations, John Paul II states that any sexual union outside of marriage is contrary to the good of the human person. Therefore, sexual unity that occurs within a relationship that lacks commitment, mutuality, permanence, and the total gift of self to the other falls beneath human dignity and distorts the "nuptial meaning" of the body and sexuality.[17]

Cohabitation is sometimes likened to "taking a car for a test drive before buying it." Such a sentiment degrades the human person because anyone "who treats a person as a means to an end does violence to the very essence of the other."[18] Further, "dignity demands that they [spouses] should be always and solely the term of a self-giving love without limitations of time or any other circumstance."[19] Thus, because of the dignity inherent to the human person, a total gift of oneself sexually in a context of conditional or limited love (even in the case of engagement) fails to treat oneself or the other as an end.[20] Rather, these relationships allow the partners to use each other as means or tools for self-satisfaction.

John Paul II, then, finds that those who cohabit, because their relationship presupposes some type of conditions to total commitment, cannot embody the unconditional love that is necessary for Christian spouses to symbolize the love of Christ for the church. Christian marriage is a representation of the faithful and indissoluble covenant love of Christ for the church, and thus cannot include any notions of being "trial" or experimental in nature. Cohabitation is beneath the dignity of the person because sexual relations ought to be placed within an indissoluble and permanent publicly recognized covenant partnership that represents Christ's love for the church.

The traditional pattern tends to view the theology and history of marriage in a linear progression that is Spirit-guided and magisterially guarded. Using Trent's canonical form as a basic interpretative structure, this approach selects supporting biblical verses, appropriate key figures throughout history, and important papal statements, and forms a coherent and systematic theology of marriage and entry into marriage. The importance of canonical form within this framework cannot be overemphasized. It provides a theological standard by which marriage can be defined and measured. Canonical form remains the standard of entry into marriage to this day. The need to define marriage as valid, to know when, and if, it took place arose within the church as it found itself increasingly involved in controlling marriage. Debates surrounding these questions of what constituted a valid marriage lasted for centuries.[21]

The current Catholic canonical understanding of marriage is that it is "brought about through the consent" of the spouses and the valid marriage is then "ratified and consummated if the parties have performed . . . the conjugal act. . . ."[22] This legal-theological understanding of marriage was offered by Gratian in the twelfth century to resolve a debate between Roman and Northern European theologians. The crux of the debate was whether a marriage exists with consent alone, or if consummation is required. Gratian's answer to this was that marriage was begun by consent and completed with sexual intercourse. This resolution did two things: "that of verifying the act and the moment that begin a marriage, and that of keeping a place for intercourse in creating a marriage."[23] In addition, Gratian's analysis highlights the fact that consent is the beginning of marriage, but not the only essential aspect. Although consent is normally understood to be the element that brings about marriage, it might be properly stated that entry into marriage begins with consent and is finished at the first act of intercourse. Without consummation, a marriage can be declared null since only a ratified and consummated marriage is indissoluble. Thus, with Gratian, the essential characteristics of marriage, or the *when* and *what*, solidified into the Catholic understanding of matrimony. This sequence (*ratum* then *consummatum*) became definitive at the Council of Trent, particularly in the decree *Tametsi*, which addressed the *how* of marriage.

Tametsi, like the work of Gratian, addressed a specific problem within the life of the church and state. At the time of its promulgation, clandestine marriage was a significant problem in the West. This issue had been troublesome for some time since there was no way to prove that a marriage did or did not exist. These unverifiable marriages left the practice of becoming married open to abuse and was devastating to many who had no way to prove that they were in fact married or not married to a certain person. *Tametsi* attempted to solve the issue of clandestine marriages by constructing a public and ecclesial form for marriage. The practical solution was to insist that all marriages contracted must be in the presence of a priest (or another person delegated by the bishop) and two or three witnesses. Any marriages that did not meet these requirements were declared null.

The development of the definition of entry into marriage and the prohibition of cohabitation become clear in light of the emphasis on the public and ecclesial nature of marriage. Since the church maintains that "marriage is brought about through the consent of the parties"[24] and that consent is to be celebrated according to canonical form, marriage takes place specifically at the moment of public consent and is consummated at the first act of intercourse. Therefore, any intimate sexual acts taking place before consent is publicly celebrated are viewed as fornication.[25] The central role of canonical form is also quite clear. It is clear then that the official teaching of the Catholic Church states that because marriage is the only suitable institution for sexual activity and begins when consent is exchanged according to canonical form, any arrangement that permits couples to cohabit intimately before "marriage" is incompatible with the faith.

In summary, the opposition to cohabitation that comes forth from this approach is founded on a "first consent then consummation" system. Consent must be publicly and liturgically celebrated according to the canonical form established by *Tametsi*. As John Paul II put it, the giving of oneself sexually without a committed gift of the whole person (marriage) leads inevitably to utilitarian motives and thus reduces the other to a means to an end.[26] Hence, cohabitation is never acceptable.

The traditional approach is open to criticism on several grounds. First, it appears obvious that historically there has not been one standard path into marriage for Catholics. Entry into marriage has been more likely to reflect local customs than universal Christian norms. Some thus accuse the church of being arbitrary in enforcing an ecclesial form that evolved as a response to a particular social problem. The Tridentine form, instituted primarily to prevent the abuses resulting from clandestine marriages, is presumed to be a matter of faith rather than a matter of disciplinary practice. This approach encourages allegiance to legal definitions of ecclesial form, rather than to a personal, human and Christian partnership of life and love.

Second, this approach is unrealistic in the present context. Many people will simply not be virginal when they marry, nor will they refrain from cohabiting, regardless of what the church teaches. For some theologians, the lack of reception of a particular teaching by a majority of the faithful calls into question the relevance of the teaching itself.[27] Moreover, many moral theologians are critical of what they perceive as an overemphasis on physical acts, rather than a consideration of the circumstances of the act, the intentions of the agent, and a focus on the good of the subject as a whole. Charles Curran, for instance, disapproves of an approach for attending to the sexual act itself, rather than to human persons as they interact with others.[28] Many contemporary ethicists are also less hasty in their condemnation of certain sexual acts as objectively wrong (intercourse before marriage, for example) or as always gravely sinful. For them, as well as many in the field of systematic theology, the bigger picture, including intention and circumstances, must come into consideration.

A Second Approach to Cohabitation

More innovative approaches to "cohabitants with an emphatic intention to marry"[29] have found proponents in the Catholic tradition and in other Christian denominations. Although many authors proposing legitimacy to types of cohabitation share common themes, a real consensus has not emerged. In reality, various positions exist concerning what types of relationships deserve reevaluation and consideration for Christians who cohabit. Some of their themes are relevant for an innovative understanding of consent and entry into marriage within the Catholic tradition.

In contrast with the first approach, which views the public and liturgical celebration of consent as the norm, these approaches offer a reevaluation of how we understand both the *what* and the *how* of marriage.

Historically, the understanding of the nature of marriage has been varied. "Christian marriage is a remarkably flexible institution."[30] Marriage customs have not been unchanging. The role of ceremonies has developed. The need for a church representative at ceremonies has changed. The function of the family in the selection of spouses has varied extensively. More recently, the understanding of marriage as a covenant, and the role of friendship and love in marriage have been newly emphasized.

Throughout history there has also been a great diversity in conditions to be met for those entering into the married state. Even the two necessary conditions of valid marriage, consent and consummation, although recurrently present in different respects throughout the history of Christian marriage, are not static, but developed into their current forms. Canonical form has not been the only manner by which a couple enters into marriage. Hence, it is not essential to what marriage is. A reevaluation of the mandatory practice of canonical form within this approach is central to its assessment of cohabitation.

For those critical of the official Catholic position, the development of ecclesial form in *Tametsi* itself is evidence for the reality of pre-nuptial cohabitation. First, *Tametsi* shows a clear break from what had been traditional practice. According to Adrian Thatcher, "For the first time in the Catholic tradition, the consent of two parties who are free to marry *is no longer enough*. . . . This adds much to the traditional teaching and represents 'a radical departure from past teaching.' "[31] This addition is quite significant. There are certainly many historical examples of ecclesial presence at weddings, such as blessings of a bishop, and the attendance of pastors; but there is a clear change after the Council of Trent in that the marriages not following canonical form are now for the first time declared invalid. This highlights the fact that canonical form could be considered more a matter of practicality than of theology since it modified how marriage was carried out rather than how marriage is understood. Or, as Lawler aptly contends, "That canonical change was well within the power of the Church to make; therefore, it is, of course, well within its power to unmake."[32]

Second, with *Tametsi*, the church specifically addressed the problem of clandestine marriages. Its formation of canonical form derived from the needs of a very particular context. Many would argue that this context no longer exists and that the church should not hold to a universal form for marriage simply because other modes of entry into marriage might be abused. The fact that our contemporary understanding of marriage has been the result of a developing tradition is an indication that the tradition could continue to develop. Since the required practice of a public ceremony to exchange consent is relatively new and is not necessarily a theological issue, a reevaluation of this practice is possible. Since the public forum for consent might be considered less a theological issue than a question of discipline, some would argue that many who cohabit on their way to the altar (for the canonically required ceremony[33]), may have already given consent in a manner similar to what has historically been regarded as marital consent within the Catholic tradition. If valid consent were given, then this fact would certainly undermine the objection that cohabitants' sexual acts were fornication. This practice would also seem to meet the requirements of Gratian's formula of *ratum et consummatum* thereby making the liturgical ceremony a public celebration of an event already underway.[34]

Although what constitutes legitimate entry into marriage may need reevalutaion, there is no firm consensus in terms of what is to be done. Most Catholic theologians who are open to the possibility of permissible cohabitation would qualify their position by assuming serious commitment, or most likely engagement, before cohabiting. Philip Keane, for example, stresses the need for "real maturity and commitment including the intention to marry when and if the social obstacles are removed" for those who might forgivably cohabit.[35] Lawler writes of the necessity of an emphatic intention to marry, but also seeks to place this step toward marriage within a publicly celebrated betrothal ceremony.[36] In this light, the engagement would be more properly seen as the beginning of marriage with a ceremony consummating the marriage.

Some theologians not only question the validity of maintaining a universal method of entering into marriage from a historical perspective, but also claim that our current cultural trends compel many to postpone marriage to a much later age. Keane, for example, writes of the financial and educational obligations that make it necessary for young people to postpone marriage until reaching their thirties in order to become stable. For Keane, this legitimizes a couple's sexual relationship since, "the intercourse's lack of public proclamation is not due to any defect in the intention of the couple; it is due rather to certain problematic characteristics of modern society."[37] Both Keane and Lawler would hold that there must be a serious commitment to marry (or an engagement); furthermore, the couple would be facing some external impediment to marriage in the form of financial or educational constraints. There is a wide range of answers to the question of which couples could excusably cohabit based on their situation of serious commitment while facing some external obstacles to marriage.[38]

A third consideration for those taking this approach is that scripture and tradition are living entities that demand critical and Spirit-led interpretation in order to find meaning for each age. In order to find meaning for those living together as a legitimate step toward marriage, the notion of fornication needs to be understood in light of the history of entry into marriage. Since canonical form (which strictly governs entry into marriage) was a development (and could thus continue to develop), a richer understanding of what fornication meant to those marrying before canonical form was obligatory could help in developing current interpretations. Our understandings of scripture and tradition on fornication may well need to be reevaluated.

Some have proposed the revival of the ancient practice of betrothal. Some argue that this practice did not require sexual abstinence before a "ceremony" where formal consent was exchanged. Since many marriage customs simply derived from various cultural customs, cohabitation might be viewed as a contemporary retrieval of the custom of betrothal. Some consider this practice a tradition that might fit those who wish to be married today, given current societal expectations.

In summary, the call for a reevaluation of cohabitation focuses on what it means to enter into marriage. The understanding of consent and consummation is not static, but has developed. The requirement that consent be given in a public ceremony was developed as a practical means to combat clandestine marriages. Thus, as a matter of practice and not theology, many question whether a disciplinary or legal notion of *ratum et consummatum* should bind our understanding in contemporary circumstances. Some maintain that couples that cohabit as a component of their transition into marriage are in fact returning to a practice that may have been licit before the Council of Trent's *Tametsi* decree. If the canonical form introduced at Trent was a departure from the previous practice of entry into marriage, it is thus not the only means of entry into marriage. If a more flexible notion of licit *ratum* is permissible, then a more flexible interpretation of licit *consummatum* might be permissible.

This pattern of innovation has some problems and limitations. This approach seems to envision as radical a break with tradition as its proponents say *Tametsi* was. Like clandestine marriage in the past, such innovations might be ripe for abuse. Moreover, many besides John Paul II have noticed that marriage has become a more individualistic, utilitarian, and materialistic, and less a communal, familial, and ecclesial event. Legitimating cohabitation could have the effect of driving human relationships further into this realm of self-satisfaction and absorption. Ultimately, such a practice might further the understanding of marriage as being only about a relationship between two people, not also about the common good, and not about children.

Even if cohabitation did become a legitimate entry into marriage, it would be difficult to determine what situations were in fact appropriate to begin sexual relations. If premarital cohabitation were tolerated on the basis of a decision based upon a sense of commitment and the firm intention to be married, would this encourage prenuptial cohabitation? How could an "emphatic intention" to marry be expressed and recognized? If a couple cannot marry due to financial or social constraints, should they be encouraged to become sexually active? Would this be a proper situation for even the remote chance of bringing new life into the relationship? If a couple is not able to afford a wedding and is not prepared to make a total commitment to each other, might it not be wise to postpone any sexual activity rather than risk having children?

Finally, it might be useful to ask whether loosening the understanding of the institution of marriage at a juncture when its failure rate is so alarmingly high would be a beneficial move. Although very recent evidence asserts that nuptial cohabiters do not seem to display a significantly high divorce rate, as is frequently claimed,[39] consenting to cohabitation may only serve to intensify the notion of impermanence within marriage. If the termination of these relationships were to be treated with gravity similar to that of marriage as suggested by Keane, we might find the busiest staff in diocesan offices that of the newly created betrothal tribunal!

These criticisms may not show the innovators wrong, but they are concerns that any innovative approach needs to deal with.

Conclusion

Although the official norm for the Catholic Church remains the Tridentine form, the "irregular" situation of many of our students or congregants may in fact be more traditional than we sometimes think. Although the official teaching of the church has not seemed to change in the recent past, the tone in some recent pastoral documents has become more charitable to those who live together before marriage. A more accurate question at this juncture seems to be whether the distinction between pre-nuptial and non-nuptial will find a more prominent place in Catholic theology.

In pastoral practice, many parishes do not demand couples to separate during their engagement if they desire to be married in the church. Many pastors seem willing to work with cohabiting couples on an individual basis, rather than offering black and white regulations or refusing to deal with cohabiting couples. Lawler, among others, has emphasized that a great deal can be done to aid cohabiting couples as they approach the church for marriage. This time can be a valuable time for instruction, and using it for that purpose can have a very constructive outcome for many couples as they prepare for marriage. The fact is that many couples choose to live together before marriage. Reviving the practice of betrothal or working with cohabiting couples does not necessarily condone the practice; it offers a practical method of dealing with an issue that is not going away. Using pastoral prudence when dealing with cohabiting couples is certainly the best and only option when facing our contemporary situation. This shift in attitude and practice will not only allow for proper preparation and instruction before marriage, it will allow those in marriage preparation to more effectively reach out to those cohabiting before marriage.

As a legal issue (leaving aside the moral considerations) it appears that cohabitation has become less of an "impediment" to entry into marriage in the recent past. In a manner parallel to that of pre-*Tametsi* times when clandestine marriages were illicit, yet valid, cohabitation should likewise be recognized as illicit, but not as a valid impediment to a public celebration. With a nuanced understanding of the history of entry into marriage, there has been a shift from rigidity and penalization when dealing with cohabiting couples to a more open and flexible style, since the prohibition against cohabitation is a matter lacking a canonical penalty. The issue of whether this should occasion a revision in the theology of marriage is not yet decided, regardless of the more pastoral approach frequently seen; but this paper has at least indicated the relevant issues in contemporary theological reflection on cohabitation.

Notes

[1]John Paul II, *Familiaris Consortio* (Boston: St. Paul Books, 1981), §75.

[2]Michael Lawler, *Marriage and the Catholic Church: Disputed Questions* (Collegeville: Liturgical Press, 2002), vii.

[3]For an example, see John Haas, "The Contemporary World," in Glenn W. Olsen, ed., *Christian Marriage: A Historical Study* (New York: Herder & Herder, 2001), 332-56.

[4]For one example, see John Shelby Spong, *Living in Sin? A Bishop Rethinks Human Sexuality* (San Francisco: Harper & Row, 1988), 40-53. For

a criticism of the "patriarchy and misogyny which permeate scripture," see Christine E. Gudorf, *Body, Sex, and Pleasure: Reconstructing Christian Sexual Ethics* (Cleveland: Pilgrim Press, 1994), 7-14.

[5]Julie Hanlon Rubio, *A Christian Theology of Marriage and Family* (Mahwah, N.J.: Paulist Press, 2003), 3, 13-18. For a discussion on the danger of excluding and condemning those who differ from the "traditional" norm of family, see Florence Caffrey Bourg, *Where Two or Three Are Gathered: Christian Families as Domestic Churches* (Notre Dame: University of Notre Dame Press, 2004), 81-84.

[6]Larry Bumpass and Hsien Hen Lu, "Trends in Cohabitation and Trends for Children's Family Contexts in the United States," *Population Studies* 54 (2000): 7.

[7]*Catechism of the Catholic Church* (New Hope, Ky.: Urbi et Orbi Communications, 1994), §2391. John Paul II states, "The Church, for her part, cannot admit such a kind of union [trial marriage] for further and original reasons which derive from faith" (*Familiaris Consortio*, §80, as cited in *Marriage Preparation and Cohabiting Couples: An Information Report on New Realities and Pastoral Practices* [Washington, D.C.: United States Catholic Conference, 1999]). Adrian Thatcher notes that among Roman Catholics in France, 50 percent of church attenders were cohabiting as they entered into first marriages. Thatcher also notes that variables exist within each denomination that affect the statistics; see his *Living Together and Christian Ethics* (Cambridge, England: Cambridge University Press, 2002), 34. Those who attend services more frequently, for example, tend to be less likely to cohabit. Robin Gill reports that among Christians characterized as in between biblical literalist and non-literalist, 50 percent agreed that cohabitation is wrong; see his *Churchgoing and Christian Ethics* (Cambridge, England: Cambridge University Press, 1999), 100.

[8]Adrian Thatcher, *Marriage after Modernity: Christian Marriage in Postmodern Times* (Sheffield, England: Sheffield Academic Press, 1999), 103.

[9]Ibid., 104.

[10]It could be argued convincingly that those who cohabit as a permanent substitute for marriage are in fact "married" since the couple may have exchanged consent, and has presumably consummated the relationship. A common-law marriage may also be viewed as similar to pre-Tridentine marriages. However, prenuptial cohabiters possess a specific and articulated desire for the sacrament of Christian marriage, while others may or may not. Those who substitute cohabitation for marriage may do so as an explicit rejection of Christian marriage. One does not want to assume anything concerning those in common-law marriages, either that they do desire marriage, or that their lifestyle is motivated by an animosity toward marriage as an institution. It seems best to address those whose intention to marry is demonstrated by engagement or an expressed desire to marry. Since this

current paper deals with those who demonstrate a desire for marriage and are in the process of becoming married, it seems fitting to deal with those described by Thatcher as being in the second group.

[11]Lawler, *Marriage and the Catholic Church*, 166.

[12]Much more could be said concerning the other issues motivating individuals to cohabit before marriage. However, from my research I conclude that the issue of fornication is a central concern of those following the traditional approach, based on the importance of physical acts within their moral theology. Thus, fornication must be the central question to address here.

[13]*Catechism of the Catholic Church*, §2391. The *Catechism* refers to *Familiaris Consortio*, §81 and the Declaration of the Congregation for the Doctrine of the Faith, *Persona Humana*, §7. The *Catechism* defines fornication as the "carnal union between an unmarried man and an unmarried woman. It is gravely contrary to the dignity of the persons and of human sexuality which is naturally ordered to the good of spouses and the generation and education of children" (§2353). All carnal sexual activity that takes place outside of the marital union is thus fornication and therefore gravely sinful.

[14]This review of John Paul II's thought is indeed cursory, but is used to provide an overview in this brief paper. Many of the principles articulated by John Paul II are also utilized in the writings of the U.S. bishops, particularly, "It [cohabitation] contradicts the meaning of a sexual relationship in marriage as the total gift of oneself in fidelity, exclusivity, and permanency" (*Marriage Preparation and Cohabiting Couples: An Informal Report on New Realities and Pastoral Practices* [Washington, D.C.: United States Catholic Conference, 1999], 1). Also see the Bishops of Pennsylvania, *Living Together: Questions and Answers Regarding Cohabitation and the Church's Moral Teaching* (Harrisburg: Pennsylvania Catholic Conference, 1999).

[15]John Paul II, *Familiaris Consortio*, §11.

[16]Ibid., §11.

[17]John Paul II, *The Theology of the Body: Human Love in the Divine Plan* (Boston: Pauline Books, 1997), 54-66. In these sections, John Paul II describes in detail what he means by the nuptial meaning of the body. He describes the profound intimacy achieved between spouses as they donate and subordinate their entire selves to each other. The deep loving communion between spouses is a result of their self-giving (which is central to what it means to be human). When speaking of the physical body he states, "The human body, oriented interiorly by the sincere gift of the person, reveals not only its masculinity and femininity on the physical plane, but reveals also such a value and such a beauty as to go beyond the purely physical dimension of sexuality" (65).

[18]Karol Wojtyla, *Love and Responsibility* (San Francisco: Ignatius Press, 1981), 27.

[19]John Paul II, *Familiaris Consortio*, §80.

[20]Cf. Pontifical Council for the Family: Guidelines for Education within

the Family, *The Truth and Meaning of Human Sexuality* 1995, §11. "When such love exists in marriage, self-giving expresses, through the body, the complementarity and totality of the gift. Married love thus becomes a power which enriches persons and makes them grow and, at the same time, it contributes to building up the civilization of love." But when the sense and meaning of gift is lacking in sexuality, a "civilization of things and not of persons" takes over, "a civilization in which persons are used in the same way as things are used. In the context of a civilization of use, woman can become an object for man, children a hindrance to parents. . . ."

[21]This is indeed a brief historical sketch. For a more in-depth analysis, see Edward Schillebeeckx, *Marriage: Human Reality and Saving Mystery*, vol. 2 (New York: Sheed & Ward, 1965). Also see Theodore Mackin, *What Is Marriage? Marriage in the Catholic Church* (New York: Paulist Press, 1982).

[22]*Code of Canon Law: Latin-English Edition* (Washington, D.C.: The Canon Law Society of America, 1983). Canons 1057 and 1061.

[23]Mackin, *What Is Marriage?*, 159.

[24]*Code of Canon Law*, Canon 1057.

[25]A very concise outline is offered in *Declaration on Certain Questions Concerning Sexual Ethics* (1975): "Nowadays many claim the right to sexual intercourse before marriage, at least for those who have a firm intention of marrying and whose love for one another, already conjugal as it were, is deemed to demand this as its natural outcome. . . . This opinion is contrary to Christian teaching, which asserts that sexual intercourse may take place only within marriage" (Charles E. Curran and Richard A. McCormick, *Dialogue about Catholic Sexual Teaching, Readings in Moral Theology No. 8* (Mahwah, N.J.: Paulist Press, 1993), 379.

[26]Not that all those who enter into marriage according to canonical form will be entirely lust-liberated and therefore never use another person as a means to an end. Rather, he highlights the self-sacrificial nature of love that ought to permeate Christian marriages and the nuptial meaning of the body. This type of love is practiced as spouses prepare for marriage and as the man and woman sacrifice the physical pleasure of their sexual union and seek the true good of the other (forming an intimate communion, avoiding use of the other), rather than seeking self-gratification.

[27]Michael G. Lawler, "Faith, Praxis, and Practical Theology: At the Interface of Sociology and Theology," *Horizons* 29, no. 2 (Fall 2002): 199-224. On page 203 he states, "A non-received teaching is not thereby false or invalid; it is merely judged by believers in practice to be not necessary at this historical time to their life in the church. . . ."

[28]For example, see Charles E. Curran, "Sexuality and Sin: A Current Appraisal," in Curran and McCormick, *Dialogue about Catholic Sexual Teaching*, 405-17; previously published in Charles E. Curran, *Contemporary Problems in Moral Theology* (Notre Dame: Fides Publishers, 1970), 159-70.

[29]Lawler, *Marriage and the Catholic Church*, 175. Also, for further

clarification of his position, see Michael G. Lawler, "Cohabitation: Past and Present Reality: A Response to Lisa Sowle Cahill," *Theological Studies 65*, no. 3 (September 2004): 625.

[30]Thatcher, *Marriage and the Catholic Church*, 119. Further, "In the case of already baptized Christians who wished to marry, the idea of celebrating these marriages with a separate church ceremony, distinct from the normal civil marriage celebrated in the family or the immediate social circle, did not at first come to mind. Christians did much the same as their non-Christian fellows, the Greeks, and the Romans, and later the Germanic, Frankish, Celtic and other peoples. The ceremonies and popular customs associated with marriage in contemporary society also formed the marriage ceremonies for baptized Christians, and of course many of these customs were eventually brought within the church's orbit" (Schillebeeckx, *Marriage*, 233). He does note that Christian spouses frequently disregarded those customs relating to pagan sacrifices.

[31]Thatcher, *Living Together and Christian Ethics*, 190.

[32]Ibid., 173.

[33]Interestingly, Thatcher asserts that "the achievement of the widespread belief that a marriage begins with a wedding was not so much a *religious* or theological, but a *class* matter" (Thatcher, *Marriage after Modernity*, 116).

[34]This is why several theologians would speak of *"pre-ceremonial"* sex rather than pre-marital sex. This position was addressed directly and condemned by the Congregation for the Doctrine of the Faith. See its review of Guindon's work "The Sexual Creators," in *Dialogue about Catholic Social Teaching*, ed. Curran and McCormick, 498-510.

[35]Philip Keane, "Heterosexual Expression, Marriage and Morality," in Curran and McCormick, 434.

[36]See Lawler, *Marriage and the Catholic Church*, 175-83. Lawler states that the sexual relationship between couples in this situation would be "far from premarital" (180).

[37]Keane, "Heterosexual Expression, Marriage and Morality," 433.

[38]The Catholic theologians discussed here are writing only about those who plan to marry. Trial marriages and serial cohabitation do not fit into this analysis.

[39]Lawler, "Cohabitation: Past and Present Reality," 623-29.

Part III

NEW HORIZONS
IN TEACHING THEOLOGY

Changing Contours of Theological Education

A Retrospective

Sandra Yocum Mize

The Origin of the College Theology Society

June 12, 2004, marked the fifty-first anniversary of the opening of a workshop at The Catholic University of America featuring contemporary perspectives "on the function and purpose of theology in the college curriculum."[1] Participants considered four distinct approaches. An explicitly Thomistic approach inculcated the habit of theological thinking and judgment. Another popular approach sought "the formation of a Christlike personality" to help students "live out intelligently their function as members of the Mystical Body of Christ." A third focused on "Church documents" to privilege "the *magisterium* of the Church." A final alternative was "to do nothing but—just keep on doing what has been done." Intense discussions followed on the challenges of teaching college theology. On the workshop's fifth day, Sister M. Rose Eileen Masterman, C.S.C., proposed founding an organization for professional development and mutual support among college theology teachers.

At the suggestion of other workshop participants, Sister Rose Eileen composed a resolution, and on 18 June 1953 a lengthy resolution met the other participants' approval. It was, the resolution noted, "the stimulating and profitable exchange of ideas concerning the common objectives, the diversified procedures, and multiple problems of the departments of Theology in our undergraduate colleges" during the workshop that inspired thoughts of forming "some national organization of college teachers of Theology comparable in academic dignity and high intellectual standards to those proposed and maintained in organizations which seek to further the advancement of other disciplines on the same level of instruction." The organization would be open to "members of the clergy and religious orders, both male and female, and of the laity, who have fulfilled the requirements for higher degrees in the Sacred Sciences or in the Philosophy of Religion or their equivalent."

The resolution expounded on the organization's potential for gaining "the esteem and respect for the department of Theology among the secularistically minded educators who not infrequently hold the dominant role in the professional evaluation of our higher institutions of learning." The resolution's final sentence moved from professional concerns to theological commitments with a reiteration of the organization's role in professionalizing teaching theology in promoting "high academic achievement" to address "the many professional problems created in a society that [neglects] . . . Theology, not only in achieving academic integration, but in the only essentially ultimate integration, namely, that of the whole man in the Mystical Body of Christ on his way to the Beatific Vision."

Appealing to the Mystical Body image placed Sr. Rose Eileen and her colleagues among Catholic intellectuals for whom that ecclesial image had evoked re-imagining the laity's contribution to the life of the church as mediators of Christ's life to an ever more imposing secular culture. The image's importance even received official sanction in Pius XII's encyclical *Mystici Corporis* (1943). Laity's effectiveness as members of Christ's Mystical Body required being theologically informed and formed, and the most obvious site for such a formation was the Catholic college. From the rank and file of those who spearheaded this unprecedented endeavor of offering lay education in theology came the founding members of a Society for Catholic College Teachers of Sacred Doctrine.

This brief summary of the College Theology Society's origins serves my contribution to this panel in two ways. First, it indicates that I am to provide a bit of historical perspective on new horizons for theological education. Second, Sister Rose Eileen's resolution highlights several contours of the changes in theological education in the United States among Catholics in the twentieth century, at least as I have come to understand it. If history is an account of change over time, I can assure you that there is no shortage of material for a history of twentieth-century Catholic theological education. I am going to mention four major loci of change in theological education: the content, the site, the demographics, and the purpose.

The Shifting Contents

The founders of the College Theology Society envisioned regular opportunities for exploring the growing variety of approaches to teaching college theology. Though the spectrum of difference was far narrower in 1953, alternatives to the neo-scholastic, highly speculative, deductive theology had been actively sought and implemented at least as early as John Montgomery Cooper's inductive approach used at The Catholic University of America in the twenties. The spectrum has, of course, broadened, and the Society's fifty years of annual publications catalogue the expanding number of interpretive frameworks and their concomitant methodologies. Existentialism, personalism, historical consciousness, social and political liberation, political theory, feminism, structuralism, post-structuralism, critical theory, and cultural studies provide a partial list. Some remain; others have been superseded or subsumed in other approaches. Almost all share a common methodological starting point—experience, perhaps the quintessential multivalent theological term. Yet, I wonder if attending to these varied approaches distracts us from a more profound source of change in Catholic theological education—the use of Scripture and participatory liturgical practices.

My choice of the phrase "use of Scripture" is deliberate because my thoughts are not on highly technical and specialized Scripture scholarship, though such scholarship is enormously important and influential in what I am about to describe. I am thinking of something more mundane and even problematic for many biblical scholars—the insertion and integration of biblical images and language into overlapping and intersecting narratives of contemporary Catholic life (inclusive of thought and practice). What happens, for example, to the stories Catholics tell themselves about who they are when the biblical images of "Kingdom of God" or "Jesus-as-the-one-who-defies-all-authorities-on-behalf-of-the-marginalized" become common theological parlance not only in textbooks and classroom lectures but in daily parish life? My historical sensibility suggests to me that the answers to this question are as varied and wide-ranging as contemporary parish life and college teaching. I pose the question not to generate a definitive answer, but to encourage reflection on the more subtle influences of the uses of Scripture.

Or again, how have changes in participatory liturgical practices over the last century inserted themselves into theological education? How are theological understandings of anthropology, sin, grace, for example, re-formed by lowering the age of first communion to seven, or gradually decreasing fasting requirement from midnight to three hours to one? How are theological understandings of incarnation and redemption re-formed with the introduction of a dialogue Mass and eventually inculturated vernacular celebrations. I also wonder about the effects of the dramatic shift in actual reception of communion from primarily an act of seeing the consecrated host, to receiving it occasionally on the tongue and carefully swallowing it, to frequent reception—now, in the hand to be placed in the mouth for chewing and swallowing with a sip of consecrated wine from a common cup? How do we as Catholic theological educators understand the return of Adoration of the Blessed Sacrament among students whose cultural context is radically different from the context out of which it originated? Or again what is being communicated in current debates about politicians receiving or not receiving Eucharist? These questions are grounded in reading materials related to theological education through much of the twentieth century. Much more can and needs to be said about the appropriation of Scripture texts and liturgical practices as the undercurrents that have subtly reshaped the contours of the landscape in which theological education takes place.

The Different Sites

There are, of course, designated sites for formal theological education on this landscape. The proposal for yet another professional society of Catholic educators arose because of a unique challenge—teaching theology not in theology's then-assumed natural habitat, the seminary, but in Catholic colleges and universities. It strikes me that the term "college" has proven most critical in the society's original name, the Society of Catholic College Teachers of Sacred Doctrine. It is after all the only word other than "society" that carried over from the original title. Neither "Catholic" nor "Teacher" appears. In 1954, the founding members had chosen the Thomistic term "sacred doctrine" as a compromise. The term communicated a "scientific" approach, i.e., one that was intellectually engaging and demanding. Yet, it avoided identification, on the one hand, with seminary education, i.e., theology, and, on the other, with advanced catechesis or sodality-like activities frequently associated with "religion." The evolution of the terms "theology," "religion," and "sacred doctrine" is remarkably complex, and what I have noted here only skims the surface.

My point here is that Sister Rose Eileen's resolution clearly identifies theology or sacred doctrine as an emerging academic discipline in the college setting. Once the presumed status of theology was as an established academic department (one that would even offer a major), it could be viewed as one among many academic disciplines housed in the college or university. Hence, the queen of the sciences had to eschew her throne. In fact, the queen sometimes has to demonstrate that she deserves any place at all in the academic court—a demand that I find hard to believe would have ever emerged if theology had remained solely in the seminary context. Of course change here is not only because theological education relocated to the college. Theology as an academic discipline developed over the last fifty years when academic culture has also changed dramatically—and not just at Catholic colleges and universities. The growth in the knowledge industry in a globalized consumer culture demands far more careful consideration than these brief comments offer.

The Changing Demographics

Change in location precipitated changes in demographics of theological education. Recollect that in 1953 the new professional organization in theology was open to anyone with the appropriate academic credentials—priests, of course, but brothers and sisters as well as, and even more significantly, lay men and women. In the 1950s the vast majority of those who taught theology were priests, sisters, and brothers—listed here in numerical descending order. But their students were obviously not limited to those preparing for ordination or even for any formal religious life as sisters or brothers; they were any and all undergraduates attending a Catholic institution of higher learning.

Today, of course, the majority of those who teach theology in Catholic colleges and universities are members of the laity. Yet, especially in the first post-conciliar generation of lay Catholic theologians, many had formation in religious communities, and many of the most influential male lay theologians had been ordained. I mention this not as a lament of some past golden age of formation or to recall the bad old days. I mention it only to highlight some of the distinctive qualities and changing contexts among those who have shaped Catholic theological education over the past fifty years. Reflecting on these demographics, it is very clear to me that those who come after them/us will be carrying very different baggage than what most of us bear.

I do not pretend to understand the implications of these generational shifts nor can I adequately address the growing significance of Latino/Latina and African American Catholics in re-forming theological education. I suspect that others' reflection on the future of theological education will speculate on teaching current traditional-age undergraduates. They also inhabit a world often difficult to comprehend. They are asked to negotiate a critical understanding of an array of possibilities (real and illusory) displayed in various popular mediums even as they continue to ask the question, "Is life worth living?"—proclaimed in the not too distant past as an unabashed affirmative declaration by one of that era's own unlikely celebrities, Fulton Sheen.

The Purposes

Changes in site and demographics have no doubt transformed the purpose of theological education. It frequently appears in the general education curriculum to educate "the whole person"—to form a Catholic secular professional rather than in an extensive specialized curriculum for the Catholic religious professional. Yet I wonder sometimes how much the purposes have changed. Recall especially the first two purposes cited in the 1953 workshop—inculcating the habit of theological thinking and judgment and forming a "Christlike personality." Most faculty members today still aspire to helping students to integrate theological perspectives within various modes of critical thinking. Many others want to form students theologically so that they might be transformed for an active life dedicated to works of mercy and justice. Of course some professors simply want to do it all in their work as theological educators—which leads me to venture into the "new horizons of theological education."

I have thought a lot of late about the image of "new horizons" in preparing these reflections. When I do a three-hundred-and-sixty-degree survey, theological education's horizons appear before me more like those of Dayton, Ohio's land and urbanscape than the desertscape of Christ in the Desert, New Mexico. An explanation is in order. Dayton's horizons are cluttered and obscured with structures—old and new. In spring, amazingly beautiful and varied foliage adds beauty and texture to the view but also obscures the horizon. Admittedly, streets running through the urbanscape do provide access to much wider horizons, even eventually to those vast, open and quite beautiful horizons of New Mexico.

Entering the Chama River Valley via a one-lane dirt road on the way to Christ in the Desert, the differences in horizons are as remarkable as the view. One sees vast, open skies, at one moment an amazing blue and at another, filled with shape-shifter cloud puffs or more ominous silvery-grey thunderheads. Then the night comes, and when clear, the sky is filled with the moon and those stars that the psalmist found impossible to count. The mesa provides an open horizon filled with mystery, jutting up into the sky, hiding from our sight what resides on its flattened top or down the other side. Lowering the eyes, one sees the light changing the mesa's colorful sides, pleated like the fiesta skirts of days gone by in colors of the earth, browns, reds, greens, grays, whites—transcendent in their earthiness. The foliage here, thanks to the Chama River, is that of dark evergreen green, with bursts of yellows, reds, and purples in the flowers that top plants and even cacti. The few buildings, flat-topped, warm adobe brown, blend into the mesas as if recalling the Anasazi cliff dwellers who carved their homes into the rock. Most days such an open horizon filled with the great beauty of mystery is only the barest of memories.

Most of the time, my theology horizon remains more like that of Dayton's urbanscape rather than New Mexico's desertscape. And like the comic superhero, the Tick, "I am easily distracted by bright shiny objects." So in trying to look to the future of theological education, I find it difficult to discern any horizon because of the current clutter on the theological landscape. I am quite frankly easily distracted by those old curricular and pedagogical structures of theological education; some of which need reclamation (not restoration), and others of which simply need removal as eyesores. The newer structures of theological education usually require as much attention as the old to ensure the needs of colleagues as well as students are well served.

This cluttered horizon calls me to the challenges of the here and now of theological education. Of course, like my view of Dayton's amazing spring foliage, I see much to commend in current theological education—especially when I see in my colleagues and certainly my students a beauty varied and frequently amazing as we abide together and flourish amidst those old and new structures. Together many of us engage in theological explorations of faith in God revealed to us in Jesus Christ and enlivened in us through the Holy Spirit and in conversations with those whose intellectual and religious commitments are defined in traditions other than Christian. On occasion, I do travel those avenues that lead toward those more open horizons where one might glimpse the transformative power of God's own love and compassion—a glimpse that is as enveloping and beautiful as any sunrise atop a New Mexico mesa. At that point, I find some connection with the hope that gives promise to the future and some connection to a past in which Sister Mary Rose Eileen Masterman had the audacity to found an academic society in search of that "ultimate integration" in the Mystical Body of Christ.

Note

[1]All quotations are taken from the document entitled "Notes on proceedings compiled by Reverend Gerald Van Ackeren, S.J., 'Workshop on the [sic] Theology and Social Sciences in Catholic College Programs,' " The Catholic University, Washington, D.C., June 1953 [Social Sciences was crossed out and Theology and Social Sciences written in] CTS collection, Box 2 ACUA.

Reading the Signs of the Times

A U.S. Hispanic Perspective on the Future of Theological Education

Miguel H. Díaz

Theological educators face an increasingly daunting challenge: How can theological education respond to the wide range of students who come from diverse intellectual, technological, social, economic, political, gender, cultural, racial, and religious backgrounds? In my professional experience, which includes teaching undergraduate and graduate students, Catholic seminarians, and lay adult Catholics in diocesan formation programs, I have often wrestled with this challenge.

Many of us might lament the fact that undergraduates, as a community of students, often lack religious literacy. As I have often joked, a number of undergraduate students would readily take bets that Noah was married to Joan of Arc! With respect to graduate students, the issue is not all that different. I have found that many graduate students come into theological education as second-career students with little formal training or background in the humanities, especially with respect to philosophy, history, sociology, and religious and theological studies. A number of these students also lack adequate training in the communication skills of reading, writing, and speaking.

To this list of lamentations, I would add the matter of teaching theology at a time when we have become increasingly mindful of the role that human contexts exercise in theological reflections. Among other things, I do not think that theological education today can ignore the significant challenges that have been offered by marginalized communities. As theological reflections continue to incorporate the challenges raised by these communities with respect to content and method, it would be unfortunate not to consider the pedagogical implications that follow from these challenges. Today, it is no longer business as usual with respect to the doing of theology, but also with respect to the teaching of theology. As theological educators, we must not only become more concerned with *who* theologizes, but also with the potential contribution of other voices to the philosophy that underlies the teaching of theology. In the following reflections, I wish to address some contemporary challenges faced in undergraduate and graduate theological education.

Some Challenges in Theological Education

In an insightful article entitled "College Theology in Historical Perspective," Patrick W. Carey traced the emergence and evolution of college theology as a discipline in the United States from the 1900s to the present.[1] Carey underscored the uniqueness of the Cooper-Russell practical approach in theological studies at the Catholic University of America in the early 1900s. Carey noted how the Cooper-Russell approach, unlike other approaches, underscored a more integral understanding of religious education that included, among other things, concern for the good and the ethical transformation of society.[2] Carey argued that this approach gradually became obsolete in the face of efforts to make theological studies more "academic" in the 1960s and 1970s.[3]

According to Carey, in attempting to make theology more academic, five problems arose that we have inherited: first, the separation of theology from spirituality; second, an overestimation of the "objective" dimension of theology that leads to a lack of integration among the intellect, the will, and emotions—anthropological aspects that constitute the human person and, as such, must be considered in theological education; third, an over-emphasis on freedom of choice with respect to theological curricula in response to a consumer culture in education; fourth, the notion that to be "academic," theology would be at its best non-committal and non-confessional in nature; and fifth, a vision that provided in the past an alternative to a rebellious generation of the 1960s that was saturated with Catholic culture, but was no longer capable of addressing the needs of the present generation of students who lack a basic fundamental background in

Christian traditions.[4] Carey concluded that we need to rethink the discipline of college theology in order to provide "a new approach that will appropriate the values of the past"[5] while meeting "the new circumstances of today."[6]

Some of Carey's concerns with undergraduate education can also be found, *mutatis mutandis*, in graduate theological education. On more than one occasion, I remember having passionate conversations with colleagues on the question of how to achieve greater integration in theological education between the mind and the spirit, praxis and theory. Honesty on our part should lead us to acknowledge that this is an issue that many of us still struggle to address on an ongoing basis.

As I have noted above, like undergraduate students, many of our graduate students have entered the field of theology with little or no prior studies in religion or theology. Like the undergraduates, these students also lack a foundational background in religious and theological studies. Moreover, given the culture of consumerism that surrounds us, it is not surprising to expect its creeping influence not only on undergraduate education, but also on graduate education. A cultural ethos that leads to overemphasize unlimited freedom of choices can be reflected in both the curricula and students of theological programs. In what remains of these brief reflections, I would like to turn my attention to the potential contribution that minority theological voices and, in particular, U.S. Hispanic theologians can make to this conversation that addresses the future of theological education in the United States.

The Contribution of U.S. Hispanic Theologians to the Future of Theological Education

One does not need to turn to official data-gathering organizations to realize that the presence of African Americans, Asians, Native Americans, and other so-called "minority" communities are disproportionately underrepresented in our student and faculty bodies.[7] One can only hope that any future re-visioning of theological education will take this reality into account. In a U.S. church that is already "catholic" with respect to its ecclesial make-up, and will hopefully one day reflect this reality across its institutional life, including its educational institutions, it is imperative that any re-visioning of theological education consider the contributions of marginalized voices.

Among these voices, the growing reflections of U.S. Hispanic theologians can offer a basis from which to begin to re-vision their contributions to theological education. Reflecting a communal, praxis-oriented, liberative, and integral approach to the human reality, U. S. Hispanic theological anthropology serves as a locus from which to initiate U.S. Hispanic models in theological education.[8] One such model that has been proposed is that of theological education as *convivencia*, a concept that can be loosely translated as "life lived communally."[9]

Drawing from the anthropological insights of U.S. Hispanic theologians, Gary Riebe-Estrella proposes to understand theology as radically rooted in communal life-experiences. Riebe-Estrella conceives the role of the U.S. Hispanic theological educator less in terms of someone who imparts information and more in terms of someone who holistically mentors students into the art of theologizing *latinamente*. To theologize in this way is to constantly seek to integrate theological themes, pedagogy, and the loci of theological education with ordinary communal experiences, especially the experiences of the poor and marginalized. "The meaning of integration," argues Riebe-Estrella, "is broadened to include not just integration among theological disciplines within the student, but also the integration of what the student is learning within the community and the church."[10]

Riebe-Estrella's approach to theological education reflects a U.S. Hispanic Catholic anthropological vision that seeks integration among human and divine realities, and among all human experiences. A philosophy of education that takes as its foundation this integral vision is not likely to precipitate problems such as those pointed out by Carey with respect to contemporary approaches in theological education. Integration in theology leaves little room for unnatural separations between theology and spirituality or between theological theory and praxis. Moreover, this integral perspective leaves little room for isolating theological education from other forms of learning. In an integral vision of theological education, the teaching of theology belongs *with* the teaching of the other human sciences, especially history, philosophy, and sociology. At a time when interdisciplinary conversations have become increasingly essential in doing and teaching theology, theological education programs, especially those that are free-standing, need to keep this in mind if they are to promote a more integral reading of the "signs of the times" among their students.

Beyond these challenges, theological education today cannot avoid addressing questions of religious plurality. In the aftermath of 9/11, we have witnessed how religious principles have driven persons to act in positive as well as negative ways against the others in their midst. Many of us have been placed face to face with what is foreign, especially with respect to religious matters. Few, however, have been given the proper tools for conversational engagement of this other. Without abandoning the particularity of its Christian traditions, Catholic theological education needs to take the initiative to invite the next generation of students to deepen and expand their appreciation for the catholicity of religious truths. In this matter, greater critical examination of the familial history of U.S. Hispanics might offer timely tools for fostering such an appreciation.

The careful study of the various forms of our ancestors' *convivencia*, that is, the grace-filled choosing as well as forced-filled living together that lies at the root of our *mestizo/mulatto* identities (particularly with respect to intercultural, interracial, and interreligious relationships among our Spanish, Jewish, Arab, Indigenous, and African ancestors) might have something of value to contribute to the human diversity that we increasingly face today. Whether as a result of conquest, expansion, immigration, or exile, the experience of living with others has profoundly shaped the history of U.S. Hispanics. This experience produced in the past and continues to birth today a particular way of being Catholic. Above all, Latino/a identity has been born in the process of living "in-between" different worlds (e.g., the Indigenous and Spanish, the African and Spanish, the Anglo and Hispanic). This dynamic process, comprised of various socio-cultural negotiations, is partly responsible for fostering openness to the other in U.S. Hispanic communities. This process has yielded a unique way of being "catholic" (e.g., living a life inclusive of the other), and has produced a particular embodiment of living the Catholic faith *latinamente*.

In facing new horizons and new challenges in theology it will be our task to continue to mentor students in the task of seeking ongoing human understanding, adoration of the living God, and transformation of the world around us. While relentless in our efforts to sustain academic rigor, we need to embrace a philosophy that promotes an integral vision willing to extend the art of theological education beyond the classroom in order to weave and include the wisdom of various Catholic traditions into the very fabric of society.

Notes

[1]Patrick W. Carey, "College Theology in Historical Perspective," *American Catholic Traditions: Resources for Renewal*, ed. Sandra Yocum Mize and William Portier (Maryknoll, N.Y.: Orbis Books, 1996), 242-71.

[2]Ibid., 249-53.

[3]Ibid., 262.

[4]Ibid., 266-68.

[5]Ibid., 268.

[6]Ibid.

[7]For such evidence see, for instance, the ATS (Association of Theological Schools) 2003-04 Fact Book contained in their web site: www.ats.edu/data/factbook.htm. See also Fernando F. Segovia, "Minority Studies and Christian Studies," in *Theological Reflections on America from the Margins: A Dream Unfinished*, ed. Eleazar S. Fernandez & Fernando F. Segovia (Maryknoll, N.Y.: Orbis Books, 2001), 1-33.

[8]On U.S. Hispanic theological anthropology, see my book, *On Being Human: U.S. Hispanic and Rahnerian Perspectives* (Maryknoll, N.Y.: Orbis Books, 2000).

[9]See Gary Riebe-Estrella, "Theological Education as *Convivencia*," in *From the Heart of Our People: Latino/a Explorations in Catholic Systematic Theology*, ed. Orlando O. Espín and Miguel H. Díaz (Maryknoll, N.Y.: Orbis Books, 1999), 209-16.

[10]Ibid., 214.

New Horizons in Theological Education

Mary Ann Hinsdale

As we look toward new horizons in theological education, three issues provide members of the College Theology Society with prescriptive challenges for our work as theological educators, if not for the next fifty years, certainly for the next twenty-five. The first issue has to do with the need to clarify our present understanding of theological education. The second issue concerns the impact of changing demographics, both of our students and of ourselves as theological educators. The growth in the number of lay theologians and of women theologians, in particular, has been greeted with enthusiasm. However, there are some additional issues regarding this demographic shift that deserve attention. The third issue concerns the need to share "best practices" with regard to undergraduate curricula and graduate student teacher preparation. In conclusion, I offer some anecdotal reflections based upon my experience over the last twenty years in a variety of contexts: seminary, undergraduate theology and Catholic studies, graduate pastoral ministry, and doctoral-level theological education.

Undergraduate Theological Education

What do we understand by "theological education," particularly at the undergraduate level? Should it be primarily academic or pastoral—or both? Do we consider theological education a "ministry"? An important first task in reflecting upon "new horizons in theological education" is to examine whether we can agree on, or whether it is even possible to have, a common, shared understanding of "theological education."

Miguel Díaz already has referred to Pat Carey's excellent essay,

"College Theology in Historical Perspective," originally presented at the 1996 meeting of the College Theology Society.[1] I, too, want to recall that essay. The problematic consequences that Carey identified as resulting from the adoption of an "academic study of religion" approach to teaching college theology in the early 1970s have been thoroughly reviewed for us by Miguel Díaz. I want to focus on just one of Carey's points; namely, the historical fact that whether one approaches college theology as "the study of religious phenomena" (i.e., neutral, objective, and descriptive, as in "religious studies"), or whether one advocates an Anselmian "faith seeking understanding" approach (i.e., "theological studies")—both religious studies and theological studies wish to be considered rigorously academic.

Both approaches want the respect of other academic disciplines in the college or university and, thus, have gradually moved away from what they considered to be "outdated pastoral functions" of college-level theology or religious studies. Certainly, most of us still hold that the goal to be rigorously academic continues to be a worthy aim of our vocation as theological educators. Nevertheless, forty years ago there was some reluctance to completely abandon "the pastoral task" in undergraduate theology and, in some ways, I believe we are still avoiding this issue.

Carey cites Bernard Cooke's address to the 1966 National Catholic Education Association to illustrate this ambivalence. Cooke argued that "the goals of deepening students' faith, promoting Christian behavior, and encouraging apostolic activities were not 'proper academic objectives' " of theology. However, Cooke did not want to eschew such goals entirely. Referring to "pastoral or fringe objectives," Cooke endorsed a pastoral role for college theology by explaining that pastoral objectives "introduce into the psychological receptivity of the student the all-important elements of the practical experience of Christianity." Thus, he asked, "Is not the experience of liturgy and the experience of the Church in apostolic action as essential an experimental foundation for theologizing as laboratory work is for the speculation of the physical sciences?"[2]

While Cooke was clearly able to distinguish between pastoral and academic roles, he did not fully separate them. That would happen a few years later when the Society of Catholic College Teachers of Sacred Doctrine changed its name to the College Theology Society, ostensibly in order to become more ecumenical and to demonstrate its academic rather than confessional allegiances. Yet, as Carey points out, "one of the chief characteristics of this academic approach was its separation from spiritual formation." This separation became institutionalized in the late 1960s and early 1970s with the development of campus ministry departments on Catholic college campuses (as distinct from the role of college chaplain, a role almost universally held by a resident Catholic priest who conducted campus liturgies and administered the sacraments). As theology and religious studies departments sought greater academic respectability, they became separated from the spiritual development of students—an area that was now the domain of campus ministry. Even today on some campuses, a line of demarcation exists that prevents campus ministers from teaching theology courses in departments of religious studies and theology.[3]

Elizabeth Johnson and Joseph Komonchak have also referred to the history of the development of the College Theology Society with respect to differentiating the teaching of college theology from the theology taught in seminaries. Yet, no one at this conference has yet ventured to say what should be the focus or content of undergraduate theology *today*. Recently, several of our colleagues have published articles in *America* and *Commonweal* that suggest that perhaps we are again at a crossroads of having to decide what we should be doing in teaching college theology and religious studies. As professors of undergraduate theology, I pose this question: do we need to shift our sights toward a new horizon regarding what we mean by "theological education"?

Here it might be well to recall some of the different meanings one can give to the meaning of "horizon." As Komonchak reminded us, a horizon can be understood as *a limiting factor*; but it can also be seen as something expansive, referring to the hopeful exercise of the imagination that attempts to scrutinize the "signs of the times" in order to prepare for the future. It is this latter sense of "horizon" that I want to recall in exploring the challenges that confront us in undergraduate theological education as we face our second half century as a professional society. Although some of us are well aware of the problematic issues in undergraduate theological education, I also want to suggest that these issues carry over into graduate theological education, since, after all, many of today's graduate students were once the "religiously illiterate" undergraduates we began to lament during the 1990s.

Two problem areas in college theology continue to surface: first, the emergence of religious fundamentalism and, second, general religious illiteracy, particularly on the part of students who were, as they tell us, "raised Catholic," and are "spiritual, but not religious." By the way, that latter phrase need not be limited to generations X and Y. As Jeremy Langford points out in *God Moments: Why Faith Really Matters to a New Generation*, this particular phrase has been heard more and more on the lips of middle-aged baby boomers as well.[4]

Varied prescriptions have been offered as a way of responding to the malaise created by these problems. Richard Gaillardetz, for example, has suggested we adopt a "dialogical apologetics," a proposal that he hopes will not only counter the overly narrow apologetics emanating from traditionalist Catholic writers, such as theologian Scott Hahn or philosopher Peter Kreeft, but will also serve as an antidote to ineffective catechesis and stand up to the challenges of Protestant biblical fundamentalists.[5] John Cavadini's solution to the problem of young adult ignorance of the faith is "a renewed pedagogy of the basics," which involves articulate, adult-level presentations of creedal affirmations, coupled with an appeal to "the sheer beauty, richness, and sophistication of Catholicism's two-thousand year-old traditions"; in short, with "formation."[6] Finally, one of our (at least for the present) "younger" theologians, Christopher Ruddy, recommends summer theology institutes, particularly for their contribution to the preparation of lay ecclesial ministers who do not have the luxury of full-time theological study. Ruddy exhorts bishops, universities, and Catholic benefactors to increase their financial support of such programs.

Although each of these proposals is commendable, no one has undertaken to suggest a programmatic scheme that includes curriculum proposals or suggested pedagogy for undergraduate college theology. I believe this work needs to be done—and it is work that belongs to those of us who call ourselves theological educators. As Sandra Yocum Mize reminded us, our students' ignorance is not a new problem. It has been nearly ten years since Pat Carey tried to get us to consider seriously the question of undergraduate theological education. The time has come to address this matter in a systematic way. If fifty years ago the issue of what should constitute theological education for the college-educated Catholic laity was deemed significant enough to warrant the founding of a professional society, fifty years later, as we face what some have referred to as the dissolution of the

"Catholic subculture" in the United States,[7] it has become a task that is *critical*, not only to our profession, but to the future of the local church itself.

The Changing Demographics of Theologians

What impact do the changing demographics of theologians have upon theological education? Both Elizabeth Johnson and Sandra Yocum Mize refer to these changing demographics in their essays. Johnson points out that the "who" doing the teaching of college theology has changed and that we need to listen to these "new voices." Certainly chief among the "new voices" who have become part of the living tradition of theological education are lay theologians, both male and female. However, in addition to ecclesiastical status (i.e., not being ordained), an additional demographic shift not often referred to is that the typical "lay theologian" is no longer a former seminarian, priest, or sister, nor even a presently vowed woman religious or religious brother.

As a college trustee, I have often listened to college admissions officers refer to certain students as "FTIACs," an acronym that stands for "first-time-in-any-college" (as opposed to transfer, or returning adult) students. Well, I would like to propose an acronym to describe the changing demographics of Catholic theologians, the NBIASCs: "never-been-in-any-seminary-or-convent." This new group of theologians is predominantly of a "post-Vatican II" generation but, perhaps even more significantly, they are not products of a religious and spiritual formation that took place in a novitiate or seminary, as was the case for many of us middle-aged lay theologians. To be sure, there are some exceptions, but I think it can safely be said that fewer and fewer theologians bring the formational background that someone who spent even six months in religious life or seminary might have received.

When I served as secretary of the Catholic Theological Society of America (1996-2003), I was frequently asked for statistics concerning the number of Catholic women theologians in comparison with male theologians. According to the most current CTSA membership database, Catholic male theologians continue to outnumber women: out of a total of 1,641 members, 481 are women, or a little less than 30 percent. Figures from the College Theology Society show a somewhat larger proportion of women members: of 1,017 CTS members,

380 (37 percent) are women. Many theologians belong to both societies, but because of different origins and different admissions requirements, the CTS also tends to have fewer clerical members than the CTSA.[8]

While most of the first women who received doctorates in theology tended to be members of religious orders, the number of non-vowed lay women receiving doctorates in theology has steadily increased over the past thirty years.[9] For example, if one examines statistics from the CTS and CTSA, the two professional societies to which most Catholic women theologians tend to belong, one finds that in the 1970s, of 55 women who earned doctorates in theology, 24 (44 percent) were non-vowed lay women and 31 (56 percent) were vowed women religious. In the 1980s, of 138 women earning doctorates, 65 (47 percent) were non-vowed lay women and 73 (52 percent) were women religious. In the 1990s, of 156 women admitted, 105 (67 percent) were non-vowed lay women and 51 (33 percent) were women religious. In the most recent four-year period, from 2000 to 2003, of the 51 women who have earned doctorates in theology, 40 (78 percent) are non-vowed lay women. As of this writing, 60 of 71 women "associate members" in the CTSA (i.e., persons who have completed all requirements for the doctoral degree except the dissertation), or 85 percent, are lay. Thus, the women who will be shaping theology in the future are predominantly non-vowed lay women.

Despite the fact that male theologians still outnumber women theologians (three to one in the case of the CTSA), the impression created by both the CTSA and CTS conventions is that women make up a considerably larger percentage of the membership than this, perhaps even 50 percent. This appears to be so because many more women than men play an active role in conventions.

Most would hold that the inclusion of women in the theological guild is a good thing; yet, it also has put a great deal of pressure on Catholic women theologians who work in academe, which remains very much "a man's world." Like the situation in most seminaries and ministerial schools of theology (even before the Vatican-mandated visitation—some would say, "inquisition"—that took place in the 1980s), women continue to be underrepresented as faculty in Catholic institutions that grant doctoral degrees in theology. A search of the websites of Catholic theology doctoral programs in the United States reveals that the number of women faculty is still quite small.[10]

If one looks at tenured women theologians, the number shrinks even more. Yet, these same women are often asked to serve on departmental and university committees in greater frequency than their male counterparts. In charting the "progress" of increasing representation of women theologians, attention also needs to be given to the equitability of "workload." The "balancing act" that women theologians who have children are called upon to perform is only beginning to be discussed in theological circles.

The questions that Claire Wolfteich raises in *Navigating New Terrain: Work and Women's Spiritual Lives*[11] deserve further reflection by the theological academy, particularly as younger lay women, both those who are married and have families and those who are single, join our ranks. A woman colleague of mine who is married and the mother of several children, for example, declared that "no woman should think about being a theologian without a dual-income family." This is a worry for several women graduate students whom I interviewed recently in preparation for the 2004 Madeleva lecture.[12]

Wolfteich's book aims to discuss two questions: "What are the spiritual and theological issues raised by women's increasing work force participation?" and "What theological and spiritual resources do religious traditions hold to address those issues?" In light of her questions, I would add this further question: "How does the work of teaching theology and doing theological scholarship influence women's sense of identity and purpose?" More specifically, we can ask how being a theologian, or "doing theology," influences their attitudes about the importance of family and religion, spheres that are traditionally dependent upon women. Wolfteich observes that today, when 60 percent of U.S. women have paying jobs (compared to 28 percent in 1940), it is important to reflect upon how work (whether in the home, in the church, or in secular jobs) *forms* women.

Work gives an experience of community and friendship, or an experience of isolation and competition. Work shapes definitions of success and fulfillment. Work presents spiritual and ethical challenges. Women form habits through their work—habits of integrity or cutting corners, habits of balance or dissipation, habits of believing they are worth something or not.[13]

Wolfteich points out that religious groups have not looked in-depth at how changing work roles shape women or how women respond creatively to their situation. I would say this is especially true for the situation of NBIASCs, especially women theologians. Conscious of the dangers of essentializing "women's experience" here, I only suggest that there needs to be a thorough reflection from the standpoint of spirituality about how women theologians integrate their vocations as theologians with their vocations as committed life-partners, whether vowed religious or married persons.[14]

The Need for Collecting "Best Practices"

In order to clarify our present understanding of theological education, the first issue I raised, I would suggest that the College Theology Society begin to collect some of our "best practices" as we seek to envision theological education for the twenty-first century. Attention should be given to the interesting Lilly-funded study, *Religion on Campus: What Religion Really Means to Today's Undergraduates*.[15] Using qualitative research methods at different types of institutions, the four authors find that the secularization hypothesis does not hold water with respect to religiously sponsored institutions. They conclude that religion is alive on college campuses. While the book is not as helpful for developing proposals for curriculum and pedagogy that address current needs in undergraduate theological education, the method employed seems to hold great possibility and is a place to begin.

In order to prognosticate about new horizons in theological education we need better data about what we are actually doing in our core courses and in our majors. Can those of us who teach in comprehensive institutions that require core courses or general education requirements in Catholic theology for undergraduates *and* offer graduate degree programs, whether ministerial or academic, really "do it all"? I believe that perhaps we are at a juncture where the College Theology Society could provide a great service in undertaking a study of "best practices" that exist in our Catholic colleges and universities that would shed more light on the state of Catholic theological education at all levels.

Emerging Issues

Other issues also deserve reflection when considering "new horizons in theological education" but, for reasons of time, I will mention them only briefly by posing some questions for further reflection. First, I have a concern about the "commodification of theology."

Increasingly, publishers seem to want "textbooks" from us, since they will have an assured market. Are important matters that deserve theological reflection going to malinger by the wayside, simply because they do not meet the market requirements?

Second, will feminist/womanist/*mujerista* theology survive? This may sound like an odd question, given that the changing demographics of theologians means more lay theologians and especially more women. I raise this question, however, despite the fact that I believe that intellectual historians of the twentieth century will judge "feminist theology" as the major contribution of women to the discipline of theology.

It has been more than one hundred and fifty years since the ordination of Antoinette Brown Blackwell in the United Church of Christ, more than one hundred years since Elizabeth Cady Stanton published *The Women's Bible*, seventy-five years since Virginia Woolf wrote "A Room of One's Own," a little more than thirty-five years since Teresa of Avila and Catherine of Siena were officially proclaimed doctors of the church, and just over thirty years since Mary Daly wrote *Beyond God the Father*. With Sheila Briggs, I think we can say that "feminist theology is no longer marginal to the discipline except in the eyes of a patriarchal ostrich with its head in the sand."[16]

And yet, it has been my experience that undergraduate theology courses (and even some graduate courses) that use the word "feminist" in the title are often under-subscribed and sometimes even have to be cancelled. And this is certainly not because the struggle for women's equality or the liberation from patriarchy has been won. Rather, it is because the words "feminist" and "feminism" have become the new "f" words. In some cases, younger women students feel that sexism is a battle their mothers had to fight, but as far as they are concerned, "there is nothing I cannot do just because I am a woman" ("OK, the church still has some silly ideas about not ordaining women, but once they find out there's no one left to do the work, they'll eventually get over it; and besides, I'm 'spiritual,' not 'religious'—so, I'm not really invested in institutions like the church"). Then, too, the likes of Rush Limbaugh and "hate radio" have practically destroyed the word with the slur "feminazi."

Anne Clifford's excellent book, *Introducing Feminist Theology*,[17] does one of the best jobs I know in debunking the myth that the post-baby boom generation no longer needs feminism. I have used her book in my classes and students have really appreciated it, but I have to admit that I call the class (which really is a class in feminist theologies) "Women and the Church."

The third issue I want to raise concerns some "first steps" that those of us who teach undergraduates might take in our attempts to restore a pastoral dimension to our work. Some years ago at a CTS convention, in the American Catholic Life and Thought Section, we discussed what we were doing in the "introductory course." I was quoted in the *National Catholic Reporter* as saying that when I began teaching college theology, I did not know I was doing "missionary work." That was a rather flippant remark, I admit. But one of the first principles of evangelization that all missionaries are exhorted to practice is to listen to the culture. I ask, with respect to our current undergraduates, do we really "listen to the culture of our students"? This is a continuing challenge that I think needs to be taken up as we move into the next stage of developing the aims of teaching college theology.

I want to share an important lesson that I learned from Dr. Helen Lewis, a woman who is both a sociologist and anthropologist, who has served as director of the Highlander Center, the alternative adult education center founded by Myles Horton that trained the pioneers of the civil rights movement (Martin Luther King, Stokely Carmichael, Rosa Parks, and others) and other leaders of poor rural communities. I pass on this advice as we begin to rethink the enterprise of undergraduate theological education. It involves what some might call "mentoring," but I prefer to call "accompaniment." Lewis never went to a conference or gave a talk without bringing a student along with her. Many of us do this with our graduate students, but I would suggest that we do this with undergraduates as well. In doing this, we can also position ourselves as "learners" who are interested in "listening to the culture."

It is no secret that "service" and "outreach" have become, in the words of the director of campus ministry at Boston College, "the new sacrament" on college campuses. Several of us have already joined student immersion trips or study-abroad trips during semester and spring breaks and I think we should continue to be involved in these endeavors. With a little creativity, I think we can come up with other collaborative experiences that would not only give us greater insight into the culture of our undergraduate (and graduate) students and provide us with greater contextual information for how to approach our classes, but such "accompaniment" experiences would also provide an opportunity for engaging the "pastoral objectives" that Bernard Cooke was ambivalent about losing some forty years ago.

I am not suggesting here that we become campus ministers or turn our classrooms into "mini-novitiates" as some of the traditionalist Catholic colleges and universities seem to be doing. On the other hand, as I listen to many of the concerns and longings of people on both sides of the generational divide, I think that those of us who call ourselves "theologians" and who claim to have "an ecclesial vocation" need to take a new look at how spiritual formation can be integrated with the academic study of undergraduate and graduate theology. It would be a bit ironic, it seems to me, if the revival of "vocation" language, so in vogue on many of our campuses due to recently received Lilly endowment grants, becomes the parlance only of career counseling centers, campus ministry, and mission and ministry offices.

Personally, I find the challenges of these new horizons in theological education invigorating and look forward to engaging the questions and suggestions I have raised. The alternative, of course, is to sit back and watch the sun set. But, as a friend of mine often reminds me, "we have to earn the sunrise." I have confidence, drawn from these last fifty years, that we are up to it.

Notes

[1]Patrick W. Carey, "College Theology in Historical Perspective," in *American Catholic Traditions*, ed. Sandra Yocum Mize and William Portier (Maryknoll, N.Y.: Orbis Books, 1996), 42-71.

[2]Bernard Cooke, "The Place of Theology in the Curriculum of the Catholic College," *NCEA Bulletin* 63 (1966): 210-13; cited by Patrick Carey in "College Theology in Historical Perspective," 262.

[3]This was true, for example, when I taught at the College of the Holy Cross (1987-2003). In schools with doctoral programs in theology, where graduate students routinely serve as instructors in required "core" courses as part of the service required for doctoral subsidy, qualified campus ministers also serve as theology teachers.

[4]Jeremy Langford, *God Moments: Why Faith Really Matters to a New Generation* (Maryknoll, N.Y.: Orbis Books, 2001). For an insightful article on the popular refrain, "I'm spiritual, but not religious," see Sandra M. Schneiders, "Religion vs. Spirituality: A Contemporary Conundrum," *Spiritus* 2 (2003): 163-85.

[5]Richard Gaillardetz, "Do We Need a New(er) Apologetics?" *America* (February 2, 2004): 26-33.

[6]John C. Cavadini, "Ignorant Catholics: The Alarming Void in Religious Education," *Commonweal* 131 (April 9, 2004): 12-14.

[7]For a provocative analysis of the implications of the "dissolution of the American Catholic subculture," see William Portier, "Here Come the Catholic Evangelicals," *Communio* 31/1 (Spring 2004): 35-66.

[8]These statistics are from the 2003 on-line directories of the CTSA (http://www.jcu.edu/ctsa/) and the CTS (http://bc.edu/cts/). The history of the CTSA is currently being written by Jeffrey Marlett of the College of St. Rose and should be available for the Society's sixtieth anniversary in 2005. Sandra Yocum Mize has written an updated history of the College Theology Society for its fiftieth anniversary in 2004 (Lanham, Md.: Rowman & Littlefield, 2005). See also John P. Boyle and Mary Ann Hinsdale, "Academic Theology: Why We Are Not What We Were," in *What's Left?*, ed. Mary Jo Weaver (Bloomington, Ind.: University of Indiana Press, 1999), 111-31.

[9]Technically, all women in the Roman Catholic church are "lay" women, since they are not ordained. In addition, "non-vowed" women is something of a misnomer, since married lay women are indeed "vowed." I resort to this terminology simply for the purpose of distinguishing the two canonical classes of "lay women."

[10]Cf. Laurie Wright Garry, "Sunsets and New Horizons," presented to the Women and Religion Section, CTS annual meeting, 2004.

[11]Claire E. Wolfteich. *Navigating New Terrain: Work and Women's Spiritual Lives* (Mahwah, N.J.: Paulist Press, 2002).

[12]See Mary Ann Hinsdale, *Women Shaping Theology* (Mahwah, N.J.: Paulist Press, 2004).

[13]Wolfteich, *Navigating New Terrain*, 4.

[14]This increasingly "lay" character of theology is the broader context in which women's work in theology needs to be assessed. But it is not only the experience of women theologians that needs to be reflected upon here. For example, when I taught in the religious studies department at the College of the Holy Cross during the 1990s, it was mostly the *men* in the department who bore the responsibility for child care during the day, since their academic schedules were more flexible than the work situations of their wives. The women in the department were either single, vowed women religious, or women whose children were grown. On snow days and teacher meeting days, the department secretary's office often took on the character of a nursery, complete with toys and diaper bags. Of course, it is a whole other issue as to why the College did not have on-campus day care or include this provision as a benefit. But the gap between the *theory* of "Catholic social teaching" and actual *practice* in Catholic institutions is a subject for another article.

[15]Conrad Cherry, Betty A. DeBerg, and Amanda Porterfield, with the assistance of William Durbin and John Schmalzbauer, *Religion on Campus:*

What Religion Really Means to Today's Undergraduates (Chapel Hill: University of North Carolina Press, 2001).

[16]Sheila Briggs, "A History of Our Own: What Would a Feminist History of Theology Look Like?" in *Horizons in Feminist Theology: Identity, Tradition and Norms*, ed. Rebecca S. Chopp and Sheila Greeve Davaney (Minneapolis: Fortress Press, 1997), 165.

[17]Anne M. Clifford, *Introducing Feminist Theology* (Maryknoll, N.Y.: Orbis Books, 2001).

Teaching Theology for the Future

James A. Donahue

Our topic—the future shape of theological teaching and learning—is most timely and important. Since its inception, the College Theology Society has always provided leadership and direction to professors of theology and religion teaching in college and university contexts, and it is fitting that at this time in history we should pause to take stock of where we have been, where we are, and, most important, where we are going.

This is a most decisive moment for theology. We live in a time when the assumptions and practices about theology and religion have undergone enormous changes. What have been until now commonly shared understandings of our work are going through significant shifts. It is time to reflect on learning and teaching theology for the future.

One of my fundamental assumptions about the work we do as theologians and professors is that our insights, our theologies, our methods, and our pedagogies are shaped by our own particular experiences as individuals and as communities. This is certainly not a shocking insight; it is the basic tenet of any contextual theology. Context, while not everything, has an enormous influence on how we go about our work.

Personally, this means that my own theological outlook has been shaped by my work as a professor of theology at the undergraduate, professional school, and graduate school levels, primarily during my fifteen years at Georgetown University, in my role as a university administrator in students affairs (as dean and vice president at Georgetown); and by my role over the past five years as president of a consortium of graduate schools of theology and seminaries at the Graduate Theological Union at Berkeley. In summary, my insights are the result of both my theoretical and intellectual involvements in the academy and in my practical involvements in university and church life. I characterize myself as a theological ethicist with very practical interests and experiences. It should be no surprise therefore that my remarks today will reflect these multiple experiences.

I want to make an important distinction: there is a fundamental difference in the way that we think about teaching theology and religion at undergraduate and graduate levels. Moreover, the differences between graduate work in theology and religion as an academic undertaking and professional training for ministry require different lenses of analyses in that each of these undertakings is intended for different purposes.

What does the religious and theological world need? And what do we as theologians need to do to prepare leaders to address the future? To answer these questions we must look at several issues that are readily apparent in our world today. They are best described as a set of dynamics that have a push-pull quality to them because we live in the midst of tensions that push and pull us in differing ways. The challenge is to find ways of developing a sense of equilibrium or integration in the midst of these forces.

First, we are *fragmented* and seek unity, both within ourselves as well as in the social world we inhabit. The *self* is being pushed and pulled in many directions—our time, our commitments, our values, our loyalties, our priorities are all stretched. At times we are forced to make compromises that do not set easy with our inner selves. Our *society*, our churches, and our religious communities are pushed and pulled as well. Our sense of community is eroding; the associations and institutions that have long kept us together now seem to be driving us apart. We find ourselves in a world of division and seeming moral relativism in which our senses of right, wrong, and responsibility get increasingly ambiguous and blurry. In the midst of this chaos, we long for integration, unity, and connectedness. We look to religion and theology for answers.

Our search for clarity and certainty in the midst of these dynamics has led many to embrace a certain kind of religious orthodoxy, or theological dogmatism, that I believe manifests at heart a religious piety that is inexcusably simplistic and reductionistic. Although such orthodoxy may serve a functional need to provide clarity and comfort, it too easily evades the more challenging work of theological and religious appropriation and construction that our times and our circumstances call for.

Second, our emerging connections through *globalization* also increase our desire for authenticity. That we are now a global world is indisputable. This coming together, made possible by new technologies and the development of communications, has proved valuable through the sharing of goods and economies, cultures and religions. However, within this larger networked community full of differing ideas, resistance has emerged. It has proved difficult to preserve the uniqueness and the particularity that protects and honors the specificity and authenticity of cultural integrity. No matter what benefits are gained from global connectedness, there is always a basic human desire to be valued, validated, and deemed worthy of acceptance for our own particular uniqueness—to be seen as our true selves. We can and should resist becoming homogenized and interchangeable parts in a global network. Thus, we pursue authenticity and claim unique identity. Again, we look to religion and theology for answers.

Third, religious *pluralism* plays an enormous role in discussions about globalization. The concept of pluralism engages fundamental questions about the relationships among varieties of forms of beliefs and raises issues of the commensurability and status of competing truth claims. Pluralism also raises basic issues of the legitimacy of religious authority in cultures and societies, as well as for individuals. Pluralism refers to the fact that the world is interpreted in multiple ways, subject to open and rational dialogue. In discussions about religious pluralism, we explore the idea of unity among differences and how to affirm our bonds of togetherness without eroding the significance of unique expressions of religious beliefs and practices.

The pushes and pulls of religious pluralism raise issues about how we understand and relate to issues of difference and otherness, religious or otherwise. Questions of authenticity and adequacy are raised as well, as individuals and groups seek to understand how their own particular construal of religious reality can be justified, embraced, and defended.

Fourth, we have a *spiritual hunger* that longs for experiences and structures of meaning, purpose, and passion. We live in a time that has been characterized as "post-denominational" in that we are seeking deep meaning and religious meaning wherever we can find it, often in the secular as well as in the sacred arenas and certainly in new forms of religious expression. Yet, we still seek in our religious denominations the values, the community support, and rituals they have traditionally provided. It is no wonder that the greatest growth in religious practices and denominations has been among the evangelical and pentecostal churches throughout the world. With their clear commitments, strong tenets, community focus, and heightened experiences of piety and devotional engagement, these groups fill a void that is frequently present in many traditions of religious practice, especially in a globalized society with its threat of homogenization. We as a people are yearning for a clear meaningful path to follow and, again, we look to religion and theology for answers.

These and other characteristics of our age necessitate a new kind of religious leadership for the academy, the churches, and the world. With this then as our context, the future direction of theological teaching and learning will need to respond to these realities. I suggest that this will and should mean different things for both undergraduate and graduate teaching.

Teaching and Learning Theology in the Undergraduate Experience

Again, the context. My assumption is that there is no singular profile of the type of student who comes to us in our undergraduate theology classes. Some have a developed understanding of their own religious traditions. Some are culturally religious with little sense of the substance of real theological issues. Some are religiously indifferent and theologically illiterate. Our role as professors, therefore, is one of introduction, not just in the introductory courses, but in the undergraduate theology curriculum as a whole. While certainly we construct our curricula with a developmental view of providing increasing sophistication in the field, our primary task throughout the undergraduate years is to teach our students the many forms of theological questions and theological issues. As teachers of theology, our task is to help them to understand the nature of what theology is, how it functions, what it does and does not do, and how it is useful for religiously and intellectually serious people to navigate the waters of religious and theological inquiry. In essence, the goal is to clarify the landscape of theology.

Key to this task is giving students the ability to make distinctions. Students all too frequently conflate religious education, catechesis, religious and theological studies, and religious faith and practice. This confusion presents a conceptual quandary for students that is far reaching, both in the classroom and academy and in the world of everyday practice. While there are several confusions that call out for clarification, and distinctions that need to be made in the theological landscape, I will suggest a few themes that I find deserve special attention in the undergraduate context.

- The distinctions between the nature and scope of theology, faith, religious beliefs and convictions, organized religion, faith traditions and denominations;
- The distinctions between theology, catechesis, and religious education;
- The relationships between theology and culture, with particular attention to how theology and religion play a role in the culture wars that dominate our social landscape;
- The theory and practice of theology;
- Distinctions between religion, faith, and spirituality;
- The idea of contextual theology;
- The relationship between theology and scripture with particular attention to issues of what constitutes an authoritative basis for religious and theological claims;
- The realities of religious pluralism and the landscape of how religious traditions engage in dialogue over issues that are central to the truth claims of each tradition;
- The sacred and secular distinctions with particular attention to a theology of revelation;
- The differences between theology and other academic disciplines.

The tools for determining what is essential to any religious or theological tradition are of critical importance for undergraduate theology. Many of our students, particularly our Catholic students, grapple with the issue of what it means to identify with a religious tradition. What does it mean to be a Catholic—not only historically, but also today? Our responsibility is to provide our students with the skills for making these determinations.

These distinctions are important in that they are essential to the realization of other goals that are central to the teaching of theology. Theology as a discipline is connected in an integral way to the practice of religion. As such, its role is to provide a means for this practice to be critically constructed and intellectually shaped. In other words, theology must enable religious practitioners to base their choices and decisions on solid criteria that can be reasoned, defended, and justified in intellectually serious ways. I would pose therefore that the goals of theology must be focused on developing our students' skills to:

- Give reasons and arguments for what constitutes the authenticity of religious experience;
- Reasonably justify the authority upon which religious claims are made;
- Develop criteria of adequacy for justifying religious convictions;
- Defend the autonomous (versus heteronomous) nature of religious claims;
- Give good reasons for what and why one believes.

While helping our students develop the skills to make distinctions and defend religious positions is an essential goal of our work, I propose that there is even a more overarching goal that we as professors must keep in mind and aim for. It is a pedagogical goal more than a substantive one, and it is simply to make our discipline engaging, interesting, and compelling. Perhaps it is an overstatement to say that one of our goals ought to be to allow our students the opportunity to fall in love with theological questions. A measure of the success for any professor is the degree to which our students are engaged in the material of our discipline. For me, this has always translated to setting as a minimum goal for my classes that my students not be bored or uninterested. I would argue that there is a committed passion in the work of theology that is intrinsic to the discipline. It would be my hope that our students would become enlivened with this passion.

Theology, Student Affairs, and Institutional Life

It has been most interesting for me to witness the role that theological questions play in the everyday practice and discourse within colleges and universities, particularly those with religious histories and identities. For many students and faculty, theology intersects their lives predominantly in matters pertaining to their everyday experiences and to the cultural and social issues that are predominant in the activities of students' lives. Institutionally these issues are typically under the purview of the Office of Student Affairs. Issues of human sexuality, cultural and racial diversity, social justice, lifestyle choices, residential living matters, sexual harassment, church oversight of academic freedom, and free speech issues are but some examples of very practical matters that occur in the everyday activities of college campuses. How colleges as institutions think about these theologically is an arena of concern that, I believe, has been far too long absent from the central concerns of many theologians and religious scholars. Faculty are quick to point out that these matters are "merely" matters for the student life staff while "real" theological thinking occurs in the classroom and in the curriculum. The problem with this view, of course, is that it misses the obvious fact that theological thinking and discourse happen with much greater frequency in the informal cultural and social ethos of an institution than in the formal rhetoric of university pronouncements and "structured" conversations and curriculum. Here is a crucial theological context we all too often overlook.

As dean and vice president for student affairs over a seven-year period at Georgetown, I watched how theology mattered in the issues of the "culture wars" that were constantly at play in the lives of the students and the institution. From issues of how "crucifixes" symbolized Catholic identity, to whether it was appropriate for Larry Flynt to speak to the students, to how human and civil rights for gays and lesbians were to be realized, to how differing meanings of "Catholic" were given voice in the university, theology as a mode of inquiry was never far from the center of the picture. Indeed, it was usually the central analytic framework for developing policy and for making both institutional and individual decisions. It is an enormous deficit, therefore, for theologians and religious scholars not to engage the issues of institutional life and bring their skills of analysis to address real and everyday problems confronting the institution. I can speak personally to both the need for and usefulness of these skills among college administrators.

Teaching and Learning Theology at the Graduate Level

Many of the issues that provide the context for undergraduate teaching are applicable as well to teaching at the graduate level. But while the context for doing theology is similar, the goals and purposes of graduate education are different. Of course, the purposes of preparing theological scholars are different from the goals sought in the theological training of future religious leaders for the churches and religious communities. I do not presume that there is singular clarity about the goals of training future religious scholars in light of today's context. However, I believe there is some agreement in the theological academy upon these issues. My remarks therefore will focus on what I consider to be some of the goals that need to be sought in theological education. These have been shaped mainly by my experience of the last four years as president of the Graduate Theological Union in Berkeley.

Since assessment and outcomes seem to be the reigning paradigm for thinking about what makes for good teaching and learning, I will simply suggest what I consider to be a set of skills and habits of thought and practice that are worthy to pursue in graduate theological education, particularly an education that is to meet the future challenges presented by our contemporary context.

The Skill of Dialogue

This includes not just the capacity to speak with others, but also to listen, to empathize, to understand, to relate, and to cross over. To know what possibilities can come out of dialogue. Understanding religious pluralism requires dialogue. The more complex questions involve determining the goals and purposes of dialogue.

The Ability to Bridge Differences

To engage in dialogue in an ecumenical and interreligious context entails the sharing of differing beliefs. Successful theological leaders must be able to identify and communicate common goals and goods in order to create bonds between people who may have inherently opposing views, and to encourage understanding across denominations and other religious traditions.

Community-Building Skills

Developing understanding across religious divides requires the ability to bring people together in search of new forms of relationship. We need structures of association and bonds of harmony, justice, and peace. This has been an achievement at the GTU, and deepening the bonds in our community will continue to be our goal.

Knowledge of History and Traditions

It seems obvious, but it cannot be forgotten: the future will be built on the past. It is essential that religious leaders know their traditions because the future will depend on creative and critical appropriations of the past.

The Knowledge of Practices

The practical realities of religious life and thought require graduates to know what exactly individuals and groups do, how they do it, and why they do it. This makes the work we do real, not just theoretical. It is integration of theory and practice that must always be the hallmark of theological education.

A Commitment to Inclusiveness

Religious leaders need to value and embrace the intrinsic worth of all people. Commitment to global, religious, racial, ethnic, gender, and sexual orientation inclusiveness is essential to the future. Inclusiveness must be fully incorporated into our curricula.

Adaptive Leadership

Graduates must possess leadership skills that use both theory and imagination to understand the dynamics of a situation at hand, to discern deeper meanings and possibilities presented in a situation, and to reframe problems and possible solutions in ways that foster collaboration and cooperation.

These skills—being able to talk with people, help them share different beliefs, bring them together, see things in historical perspective, understand religious practices, value all people, and lead effectively—are essential to our world.

Conclusion

The College Theology Society is fulfilling its mission when it engages its members in the discourse that is critical to the times. It does this as it focuses its attention on what the theological challenges of the present are, how the insights and resources from the past can be appropriated to address present challenges, and when it seeks to provide resources for thinking theologically about our future. I hope that my comments are helpful in enabling us to achieve this task as we explore new horizons in undergraduate and graduate teaching of religion and theology.

A New Direction
in Teaching Global Solidarity

Partnering with Catholic Relief Services

Suzanne C. Toton and *Ismael Muvingi*

"Global Poverty, Liberation Theology and the Struggle for Justice" is a theology/religious studies course that has been taught regularly at Villanova University for more than twenty-five years. Yet it is always "under construction." For example, the terms "first," "second" and "third" worlds, once used to categorize the world's nations, are now obsolete. Gross national product (GNP) is no longer a reliable indicator of progress in poverty reduction. While the 1974 World Food Conference pledged to end hunger by the end of the decade, now the Millennium Goals aim at cutting poverty and hunger in half by 2015. HIV/AIDS was almost unknown in the early years of the course; now it is the leading cause of death in Africa and the fourth leading cause of death worldwide. And today our world is not merely interdependent, but globalized. Our lives are connected as never before through information and communications technology, trade, investment, and powerful global institutions.

The Christian theological perspectives that inform, critique, and clarify moral responsibility in these areas have also changed. Latin American liberation theology, contextual theologies from Africa and Asia, theologies that address the struggle of poor women, the destruction of the environment, and topics such as human rights are being rethought in light of a globalization that respects neither cultures nor borders. Even Catholic social teaching, no longer the church's best kept secret (as Peter Henriot and colleagues once put it), seems more to whisper than speak powerfully and prophetically to today's global reality.

Our pedagogy, which took its inspiration from Paulo Freire and settled into consciousness-raising and service learning, has been shaken to its very core by the radical witness of the martyrs of the San José Simeon Canas University of Central America (UCA) in El Salvador. UCA committed itself at every level to educate about the social reality of which it is a part, to enter into solidarity with the poor and marginalized, and to work to shape a more compassionate, just, and peaceful social order. The witness of UCA poses a great challenge to theologians and ethicists who are committed to furthering global justice through the academic enterprise.

Is it possible to do more than educate *about* injustice and the responsibility of Christians to eradicate it? Can solidarity be experienced and cultivated within the structure of an academic course? I believe it is possible, but only if we are willing to push the boundaries of traditional pedagogy and also enter into new company that challenges us to see, understand, and respond in new and more compelling ways.

A partnership between my Global Poverty course and Catholic Relief Services (CRS) clearly brought my students into unimagined company. It enabled them to discover new ways to conceive solidarity and to act in solidarity with the poor and marginalized of the global community—all within the parameters of a course in Christian social ethics.

The Theological Challenge

In *The Principle of Mercy*, Jon Sobrino laid the theological foundation for our collaboration with CRS.[1] In this powerful book, Sobrino wrestled with the concept of mercy. He drew on his experience of the thousands of people from all over the world who went to El Salvador during its twelve-year civil war, and of thousands more who could not travel to El Salvador to investigate the situation, but who sent assistance nonetheless. They came from all walks of life, all economic classes, and all religious denominations. They included church officials, priests, men and women religious, lay people, theologians, journalists, labor leaders, politicians, and representatives of human rights organizations.

Sobrino was intrigued by the nature of their response. When material aid was sent, even it did not have the characteristic "feel" of contributions that typically flow into a country after a tragedy or natural disaster. Sobrino chose the term "solidarity" because the response seemed to have more depth; it was a matter of conscience; it was relational, involving a mutual giving and receiving; and more important, it was ongoing. In addition to financial assistance, the "donors" wrote letters, made official statements, published articles, circulated theological and pastoral writings from and about El Salvador, shared information, organized demonstrations, testified before Congress, and held prayer services. Moreover, it continued throughout the war and, for many, continues today. It reminded Sobrino of St. Paul's admonition to "bear with one another."

Sobrino said that while we may think of these as works of mercy, these actions were more. Those who responded, individually, collectively, and institutionally to the poor in El Salvador were *in solidarity* with them. Sobrino argued that the gospel calls Christians to do more than works of mercy; our lives must be molded by mercy. Mercy must become the *structuring principle* of our lives and institutions. Mercy must drive us to shape a compassionate, just, and peaceful society. According to Sobrino:

> This world is ever ready to applaud, or at least tolerate, works of mercy. What this world will not tolerate is a church molded by the principle of mercy, which leads that church to denounce robbers who victimize, to lay bare the lie that conceals oppression, and to encourage victims to win their freedom from culprits. In other words, the robbers who inhabit this anti-merciful world tolerate the tending of wounds, but not the true healing of the wounded.[2]

In Jesus' parable, the Good Samaritan allowed himself to be moved by the suffering of the man who lay dying along the side of the road. He interiorized the other's suffering, and it drove him to take action. Sobrino argues that the place of the church, and our place as Christians, is by the side of the road with the victims of this world. Sobrino finds that a church molded by mercy defends and encourages victims, exposes and denounces robbers, and reveals the truth about what is happening. It stands in solidarity with victims to help secure their God-given rights.

Given the power of Sobrino's theology and the challenge posed by the radical witness of UCA, the practical challenge remained: how could we experience, understand, and express solidarity within the parameters of an academic course? In writing on the mission of the university, Ignacio Ellacuría, S.J., the martyred president of UCA, pointed us in the right direction. He argued that while it was impossible to physically move the university closer to the poor, it must do its research, teaching, and carry out its social projects from the social location of the poor or, as he put it, from the "theoretical locus of the poor."[3] That social location, he believed, was essential to keep the university focused and faithful to its mission. "Ellacuría used to say that we think and write and do research at a desk. . . . But we don't think from the desk. . . . We think or we try to think from the crosses of the world."[4] Ellacuría also argued that the university must put itself in relationship with the "poor-with-spirit,"[5] that is, with those who have not resigned themselves to oppression and who refuse to allow the forces of death to have the final word. Thus the real challenge was how to think and do our research from the social location of the poor without going to the "third world," and how to put ourselves in relationship with the poor, the "poor-with-spirit," and with those who struggle with them against the forces that deny the poor their lives.

An Opportunity for Response

The opportunity presented itself in an offer made by Eileen Emerson, the Church Outreach Coordinator for Catholic Relief Services (CRS), at a meeting of the Association of Catholic Colleges and Universities Wrap-Around to the annual Social Ministry Gathering in February 2002. Emerson announced that CRS wanted to make itself and its resources available to Catholic colleges and universities. As the institutional link between the U.S. Catholic Church and the world's poor, CRS works to address the suffering of the poor.[6] It also provides a vehicle for learning about the suffering of the marginalized and the specific ways by which the church enters into solidarity with them. CRS offers U.S. Catholics opportunities to participate in the global work of furthering compassion, justice, and peace.

CRS made its offer in the context of its newly defined mission and a new Africa Campaign. Today CRS defines its mission in terms of a dual constituency: to serve the poor and marginalized overseas through relief, development, and advocacy, and to generate solidarity with them in the U.S. Catholic population—solidarity that will eventuate in structural change. Because of the rapid increase in poverty, the spread of HIV/AIDS, and war, particularly in sub-Saharan Africa, CRS had decided to give priority to that region by launching an Africa Campaign, "Africa Rising: Hope and Healing," in 2000. The campaign's purpose was to educate and mobilize the U.S. Catholic constituency to advocate for policy changes toward Africa.

CRS collaborates with partner agencies overseas and responds to human suffering and the struggle for justice and peace regardless of racial, ethnic, national, or religious differences. CRS's relief and development work and its educational and advocacy efforts reflect Catholic social thought in its embodied, living form. As CRS witnesses to the tradition in challenging circumstances, the principles of Catholic social teaching are not simply applied; they assume greater depth and breadth of meaning, and they develop and evolve.

CRS publicly witnesses to one of the most fundamental truths of our faith: the sacredness of life. Its work, particularly with the weakest and most vulnerable—for example, the victims of war, natural disasters, famines, HIV/AIDS, and those struggling for justice and peace—speaks this truth where it most needs to be spoken. The work of CRS overseas and its programs of education and advocacy at home serve to remind the global society that no one's life, no matter how weak or vulnerable, different or distant, is to be neglected or wasted.

Could building a relationship with CRS help my students gain insight into the various ways this fundamental truth of faith can be witnessed to and also advanced in the larger society? What could be the possible advantages in having students collaborate directly with CRS?

Building a relationship between CRS and the students could enable the students not only to grasp better the public and political dimensions of faith and the call to faithful citizenship, but also to have the opportunity to put those dimensions into practice. Our study of development would benefit considerably from learning about CRS's experience as it carried out development activities in specific communities throughout the poorer regions of the world. Our definitions and assumptions about what development is and how it takes place would be challenged. We would gain insight into the impact of macro-development policies on the micro level. The need to address the development agenda would take on greater moral urgency. The vision of the Christian tradition and Catholic social teaching could come alive for my students in new and compelling ways.

The U.S. Catholic Church expresses its preferential option for the poor *institutionally* through CRS. An institutional commitment can be extraordinarily effective because of the resources that can be harnessed and the leveraging that is possible through a broad sphere of influence. The option for the poor, when concretized, can in turn inform and deepen the institution's original commitment and take it to deeper levels. The students could see this, for example, in CRS's decision to launch its Africa Campaign and in its shift in direction to commit to work both abroad and at home. The students could learn about the importance of institutional commitments, for resources and strategies not available to individuals can be utilized by institutions.

The work of CRS could vividly demonstrate to the students that the common good cannot be equated only with the good of our own society. Students could gain more insight into the specific conditions necessary for the poor to realize their God-given rights to life and dignity. They could also become more conscious of how decisions by international institutions, nations, banks, businesses, consumers, and citizens impact the global society and particularly the poor. Whether it would be promoting a new trade agreement such as CAFTA (Central American Free Trade Association) or seeking new funding to fight HIV/AIDS, my hope was that students would get into the habit of asking what the specific impact of legislation would be on the poor.

The experience of CRS at the grassroots level places it in a unique position to inform and press the U.S. Catholic Church and the larger public into action. Our students could gain insight into how solidarity is generated and sustained by observing how CRS uses its experience to educate in dioceses, parishes, and schools, to engage the media, to raise funds, and to advocate for policy change. In addition, a relationship with the CRS staff, committed at home and overseas to build a more just, compassionate, and peaceful global society, could give students entry into a larger community of faith that would endure after they left my course and the university.

In its document, *Faithful Citizenship*, the U.S. Conference of Catholic Bishops states that the church has an important role to play in public life.[7] The Catholic community is to be a community of conscience and use its citizenship to build a culture of life. Catholics have not only the right but a responsibility to participate in and shape the public and political arenas. The bishops write, "Responsible citizenship is a virtue and participation in the political process a moral obligation."[8] Collaborating with CRS would provide ways for my students to better understand and express their solidarity through exercising their citizenship.

The Relationship Concretized

To test the waters, I took a student delegation the first week of the semester to the national office of CRS in Baltimore, a two-hour drive from Villanova's campus. The purpose was to see CRS's headquarters, meet some of the staff, get an overview of CRS's mission and work overseas and at home, and to be introduced to the Africa Campaign. This meeting had several other objectives: to determine a realistic level of student interest and enthusiasm, to brainstorm on how best to integrate the relationship with CRS into the course, and to begin to consider in more detail the components of a legislative advocacy project. The level of interest, enthusiasm, and ideas generated by the student delegates was so high that I worried it would raise undue expectations.

I also needed to make sure that the course material was sufficiently covered so that the students would get the most out of the CRS experience. This included a solid foundation in Catholic social thought and a working knowledge of papal documents that spoke to the problem of underdevelopment. Because the course attempted to follow the methodology of Latin American liberation theology, it was important for students to understand that methodology and also some of the key theological concepts that inform this school of theology. The United Nations Development Program (UNDP) reports supplied the most up-to-date data on poverty as well as the indicators the agency employs to define and measure progress. Students were given a solid introduction to and critiques of the Bretton Woods institutions of the World Bank Group and the International Monetary Fund, as well as the General Agreement on Tariffs and Trade, the World Trade Organization, and the expansion of transnational corporations. Special attention was given in the course to the phenomena of the expansion of transnational corporations, globalization, and its potential to set back or improve conditions for the poor; third-world debt and efforts to reduce it, and unemployment, underemployment, and immigration.

Several weeks into the course, we launched our partnership with

CRS by taking the entire class for an all-day seminar to the CRS headquarters in Baltimore.[9] At the end of the day, the students said they were "pumped" and ready to go! We maintained the momentum by using the CRS website. Students were required to visit it weekly, to explore a different component with each visit, and also to pay special attention to CRS's advocacy initiatives.[10]

A key purpose in partnering with CRS was to build and experience solidarity through advocacy. This took concrete form in the legislative advocacy project. Given the three-prong focus of the Africa Campaign on increasing aid, peace-building, and stemming the spread of HIV/AIDS, students were instructed to form groups based on the issues that most interested them and also the states, congressional districts, or regions of the country that were represented in the class. After a fair amount of negotiating, the legislative groups fell into place. Each group then was to research its chosen legislative issue, beginning with material provided by CRS. Students were free to divide the research tasks among themselves. They were to keep in mind that the purpose of their research was not to produce a term paper, but to present a clear, logical, succinct, and compelling case to their legislator. They were also required to develop a one-page executive summary with additional resources and contact information that would be left with the legislator. One surprising development was the close working relationship students developed with CRS staff. The staff provided additional material and encouraged the students to call and e-mail for clarifications and questions. During the same two-week period in April, the groups were required to make an appointment with a legislator of their choosing. A student from each group was responsible for scheduling the appointment and gathering background information on the legislator, including his/her voting record on similar legislation.

With their advocacy visits fast approaching, my seemingly confident students developed a collective case of "cold feet." Assurances from me failed to convince them that they knew more than most Americans about their respective issues. They were certain no legislator or aide would listen to a group of students or, if they got a hearing, they would not be taken seriously. The students were afraid that the legislator might try to "trip them up" and make them look foolish. And, finally, they worried that their positions might simply be "wrong." On hearing this, I must admit that I began to worry that the project would fall flat on its face before even getting to Capitol

Hill. But I also knew, and reminded the students, that we had a relationship and agreement with CRS that was important to honor.

I contacted NETWORK, the Catholic Social Justice Lobby, which over its thirty-year history has trained thousands of people to lobby effectively. We arranged a conference call for the next regularly scheduled class meeting. NETWORK had never done this before with a class of students and neither had I, but it worked exceptionally well. After their "crash course" in the mechanics of lobbying, the students felt more confident. Their final assignment before meeting with their legislators was to practice their presentation and role play, keeping in mind the objections they were sure to meet.

The first group of students met with James Greenwood (R-Pennsylvania, 8th District) at his district office in Doylestown. They asked Representative Greenwood to support the allocation of $700 million of the $27 billion Emergency Supplemental Fund to the 2002 budget to address the HIV/AIDS pandemic in southern Africa. Since funds from the Emergency Supplemental Fund were to be distributed under three categories—homeland security, war measures, and helping friendly nations—the students argued that stemming the spread of HIV/AIDS in Africa clearly came under the category of helping friendly nations. The students reported that the congressman shared their concern for stemming the spread of HIV/AIDS in Africa, however, he was reluctant to use funds from the Emergency Supplemental Fund for that purpose. In his judgment, there was no clear connection between stemming HIV/AIDS and the war on terrorism. The students reported that when they attempted to make the connection, Greenwood turned a deaf ear, and told them that with our nation's mounting deficit he was reluctant to fund new initiatives without finding new sources of revenue. He asked them directly whether they would be willing to have their student loans cut or if their parents would be willing to pay higher taxes to fund HIV/AIDS initiatives in Africa. He as much as said, "Don't ask me for money if you can't come up with a viable new source for funds."

The students were a bit "thrown" by Greenwood's response and also by their inability to move the discussion forward. Nevertheless, they felt that Representative Greenwood was basically a "nice person" who felt his hands were tied. Even though they made little headway with Greenwood, they felt the meeting was a good experience, principally because it surfaced the nature of some of the opposition. When they reported on their meeting to the class, however, the class reacted by saying that "nice person or not, Greenwood was attempting to 'snow' them and they should not have let him off the hook so easily." The students in the Greenwood group recovered their footing in their thank-you letter to the congressman in which they explained in greater detail the connection between fighting terrorism and stemming HIV/AIDS in Africa and where the funds might come from.

A second group met with the aide to Eric Cantor (R-Virginia, 7th District) in Cantor's Washington office. Expecting to be challenged after hearing the report of the students in the Greenwood group, these students were surprised to find that Cantor's aide knew very little about the Emergency Supplemental Fund. Having learned from the NETWORK briefing that this is sometimes the case, the students quickly adapted and used the meeting as an opportunity to provide the aide with information about the Emergency Supplemental Fund, the HIV/AIDS situation in Africa, and the importance of our nation exercising leadership to fight AIDS. When they asked the aide directly how the congressman might respond to using funds from the Emergency Supplemental Fund, he was noncommittal. While this meeting was not particularly satisfying, the students did come away feeling that they had been prepared and that they had acted professionally. They also recognized that their meeting was, nevertheless, important for the experience and its educational value on both ends.

The third group that met on HIV/AIDS and aid to Africa had a very different experience. They met with the aide to Representative Christopher Smith (R-New Jersey, 4th District). Unbeknownst to them the congressman's aide was a Villanova graduate. He offered to meet them on campus before an alumni function. The students were exceptionally prepared for this meeting: they had reserved a private room in the student center and prepared a PowerPoint presentation. Having done their research, they knew that Congressman Smith had introduced, co-sponsored, and supported major legislation to address the spread of HIV/AIDS, to increase funding for micro-enterprise loans for the very poor, and to expand the Highly Indebted Poor Country (HIPC) debt relief program. The aide was informed, showed genuine interest in the students' presentation, and engaged them in spirited discussion. But he too had not considered using a portion of the Emergency Supplemental Fund for addressing the HIV/AIDS crisis in Africa. The students felt the meeting was a good exchange. They felt complimented by the aide's remark that he wished other constituents were as informed and prepared as they, and he suggested that they keep in contact with him.

The final group of students met with an aide to Senator Paul Sarbanes (D-Maryland) on the Sudan Peace Act. They expressed concern over the Khartoum government's "depopulation" and the forced acculturation of the civilian population of southern Sudan for the purposes of gaining control of and profiting from newly discovered oil and gas reserves. They noted that the oil and gas revenues were being used to strengthen the Sudanese military, enabling it to carry out its campaign of terror in the region. While they applauded Senator Sarbanes's interest in Sudan and his support for the Sudan Peace Act, Senate Bill 180, the students specifically requested the senator's support of Sections 8 and 9 of the bill, which required full financial disclosure of oil and gas transactions between foreign companies and the Sudanese government and, in the event of noncompliance, sanctions that would effectively bar these companies from trading in the U.S. market. The aide told them that the senator was in "general" support of the bill, however, she was certain he would not play a more active role in promoting it. She stated that as chair of the Senate Banking Committee, Sarbanes had much more pressing matters to deal with, such as the Enron scandal. She recommended that they contact leading proponents or opponents of the bill rather than asking more of Sarbanes. While they were somewhat discouraged by the reception from the senator's aide, the students felt that they accomplished some of what they set out to do. They also learned much more about the issue, the strengths and weaknesses of their approach, and what they would do next time to be more effective.

Outcomes

The advocacy project had several positive results. First, the legislators and their aides heard from students, a constituency they usually do not hear from. This should help to dispel the attitude that today's youth are uninterested in political and global issues. In addition, the students did not simply "breeze in." They took their meetings seriously; they were informed, well-prepared, and articulate. In addition, the students alerted their legislators and aides to major issues of which they were not aware. And they educated, engaged in dialogue, did presentations, and left information that included contact names, organizations, and websites for follow-up.

In each meeting the students stated that they were working in partnership with Catholic Relief Services. They explained what CRS is and the nature of its work. They also informed them of the position of the U.S. Catholic Church on the issues they raised. Finally, in my judgment, this project alerted legislators to the fact that global education is gaining significance in the curriculum of Catholic colleges and universities as is education for advocacy. And it is important for them to know that their various positions are being monitored.

In preparing their cases, the students quickly learned what they knew and did not know about the issues. The pressure of the legislative meeting forced them to find answers. They had to work collaboratively and efficiently and plan strategically. They were forced to come to terms with their fears of inadequacy and of not being taken seriously. Because they had researched who their legislators were and what positions they held, they gained important information they would not necessarily have acquired during the course of the semester. It also alerted them to the fact that their position might not be received warmly, and they prepared for objections.

This approach also surfaced differences of opinion among students in the group. These had to be addressed and resolved before meeting their legislators. The legislative meeting forced them to think on their feet. Because they engaged in advocacy, advocacy itself no longer seemed overwhelming. It was not something only the most informed adults or very powerful people do. They jumped into the water and did not drown; they came to the surface; some floated and others swam. There was not one group or student who did not express eagerness to try it again. They learned that there was something that could be done about the issues we studied during the semester and that they could be part of the action. More important, they now understood that advocacy is a serious and significant way of entering into solidarity with the poor and marginalized. And, finally, they experienced being in the company of faith, that is, in the company of men and women at home and overseas who not only believe in justice, compassion, and peace but are invested in its creation.

The outcome of the advocacy project was also positive for CRS. CRS is all too aware of the fact that legislators who are put into office by their constituents do not answer to non-governmental organizations such as CRS, however commendable their work. Moving legislators on social justice issues, especially international ones, requires that such issues be owned by constituents. Thus, the students directly contributed to the work of CRS.

Replicability of the Learning Model

While the easy commute from Villanova to Washington, D.C., and to Baltimore certainly made field trips possible, this project is replicable nonetheless. In this age of information and communications technology, distance is not a factor. Faculty and students can easily access the work of CRS or other agencies engaged in the work of social justice and peace through the internet. They can tap their rich resources—web, print, audio-visual, and speakers—and integrate them into courses and programs. Virtually every agency today engages in legislative advocacy and provides material and assistance to do this effectively. While a personal visit to legislators in Washington, D.C., is a thrilling experience, how frequently can that trip be made? In reality, advocacy is exercised day in and day out through phone calls, letters, and e-mail, which in themselves are effective. Moreover, congressional representatives have local offices in their districts that are accessible.

In addition to CRS, the Catholic Campaign for Human Development (CCHD), the Bishops' Office of Social Development and World Peace, and Catholic Charities are eager to make their resources available to and collaborate with Catholic colleges and universities. CRS, CCHD, and Catholic Charities have regional offices and some even have local offices. The barrier is not distance; it has more to do with commitment, imagination, and a willingness to experiment and take risks.

The implications of this initiative and others around the country for building solidarity within the larger university are just beginning to unfold. CRS and a number of universities, including Villanova, are beginning to explore a faculty fellows program in which faculty can contribute to and be enlisted in CRS's research needs and advocacy efforts. CRS's vast experience and relationships can also be tapped for a faculty's own research projects. Law students in clinical programs can assist CRS in international law or human rights cases. CRS can contribute toward educating and training nursing students who volunteer or plan to work overseas. CRS can provide opportunities for business faculty and students to explore in greater depth issues such as the impact of extractive industries, especially oil and mining, on the poor, micro-enterprises, and socially responsible investment. In the case of micro-enterprises, field trips are certainly within the realm of possibility. There are similar opportunities for faculty and students in engineering or environmental studies. Next semester, a Villanova class of environmental studies students will visit a CRS site in Ecuador during spring break to observe environmentally sustainable agriculture.

These and others initiatives hold the promise of bringing the university, faculty, and students into deeper relationships with the poor and marginalized, entering into solidarity with them, and together working to build a more compassionate, just, and peaceful global order. When all is said and done, if that is not the end purpose of the Catholic college and university, what is?

Notes

[1] Jon Sobrino, *The Principle of Mercy: Taking the Crucified People from the Cross* (Maryknoll, N.Y.: Orbis Books, 1994).

[2] Ibid., 23.

[3] Ignacio Ellacuría, S.J., "The University, Human Rights, and the Poor Majority," in *Towards a Society That Serves Its People: The Intellectual Contribution of El Salvador's Murdered Jesuits*, ed. John Hassett and Hugh Lacey (Washington, D.C.: Georgetown University Press, 1991), 213.

[4] Jon Sobrino, S.J., "The Cost of Speaking the Truth: The Martyrs of Central America, El Salvador," *The Journal of Peace and Justice Studies* 3 (1991): 9.

[5] Ignacio Ellacuría, S.J., "Utopia and Prophecy in Latin America," in *Mysterium Liberationis: Fundamental Concepts in Liberation Theology*, ed. Ignacio Ellacuría and Jon Sobrino (Maryknoll, N.Y.: Orbis Books, 1993), 303.

[6] CRS is the official relief and development agency of the United States Catholic Church. Founded in 1943 to assist European refugees during World War II, in the last sixty years its work has extended to ninety-four countries worldwide, providing emergency relief, promoting economic and social development, and furthering justice and peace.

Since its inception, CRS's view of itself has evolved concomitant with both the state of international affairs and the thinking in the field of development. While the need for emergency relief persists, people in "non-emergency" but desperate situations also need support not only to survive, but to try and work their way out of the desperation of poverty. With changes in the church and the world brought about by Vatican II, the end of the Cold War and its aftermath, resulting in unstable states and eventually globalization, CRS came to recognize that without true systemic change and a more peaceful milieu, long-term development would simply not happen. Thus the agency, in addition to providing relief, set out to work for systemic change and building right relationships that would lead to just and peaceful societies. The principles of Catholic social teaching that call for the dignity and equality of the human person, solidarity, the rights and responsibilities of every person to work for the common good provided the perfect framework for doing that. Given this development in its own thinking and work, CRS began to realize that the poor could no longer be its only constituency. It also needed to educate the affluent and bring them into solidarity with the poor and marginalized.

[7] *Faithful Citizenship: A Catholic Call to Political Responsibility* (Washington, D.C.: United States Catholic Conference of Bishops, 2003).

[8] Ibid., 9.

[9] The content was as follows: Emerson gave a history of the agency, a description of where and how it works overseas, and an explanation of its dual constituency model. Next, Ismael Muvingi, then coordinator of CRS's Africa Campaign, gave an overview of the campaign, its goals, and materials. Dan Griffin, from the Sudan desk, gave an overview of the history of the war in the Sudan and the efforts to bring peace to the region. Jennifer Dingle, who works in direct marketing, and Christopher Lee, who works in corporation/foundation relations, spoke about fundraising. After lunch students participated in a community-banking simulation game CRS was piloting. They also toured the CRS offices to get a better sense of where CRS works and its support staff. We then divided the group into the "pillar" issues of the Africa Campaign: direct aid, peace-building, and HIV/AIDS. Each group was given a presentation by an expert in that area. Then the CRS Coordinator for Advocacy Initiatives on Africa, Pam Font-Gabel, laid out the legislative issues CRS is working on. And finally, Amy Rumano and Melissa Christ from the CRS Recruitment Team spoke to the students about careers in international development.

[10] I made every effort to integrate CRS's Africa Campaign material into the course. For example, in the section on Catholic social teaching we read the U.S. Catholic bishops' statement "A Call to Solidarity with Africa" and CRS's powerful new mission statement, "Solidarity Will Transform the World." In my introduction to development we read CRS's pamphlet, "Africa Rising! Hope and Healing," which introduces the campaign, and also its pamphlet on HIV/AIDS programs in Africa. For the section on trade we read a paper by Ian Gary, CRS's Strategic Issues Advisor, entitled, "Extractive Industries in Africa," and a pamphlet on peace-building activities. Finally, for the section on foreign assistance, we read a short paper, "Africa Rising! Hope and Healing: Poverty in the Midst of Plenty."

Contributors

J. Matthew Ashley is associate professor of systematic theology at the University of Notre Dame. His most recent book is *Interruptions: Mysticism, Politics, and Theology in the Work of Johann Baptist Metz* (University of Notre Dame Press, 1998).

Michael Horace Barnes is professor of religious studies at the University of Dayton. He has edited two CTS annual volumes. His *Stages of Thought: The Co-Evolution of Religious Thought and Science* (Oxford, 2000) received the CTS annual book award in 2001.

Anne M. Clifford, C.S.J. is associate professor of theology at Duquesne University. She has co-edited a CTS annual volume and is the author of *Introducing Feminist Theology* (Orbis Books, 2001).

Miguel H. Díaz is associate professor of theology at the College of Saint Benedict/St. John's University. His most recent book is *On Being Human: U.S. Hispanic and Rahnerian Perspectives* (Orbis Books, 2001).

James A. Donahue is president and professor of ethics at the Graduate Theological Union in Berkeley. He is the author of *Ethics across the Curriculum: A Practice-Based Approach* (Lanham, Md.: Lexington Books, 2003).

Elizabeth T. Groppe is assistant professor of systematic theology at Xavier University in Cincinnati. Her dissertation was published as *Yves Congar's Theology of the Holy Spirit* (New York: Oxford, 2004).

Steven R. Harmon is associate professor of Christian theology at Campbell University Divinity School, Buies Creek, North Carolina. He is the author of *Every Knee Should Bow: Biblical Rationales for Universal Salvation in Early Christian Thought* (Lanham, Md.: University Press of America, 2003).

Mary Ann Hinsdale, I.H.M. is associate professor of theology at Boston College. She received the CTS best book award in 1987 and the best article award in 2002 and has co-edited a CTS annual volume. Her Madeleva Lecture, *Women Shaping Theology,* is forthcoming from Paulist Press.

Elizabeth A. Johnson is Distinguished Professor of Theology at Fordham University. Johnson's *Truly Our Sister* won the CTS annual book award in 2004. Her most recent book is *Dangerous Memories: A Mosaic of Mary in Scripture* (Continuum, 2004).

Sally Kenel is associate professor and assistant chair in the Department of Theology and Religious Studies at St. John's University in New York. Her current research is centered on the interface of theology and ecology.

Joseph A. Komonchak is Ordinary Professor in the School of Theology and Religious Studies at The Catholic University of America where he holds the John C. and Gertrude P. Hubbard Chair in Religious Studies. He is the chief editor of *The New Dictionary of Theology* (Michael Glazier, 1987) and editor of the English edition of the five-volume *History of Vatican II* (Orbis Books).

Colleen M. Mallon, O.P. is assistant professor of theology and religious studies at St. John's University, New York. She wrote "Ecclesial Discipleship: Applying the Requirements of the Gospel to the Church as Social Institution" (*Louvain Studies* 28, 2003).

Ismael Muvingi is a candidate for the Ph.D. in conflict analysis and resolution at George Mason University. He was an institutional relations officer and director of the Africa Campaign at Catholic Relief Services and is now an instructor in conflict resolution at

Canadian Mennonite University, Winnipeg. His research centers on resource extraction and conflict.

Norbert Rigali, S.J. is professor emeritus of theology and religious studies at the University of San Diego. His research and teaching centers on the foundations of Christian ethics.

Terrence W. Tilley is professor of religious studies at the University of Dayton. His *Story Theology* won the CTS annual book award in 1986. His most recent book is *History, Theology and Faith: Dissolving the Modern Problematic* (Orbis Books, 2004).

Suzanne C. Toton is associate professor of theology/religious studies and on the staff of the Center for Peace and Justice Education at Villanova University. Her next book *Justice Education: From Charity to Solidarity*, is forthcoming from Marquette University Press.

Randall Jay Woodard is a candidate for the Ph.D. in systematic theology at Duquesne University. His areas of interest include sacramental theology, marriage, and family.

Sandra Yocum Mize is department chair and associate professor of religious studies at the University of Dayton. She co-edited *American Catholic Traditions: Resources for Renewal*, CTS Annual Publication 42 (Orbis Books, 1997) and is the author of a history of the CTS (Sheed & Ward, forthcoming).